The case for
CREATIONISM

The case for CREATIONISM

by
Colin Mitchell

Copyright ©1994 Colin Mitchell
First published 1994

ISBN 1-873796 35 8

Published by
Autumn House Limited
Alma Park, Grantham, Lincs., NG31 9SL, England

The case for
CREATIONISM

CONTENTS

FIGURES IN TEXT

ACKNOWLEDGEMENTS

My thanks are due to Pastor Eric Lowe and Drs. Mart de Groot, Hugh Dunton, David Marshall, Leofric Rhodes, Albert Waite, and John Walton for valuable advice leading to necessary corrections and improvements of the text, and to Mr. David Cheng for Chinese translations. I also would like to thank the members of my family, especially my wife Clemency and also Patrick, Stacy, and Laura Mitchell for advice and help.

I acknowledge with thanks the following organizations for permission to reproduce figures: Oxford University Press for 2.1, Creation-Life Publishers for 8.1, Prentice-Hall for 8.2, Chapman and Hall for the Ichthyostega diagram in 9.1, and the American Association for the Advancement of Science for 11.2. Figure 11.1 was taken from a tourist map of Beijing. Figure N.1 was inspired by Bowden (1983).

Every effort has been made to contact organizations and individuals to obtain permission to reproduce material and we apologize for any that may have been omitted from this list.

PART I

PHILOSOPHICAL AND HISTORICAL BACKGROUND

CHAPTER 1

WORLD-VIEWS, EVOLUTION, AND THE 1990s ETHOS

1.1 EVOLUTION AND WORLD-VIEW

Our actions are based on our beliefs, and the collective actions of groups and societies are based on their collective beliefs. Such collective beliefs constitute a world-view. This can be defined as the whole complex of ideas held by a society or group by which they relate themselves to the cosmos. Our world-view to a large extent governs our behaviour. In order to understand behaviour, we must understand the beliefs which underlie it.

Much that we do today derives from scientific ideas which have developed over the past century and a half. An important component of this is Darwin's theory of evolution. It is therefore important to understand what it says, how it arose, and what its effects have been. This book begins by considering the last of these. We can best appreciate the relevance of the pros and cons of the theory when we see the range of its effects on the beliefs and actions of our own society.

World-views consist of sets of paradigms. These are smaller sets of interrelated ideas which together form the whole. The European medieval world-view, for instance, included such paradigms as belief in the Christian revelation, the divinely-ordained authority of Church and State, and the finality of Greek science. The Renaissance modified this by reintroducing a paradigm of classical culture.

History shows a persistent human search for a *unitary* world-view which co-ordinates ethics and science into a single explanatory system. Some periods have seemed to approach this objective. For example, the Roman Empire under the Antonines and Europe at the height of the Middle Ages appear to have achieved a sort of synthesis, but this did not extend beyond their boundaries and was never universally accepted within them. The same search for a unitary world-view continues today, and has Darwin's Theory of Evolution as one of its basic paradigms.

At any time there seem to be three sorts of paradigm: those that contribute to the current world-view, those that can be harmonized with it, and those that cannot be harmonized with it. The third category, if pursued, can generate a change in the world-view, sometimes called a 'gestalt switch'.[1]

The theory of evolution was such a paradigm. It was largely instrumental in causing a revolution in the scientific view of origins. This undermined the Victorian world-view and was largely responsible for the gestalt switch to today's evolution-dominated world-view.

Darwin's theory is twofold: a special theory of intraspecific micro-evolution and a general theory of transspecific macro-evolution. Micro-evolution teaches that the survival of the fittest by natural selection caused significant changes to occur within many types of living creature. He obtained convincing evidence for this on the voyage of the *Beagle*, and it was abundantly confirmed by subsequent work. Geographical isolation was seen to cause species to develop divergently in different environments and ultimately to deny them the ability to breed with cousins. Such changes have been claimed, for example, for the peppered moth, the European gull, the *Drosophila* fruit fly.

Macro-evolution goes much farther. It states that all living things have arisen by a naturalistic, mechanistic, evolutionary process from a single living source which itself rose by a similar process from a dead inanimate world. It has been called the 'amoeba-man theory'. It goes beyond the limited variations of micro-evolution. It transgresses the limits of what the King James Version of the Bible calls 'kinds'. This word is a translation of the Hebrew word *min* which is used to describe the main divisions of plants and animals. It is not possible to tie this term to a specific scientific definition. In Genesis 1 it refers to broad groups such as fruit trees, herbs, cattle, and fowls. In Leviticus 11 and Deuteronomy 14 it concerns somewhat narrower classes such as beetles, storks, mice, and tortoises. It is never used of humans. It seems most reasonable to conclude that a 'kind', when applied to the animal kingdom approximates to a group of creatures that are interfertile where the chromosomes of both parents contribute to the offspring, and therefore can hybridize. Hereinafter, the word 'evolution' will be used in the sense of macroevolution which transgresses these limits.

The idea of macro-evolution questioned the biblical record in a way that few earlier scientific ideas had done. If all life was ultimately descended from simple monocellular creatures, humans were not created by a special divine act, but were the product of a long random process, and the Earth must be more than a few thousand years old.

The theory appeared in an environment which already questioned biblical authority in science. The eighteenth-century Deists rejected the Bible as a source of knowledge, looking to mankind's own powers of reasoning to determine what we should believe and how we should act. They did not disbelieve in God but restricted His role simply to the opening acts of creation, after which the world operated as a vast machine controlled by scientific laws, such as Newton's law of motions.

Biblical authority had also long been questioned by geologists. The early nineteenth century witnessed a debate between Vulcanists, who saw volcanic activity as the dominant factor in forming the Earth's landscapes, and Neptunists who ascribed them mainly to a flood.

Evolution's intellectual triumph has led to the acceptance of its ethical and philosophical implications. It has altered our whole world-view. The change in the idea of the fixity of species has led to a change in our view of the nature of truth and ethics. It has led to a belief in the conditionality of moral principles and encouraged the acceptance of 'situation ethics'. We have lost concept of absolutes. Where there are no absolutes there can be no truth; where there is no truth there can be no justice; and where there is no justice there can be no hope. Thus an absence of absolutes leads to a paradigm change that Schaeffer[2] called falling below a 'line of despair'. The change in thinking has been profound and world-wide.

It came after about 1890 in Europe and after about 1935 in the USA. Before these dates people had operated on suppositions essentially the same as the Christian's. Absolutes counted. If something was true, the opposite was false. If one told somebody to be good, they might not obey, but at least they knew what one meant. Or if one said something like 'this is true', it would be taken in an absolute sense. Since these dates, however, terms such as 'good' and 'true' have lost meaning, and have become relative and conditional.[3] The criteria of virtue and merit have become evolutionary success or practicality rather than accordance with absolute standards.

Geographically the change occurred first in Germany, then on the rest of the Continent, then in Britain, then the USA. Socially it occurred first among intellectuals, then among workers, then in the bourgeoisie. Intellectually it began in science and then moved to philosophy, the arts, general culture, education and, last of all, to theology.

1.2 CONSEQUENCES OF THE EVOLUTIONARY WORLD-VIEW

Certain specific consequences have followed from the acceptance of evolution.

In science, humanity is seen as not differing fundamentally from animals. Not only our physical characteristics but also our mental and moral outlook have all evolved. We do not differ from animals in kind, only in degree. Nature is a struggle. Cells and organisms do not collaborate but compete and fight. Progress is random, deriving from natural selection and the survival of the fittest.

In philosophy, the change can be seen in the destruction

of the concept of fixity, an absence of absolutes. As natural forms change, so does knowledge and reality. Ethics develop from situations. There is a generally hopeful view of human progress, a belief that we are moving forwards and upwards. Conflicts between individuals and groups may sometimes be justified on the ground that this is the path of evolutionary progress.

In music and the arts, there has been a loss of structure. The emphasis is on personal experience and expression. There is a frustrating search for universals. Because absolutes have been lost, there is a striving for something to take their place. Picasso, for instance, changed his forms of self-expression throughout his life. He saw a solution in the Marxist synthesis, but towards the end of his life tended to retreat into hedonism. Van Gogh, Gauguin, and Munch all in different ways illustrate a search for the lost universal, but moved towards despair in not finding it. Modern music and drama tend to favour unconstrained self expression and show an absence of structure. The criteria of merit are the originality and forcefulness of the imagery.

In psychology, human behaviour patterns are seen as deriving from animal origins. Freud's emphasis on the sexual explanation of psychology was based on this idea. Appleton,[4] for instance, has suggested that our aesthetic reactions to the environment are atavistic, deriving from a remote animal ancestry. We evaluate landscape features from the point of view of their suitability as prospects for finding food and necessities, or as refuges from danger.

In the social sciences, the concept of sin is rejected. Man is seen as basically good. His circumstances are determined by economic needs. His relationship to his environment is analogous to that of animals to their habitats, without a supernatural component. Evolutionary success through natural selection and survival of the fittest becomes the social as well as the biological imperative. Consequently, the emphasis in practical work is shifted away from personal regeneration towards the improvement of relationships and 'social engineering'. Our responsibility to our society comes to precede, and where necessary to replace, any higher claim.

In business, there is a tendency to esteem strife and selfish competition. Two well-known industrialists who became outstanding philanthropists illustrate this. Andrew Carnegie was first deeply troubled by the consequences of evolutionary theory, but came to accept it as desirable when he saw the law of competition as biological. He said, 'It is clear we cannot evade it. While the law may sometimes be hard for the individual, it is best for the race.'

John D. Rockefeller said:

'The growth of a large business is merely the survival of the fittest. The "American Beauty" rose could be produced in splendour and fragrance which brings cheer to the beholder only by sacrificing the buds which grew up around it. It is not a lethal tendency in business, it is merely the working out of the law of nature and the law of God.'[5]

In education, the emphasis shifts from moral training to self-expression. The child is seen as basically good. Behavioural deviations are due to bad circumstances. Teaching emphasizes the practicalities of this world rather than eternity. Discipline is utilitarian rather than moral. Haeckel, as long ago as 1879, sought an evolution-based religion for schools in place of Christianity, because he believed that the chosen minority who survived the evolutionary struggle were not only the fittest but the best. This can be contrasted with a statement attributed to the Duke of Wellington that 'education without religion makes men into clever devils', which is grounded in the opposite belief that intelligence can be dangerous when divorced from moral principle.

There has always been a tendency for universities, first founded to teach religion, to become secularized. This process has accelerated over the past decades. Within academic disciplines the penetration of evolutionary thought has led to secularization, first of the sciences, then of the social sciences, and now increasingly of liberal arts subjects such as languages and literature. This is because the secularization of science leads to the appearance of the same ideas in non-scientific writing. Early examples of this trend in literature were Wells, Shaw, and Ibsen.

Evolution has, by its emphasis on random processes, encouraged the concept of a world without God. This has had three discernible results in modern fiction and drama. First, it has contributed to a widespread avoidance of moral absolutes, so that attitudes and behaviour which in the past would have been considered taboo, have become acceptable. Secondly, it has encouraged a stress on social, rather than individual, morality; organizational restructuring rather than personal redemption. This inspired some socially idealistic literature and drama, especially in Communist countries, but its inadequacy in practise to solve many human problems formed a theme for such novels as Conrad's *Heart of Darkness*,[6] Orwell's *Animal Farm*[7] and Golding's *Lord of the Flies*.[8] In these, an underlying human bestiality dooms utopian idealism to failure. Thirdly a belief in evolution is linked to Existentialism through its scientific justification of a purposeless world. It has thus indirectly influenced fiction which draws its inspiration from Existentialism. This can be seen in the novels of Orwell, Franz Kafka, Albert Camus and Simone de Beauvoir, and the plays and novels of Jean-Paul Sartre and Samuel Beckett. Kafka's *The Castle*[9] and *The Trial*[10] and Orwell's *1984*,[11] for instance, illustrate a final effect of Existentialism — a failure to establish personality, a sort of reduction to nothingness.

Evolution has had a profound influence on politics and war. A philosophical justification for authoritarianism had come from Rousseau's concept of the 'general will'. This was a consensus to be determined by majority voice. Once determined all must obey it. It provided a rationale for the authoritarianism of the French revolutionary government. Evolution has probably increased the potential of this concept for oppressive ruthlessness by implicitly accepting that ends justify means — that it is creditable to be unscrupulous in a good cause.

In every European country between 1870 and 1914 there was a war party demanding armaments, an individualist party demanding ruthless competition, an imperialist party demanding a free hand over backward peoples, a socialist party demanding the conquest of power, and a racialist party demanding internal purges against aliens. All of them, when appeals to greed or glory failed, or even before, invoked Spencer and Darwin as providing the scientific justification. War itself was regarded as beneficial. Earlier commanders such as Napoleon, Nelson, and Wellington had seen war at first hand and described it for what it was, in simple, unpleasant words. By contrast some writers in the second half of the nineteenth century poeticized war and luxuriated in the prospect of it. They took it for granted that all struggles were struggles for life and the death of the loser its 'natural' goal. The ability of English colonists to defeat and kill native Australians was, for instance, regarded by some as a mark of their superiority.[12]

An evolution-influenced view was characteristic of the political extremes, both left and right.

Engels believed strongly in evolution:

'Nature works dialectically and not metaphysically. . . . In this connection Darwin must be named before all others. He dealt the metaphysical conception of Nature the heaviest blow by his proof that all organic beings, plants, animals, and man himself are the products of a process of evolution going on through millions of years.'[13]

Karl Marx believed that religion was mainly a social phenomenon resulting from social structures, and would collapse when they did. It was therefore undesirable. His ideas had considerable affinities with Darwin's. Both thought they had discovered the basic law of development, and that struggle was the means. Both supposed that nothing good is really lost in this struggle, and that things happen automatically and for the best[14]. Marx preached a doctrine of philosophical materialism, which his successors called 'dialectical materialism'.[15] This claimed that quantitative changes in matter also yield qualitative changes (for example the emergence of mind); that nature is a result of contradictory opposites; and that the result of one opposite (thesis) clashing with another (antithesis) is a synthesis that preserves and transcends the opposites. This view has clear affinities to the evolutionary theory. It is no surprise, therefore, that Marx saw Darwin's *Origin* as very important since it provided a basis in natural science for this historical process. He sought permission to dedicate *Das Kapital* to him, which Darwin declined.

In pre-World War II Europe, Social Darwinism was a commonly held philosophy. Its underlying idea was that in the course of a ruthless competition and battle, a natural selection takes place which prevents or offsets aberrations and makes for a proper balance between population and available resources. According to the immutable laws of heredity, the unfit cannot be educated and therefore must be eliminated.[16]

In Russia, Darwinism was seen as explaining the evolutionary triumph of the proletariat over the capitalists. The inhuman atrocities connected with the October Revolution and the later collectivization of the farms were carried out in the name of science. Courses on Darwinism were given at universities, and popular lectures to the workers. In World War II, systematic compulsory lectures on Darwinism were given even to prisoners of war. In the light of this constant indoctrination, it becomes easier to understand the lack of feeling, and the scientific detachment which became characteristic of many Russian soldiers. Even the horrors of the Hitler camps were hardly as terrible as the revelations about Soviet camps and the deportation of Poles. Zoe Zajdlerowa[17] speaks with deep feeling about the almost total lack of humanity displayed by Russian soldiers engaged in this work. She describes such deportations by rail in these words:

'I have searched in vain through masses of evidence for

records of anything approaching humanity being shown by any soldiers on any of these trains. I have a record of one man passing an extra bucket of water and five other records of doors being opened for a short period, some ten minutes or so, to let some air in; and this only after the most urgent entreaty and from caprice, not in any way furnishing a precedent for other occasions. This question has preoccupied me profoundly. Throughout my work on this book, work which has occupied several years, I have searched the evidence exhaustively on this point. I have also put the question to every single person with whom I have talked. It has been of immense importance to me, of an importance greater than I can possibly express, to discover that some instinct of humanity did survive somehow. The answer invariably given to me has been that it did not.'

This must indict the Marxist philosophy on which Soviet society was based. Since this has roots in evolution, there seems to be a linkage between evolutionary ideas and such inhumanities. The collapse of political Communism since 1989 may be explained as to some extent a revulsion against a philosophy which has such effects.[18]

At the opposite political pole, Mussolini's attitude was completely dominated by evolution. In public utterances he repeatedly used the Darwinian catchwords while he mocked at perpetual peace, lest it should hinder the evolutionary process. For him the reluctance of England to engage in war only proved the evolutionary decadence of the British Empire.[19]

In England at the turn of the century Karl Pearson wrote, 'You pray for a time when the swords shall be turned into ploughshares, but believe me when that day comes man will no longer progress.'[20] Evolution was thus seen as something creditable. Nietzsche saw Christianity's defence of the weak as retrograde and as reversing the beneficial effects of natural selection.

'Christianity is the *reverse* of the principle of *selection*. If the degenerate and the sick man ("the Christian") is to be of the same value as the healthy man ("the pagan"), or if he is even to be valued higher than the latter, . . . the natural course of evolution is thwarted and the unnatural becomes law.'[21]

Even the losers in war recognized the merit of this process. Renan, smarting under the defeat of his country in the Franco-Prussian War of 1870, declared that 'war is in a way one of the conditions of progress, the cut of the whip which prevents a country from going to sleep'.[22]

Prince Bülow, later the German Chancellor, spoke along the same lines when he said, 'We must realize that there is no such thing as permanent peace, and must remember Moltke's words: "Permanent peace is a dream and even a beautiful one. War is an element of the order of the world established by God in God's scheme of the world." '[23] Adolf Hitler in *Mein Kampf* wrote, 'He who lives must fight; he who does not wish to fight in this world, where permanent struggle is the law of life, has not the right to exist.'[24] Immorality, craftiness, ruthlessness and brutality are thus raised into virtues. Euthanasia of unproductive individuals is justified.

In translating these concepts into grim reality, some idea of the mentality of the Nazi leadership can be gauged from the remarks of Heinrich Himmler during World War II to SS leaders:

'The SS man is to be guided by one principle alone: honesty, decency, loyalty, and friendship towards those of our blood, and to no one else. What happens to the Russians or the Czechs is a matter of total indifference to me. . . . Whether other peoples live in plenty or starve to death interests me only in so far as we need them as slaves for our culture; for the rest it does not interest me.'[25]

Recent European history has seen the consequences of these ideas.

Theology was the original mainstay of creationist beliefs in the Christian world. But it became deeply influenced by evolutionary ideas. Although the appearance of *Origin* provoked violent controversy, attempts were soon made to show it was compatible with religious faith.

The concept of the Bible as a special authoritative revelation gradually yielded before the impact of evolutionary thought. The proponents of evolution suggested that all religions were the result of an automatic developmental process, and the Bible was a product of natural evolution — a collection of books displaying man's progressive understanding of God. This new interpretation became allied with the theological movement called higher criticism, which called for a complete repudiation of the concept of the complete inspiration of the Bible. The principles of historical criticism were applied to the Bible, and its books became regarded as human and fallible, with the mistakes and contradictions that often characterize ancient writings. The history of Israel came to be seen as representing various stages through which Hebrews went in their quest for God.[26]

These views came to be espoused by the movement generally known as Modernism, typically expressed by Harry Emerson Fosdick:[27]

'We know that every idea in the Bible started from primitive and childlike origins and, with however many setbacks and delays, grew in scope and height towards the culmination of Christ's Gospel.'

This changed view of the Bible led to a radical transformation of the old Christian position on the source of religious authority. Instead of being bound by what was written, the Christian could use the Scriptures in subjection to his own reason, the latter being the ultimate guide in cases of doubt.

This fundamentally reduced the place of Jesus Christ. He was seen mainly as providing the example and inspiration for ethical living. The stress was on His humanitarian teachings and a social gospel which alleviated suffering in harmony with the inevitable progress fostered by evolution. Concern was concentrated on this life, more or less repudiating the life to come.

The changed theology also brought a new attitude to

non-Christian religions. Since all religions were evolutionary products, none could be considered right to the exclusion of others. This, coupled with the realization of great material and social needs of much of the world, contributed to a shift of missionary emphasis towards establishing hospitals, developing agricultural programmes, and fostering education.[28] These had previously been seen as the fruit rather than the root of religious regeneration. They were now increasingly seen as the path to such regeneration.

Finally, evolution contributed to a changed attitude to biblical research. This became more detached and critical, and less aimed at discovering hitherto unrevealed truths in the text. The early nineteenth century had seen a great revival of Bible study, notably in connection with prophetic interpretation. This had been associated with a far-reaching religious awakening and a foundation of the Baptist, Wesleyan, and Anglican missionary societies.[29] A lessened interest since the mid-nineteenth century has coincided with the triumph of Darwinism.

1.3 SUMMARY

The behaviour of societies depends on their world-view. A change in this can result from a change in one of the major paradigms which composes it. The theory of evolution in the mid-nineteenth century caused such a change. Until then, mankind had generally believed that all major types of living thing were separately created a few thousand years ago. Since then, they have generally believed that all were descended from the simplest organisms by a process of evolution over millions of years. This change has had profound and far-reaching effects on all aspects of human thinking and behaviour. These effects can be seen in changed views in science, philosophy, music, the arts, psychology, the social sciences, education, politics, and theology.

REFERENCES
[1] eg Kuhn 1962, page 117. [2] 1969, page 20f. [3] Ibid, pages 41-44. [4] 1975, pages 65-68. [5] quotation from Clark 1972b, page 106. [6] 1917. [7] 1951. [8] 1965. [9] 1986. [10] 1955. [11] 1980. [12] Barzun 1958, pages

92-95. [13] Engels 1975, quoted by Keane 1991, page 218. [14] Barzun 1958, page 100. [15] Chadwick 1975, page 59. [16] Keane 1991, page 216. [17] 1989, page 71. [18] Clark 1972b, page 112f. [19] ibid, page 115. [20] Clark 1972b, page 114. [21] Brinton 1941, page 146. [22] quoted by Barzun 1958, page 93. [23] Hayes 1941, page 340; Barzun 1942, page 101. [24] quoted by Clark 1972b, page 116. [25] quoted by Keane 1991, page 217. [26] Zimmerman 1966, pages 173, 174. [27] 1926, page 11. [28] Zimmerman 1959, pages 175, 177. [29] Froom, vol. 3, pages 265, 266.

CHAPTER 2

THE DEVELOPMENT OF THE PRESENT WESTERN WORLD-VIEW

2.1 PRE-CONDITIONS IN THE WESTERN WORLD-VIEW

Evolutionary theory could only gain acceptance where certain basic assumptions about the cosmos, and certain socio-economic conditions, themselves largely a result of those assumptions, were present. Two such assumptions were: a. that the universe was rational and governed by unchanging and predictable natural laws in which the linkage of cause and effect was automatic and observable, and b. that ethical questions were separate from scientific and that the latter could be pursued without reference to the former.

The belief in a rational universe derived from Hebrew and Greek roots which saw it as created and regulated by rational and knowable deities. Beyond this, these two world-views differed profoundly. Hebrew religion was monotheistic and required absolute moral response. Greek religion was polytheistic and required reason and moderation to approach a pantheon of anthropomorphic and sometimes inharmonious deities. The former gave rise to a dominantly ethical and religious, and the latter to a dominantly rational and scientific, world-view. This difference had long-term repercussions in the reception of the evolutionary theory.

Attempts have been made to synthesize the two. The final pre-Christian endeavour in this direction was that by Philo of Alexandria (c20 BC–AD 50). Philo was a devout and learned Jew who was also deeply imbued with Greek culture, although as a Platonist the tendency of his philosophy was away from observational science.[1] His chief aim was to recommend Judaism to the respect, and if possible the acceptance of the Greeks. His method was to use a twofold interpretation of the Scriptures — the literal and the allegorical. He believed that the literal must be held fast, but sometimes the allegorical gave a truer sense. He allegorized Scripture to make it speak the language of Greek philosophy. Perhaps his best known allegory, because it is a defence of the use of pagan philosophy in Hebrew and Christian theology, is the one concerning the newly emancipated Jewish slaves who borrowed or asked jewels of the Egyptians before marching eastwards. Egyptian, explains Philo, means Greeks; and since jewels are precious possessions, they represent the precious Greek philosophy; that the Jews asked for and took them means that any child of God may make use of Greek philosophy.[2] Such a far-fetched interpretation underlines the difficulty of harmonizing the two systems.

Philo also developed the Stoic doctrine of the *logos* as a cosmic principle of order and harmony, seeing it as the pattern or power by which God impinged on the world, and the unifying principle behind the diversity of natural phenomena. Although a contemporary of Christ, his writings completely omit the changed concept of the logos which resulted from its application to Jesus as both the Creator[3] and the one who 'was made flesh and dwelt among us'.[4]

After Philo, the task of harmonizing the Scriptures with science fell on the Church, while Eastern Judaism moved farther and farther away from the direction which the New Testament had taken up in unfolding the spiritual elements of the Old.

The acceptance of Christianity as the religion of the Roman Empire was accompanied by a continuing decline in scientific effort. This seems to have been largely due to the influence of Augustine of Hippo (AD354–430). His immense theological prestige, derived from his systematization of Catholic doctrine, brought acceptance of his scientific views. These were derived largely from Neo-Platonism,

FIGURE 2.1. Epitome of the doctrine of macrocosm and microcosm. A series of concentric circles recalls the concentric spheres of the older astronomy with World, Year, and Man as centre. An outer circle bears the names of the four elements; within them are four seasons; and within them again the four humours. On either side of each element is the name of one of the 'qualities', caught in the strand that weaves together all the items of the theory. The outermost circle that is not caught in the web is the rampart between the world that we know and the heavenly world of which we have no direct knowledge.   Source: Singer 1966, page 135.

a philosophy developed by Plotinus (AD 207–270). As its name suggests, its main emphasis was on reviving Plato's philosophical ideas. These were distinctive in seeing introspection as the path to truth and in disdaining scientific observation. Plato saw mathematics as superior to other types of study because it was abstract and underived from anything in the visible world. Through Augustine's influence Neo-platonism came to dominate the Christian view of the natural world.

It viewed the world as a circle with man ('microcosm') at the centre and other circles concentrically outside this, in order: the four humours, the four seasons, and the four elements, the extremity being the universe ('macrocosm'). All were bonded together into a synthesis as shown on Figure 2.1. The centre contains the 'Idea', or 'Form', which is almost personified. This controls the natural world which, like all matter, is evil. This is almost personified. Matter is evil. It may at times break away from Idea and become involved in discord, strife, or even chaos, from which it can only return by further contact with Idea. Thus mankind must seek to free itself from contamination with matter.

The natural creation was seen as only a background to the human spiritual pilgrimage, not meriting independent enquiry. This view remained dominant for over 1,200 years, until the seventeenth century. It had the effect of subordinating scientific observation to ancient authority, causing it to be neglected.

The reversal of the medieval world-view was largely due to Thomas Aquinas (1227–74). He did two things. First, he completed the work of his teacher, Albertus Magnus, in reintroducing Aristotle into the University of Paris, then Europe's leading intellectual centre. Aristotle differed from Plato in being a keen observer, and some of his observations of phenomena such as climate and animals have remained of value to this day. His reintroduction re-established observation as a path to scientific truth. This met severe theological opposition because of the threat it posed to the Augustinian synthesis.

Secondly, Aquinas contended that observations of nature could proceed independently of faith because human reason was unaffected by the Fall. This made reason autonomous, allowed unfettered thought, and brought scientific advances, but tended to detach science from ethical moorings. This concept of autonomous human reason paved the way for the Renaissance. This began in Italy in the fourteenth century, reviving the intellectual perspectives of the classical age. Science became a popular cultural activity. The Renaissance was not anti-religious, but it revived the distinction between religious and secular knowledge which had become obscured in the Middle Ages. The medieval world had seen natural phenomena as secondary and derivative aspects of spiritual realities. Even Aquinas' reintroduction of Aristotle had made relatively little impact because it only formed a part of his total theological system. As time passed, the formulation and verification of scientific hypotheses gradually reduced the role of supernatural agencies. Explanations were strictly in thisworldly terms. This reduced the practical utility of religion although many scientists still found their inspiration from it.

The Reformation, with its return to Bible study, revived the distinction between Christianity and culture which the medieval synthesis had obscured. It also encouraged a wider range of independent thought. This contributed to the advance of observational science and free enquiry rather than appeals to the classics. Far from emphasis on the Bible being restrictive on scientific thought, it is notable how many prominent scientists had a Protestant background. When the Royal Society, for instance, was established in 1662, 90 per cent of its foundation members were Puritans or had Puritan connections.[5] No conflict was seen between science and Scripture.

The Enlightenment was the philosophical movement which followed in the eighteenth century. It came in the aftermath of the debilitating seventeenth century wars of religion, which had sunk the legal and moral authority of religious institutions and functionaries to a low ebb. It stressed the importance of reason and the critical reappraisal of existing ideas and social institutions. It witnessed significant scientific advances, notably Newton's theory of planetary motions. Newton was devoutly religious and wrote extensively on the Bible. But one consequence of these scientific discoveries was to emphasize a mechanical view of causation in nature. This tended to diminish the role of the supernatural in the popular estimation.

The Enlightenment further accelerated a separation of science from religious moorings by breaking the basic Christian consensus which the Reformation crisis had left fragile but intact. Christianity became not only ignored but actively contradicted. Critics such as Voltaire and Hume, although few in numbers, had a wide influence. The Christian world-view, although it remained dominant, ceased to be normative. The Enlightenment left a legacy of secular humanism, which has generally persisted as a dominant world-view to this day.[6] The effect of these historical processes was to leave an intellectual environment in which the Church had lost scientific influence and there was a weakened linkage between religious truth and scientific discovery. This further prepared the ground for the acceptance of the evolution theory.

2.2 THE BEGINNINGS OF THE EVOLUTION THEORY

We must now turn to the origins of the theory itself. The first person to set down an evolutionary explanation of the origin of species was Georges Buffon (1707–88). He saw geological strata as representing historical stages, and his idea that certain species had been lost allowed the study of palaeontology to proceed with a ready-made explanation of the large gaps between fossil and living forms.[7]

Lamarck (1744–1829) sought to discover a universal law which would incorporate all the various sciences into one great systematic materialistic framework. His central theme was that there were 'subtle and ever-moving fluids' which were 'excited' and by which the organs of animals were gradually adapted to their environment. These characteristics were then passed on to their offspring. He also believed that the continents had been built up by inundations of the sea and that nature had had unlimited time to accomplish her task of transforming living organisms. His view was thus materialistic. It differed both from the Darwinian theory and modern science in its belief in a speculative animal biochemistry which was able to effect the inheritance of acquired characteristics. For these reasons it has only historical interest today.

Georges Cuvier (1769–1832) became an authority on living and fossil animals. He rejected Lamarck's ideas on evolution, claiming that the fossil evidence did not show a consistent slow transformation of one species into another. He believed in a series of catastrophes after each of which animals were replaced by newly-created species.

Erasmus Darwin (1731–1802), grandfather of Charles, set out ideas of evolution similar to those of Lamarck in his book *Zoonomia*.[8] He believed that the universe had been formed from an initial explosion (analogous to the modern idea of the 'Big-Bang', which is conceived to have been the mighty explosion of matter which started the universe), and a belief in the continual transformation of animals from one species to another by adapting to their environment in a purposive way, without supernatural direction. His views were known as Darwinism even before his grandson Charles was born, but did not receive wide acceptance at the time. This was because they were not backed by a body of evidence such as that which Charles later sought to provide.

Robert Malthus (1766–1834) foreshadowed evolution theory with his study of populations.[9] Since humans can double their numbers at least once in twenty-five years, and since the supply of food can only increase in arithmetical ratio, it naturally follows that increase of population must always be checked by lack of food. But, except in cases of famine, this check is never operative, and control of population growth is due to 'moral restraint, vice, and misery'. The constant increase in population beyond the means of subsistence, drives down wages, increases the price of food, and has the effect of lowering the marriage and birth rates. This situation in turn stimulates renewed agricultural enterprise, increasing the means of subsistence. This swells the marriage and birth rates, raising the population, once again provoking a shortage of food, and so on. There are limits beyond which no population can be varied by breeding, and so the human race will not progress towards a perfect state but will be trapped in this cycle. When Darwin later came to formulate his theory, he was strongly influenced by this argument, but reached an opposite conclusion from it. Malthus believed that the only solution to population pressures on resources was moral restraint, which was also a Christian duty. Darwin, by contrast, concluded that the struggle for existence would enable the fittest to survive and produce a continual progression of improving species. He thus used Malthus's idea to point to conclusions almost the reverse of those which Malthus himself advocated.

In 1844 Robert Chambers published anonymously a book entitled *Vestiges of the Natural History of Creation* in which he set out evolutionary views, although he stated that the process was in control of 'the One Eternal and Unchangeable'. Today this would be called theistic evolution. The book was very popular. Four editions appeared in the first seven months and then it came out annually for the next ten years. It was strongly criticized at the time, but Darwin, in later editions of *Origin*, said it was a valuable precursor of his own work in calling attention to the subject, removing prejudice, and thus preparing the ground for analogous views.[10]

2.3 GEOLOGICAL PRECURSORS

The biblical time scale of a few thousand years appeared far too short for evolution to have operated. A time in millions of years was provided by the Uniformitarian Theory of geology.

The eighteenth century had seen a debate between *Neptunism* and *Vulcanism*, over the question of whether the oceans or volcanoes were the dominant force which had moulded the landscape. The former was advocated by Abraham Werner (1750–1817) who emphasized the mechanical and chemical action of flood waters. James Hutton (1726–97) taught the Vulcanist theory which emphasized the importance of heat on the earth's formation. Because both these theories involved vast, rather rapid, changes they were called *Catastrophist*. Hutton was also the original proposer of Uniformitarianism. This taught that sedimentary strata were laid down slowly over long periods by the ordinary forces of rain, frost, moving water, etc., acting as they do today. Hutton claimed that exposed strata are weathered and eroded into lakes or the sea, eventually settling to form new strata. These could be hardened by pressure and heat and uplifted to form new mountain areas, to commence the cycle all over again. This continuous cycle of events would take an immense time — millions of years.

Charles Lyell (1797–1875) first published his influential three-volume *Principles of Geology*, advocating the uniformitarian theory, in 1830. The book was immediately popular and in twenty years had led to its general acceptance and a rejection of Catastrophism. He was working on the twelfth edition when he died. It remains the basic background to geological teaching today. Its central theme is the uniformity of geological processes. In his conclusion to Volume 1 Lyell[11] categorically rejects a catastrophist view, but on moral rather than scientific grounds:

'Never was there a dogma more calculated to foster indolence, and to blunt the keen edge of curiosity, than this assumption of discordance between the ancient and existing causes of change. It produced a state of mind unfavourable in the highest degree to the candid acceptance of those minute but incessant alterations which every part of the earth's surface is undergoing. . . . For this reason all theories are rejected which involve the assumption of sudden and violent catastrophes and revolutions of the whole earth and its inhabitants — theories which are restrained by no reference to existing analogies, and in which the desire is manifested to cut, rather than patiently to untie, the Gordian knot.'

Uniformitarianism was made even more acceptable by the 'Tranquil Theory', first suggested by the Swedish botanist Carolus Linnaeus (1707–78) and introduced to the British public by John Fleming, Professor of Natural Philosophy in Aberdeen, in 1826.[12] This claimed that the Mosaic narrative taught only a gradual rise of flood waters, destroying neither soil nor vegetation. It was therefore quite reasonable to suppose that no traces of a biblical Flood remained.

2.4 CHARLES DARWIN

Charles Darwin was born in Shrewsbury on 12 February 1809, the same day as Abraham Lincoln. His maternal grandfather was Josiah Wedgwood, maker of the famous Wedgwood chinaware. His paternal grandfather was Erasmus Darwin, his father was a highly successful physician. As a young man Charles showed promise and aided his father in his duties. In 1825 he went to Edinburgh to study medicine. But he took no interest in his studies and was a failure. Looking for an alternative he was recommended to study theology. He went to Cambridge, but though he completed his degree, his interests had again drifted away and he decided not to be ordained. He later admitted that his time at Cambridge 'was wasted, as far as the academic studies were concerned, as completely as at Edinburgh and at school'.[13]

He became interested in geology in 1831 during his last year at Cambridge when he became friendly with Adam Sedgwick (1785–1873), the professor of Geology, who in that same year became a Fellow of the Royal Society and President of the Geological Society. Under Sedgwick's influence he was first a Catastrophist. He also became friendly with the Professor of Botany, the Reverend John Stevens Henslow, who recommended him for the post of naturalist on the *Beagle*, which was sailing to make more accurate navigational charts. He accepted the post. The voyage had a profound effect not only on his own life, but upon the whole subsequent history of science.

Just before he sailed, Henslow gave him a copy of the first volume of *Lyell's Principles of Geology* with the advice that he should not believe its contents! When reading the book, however, he became an enthusiastic convert and based all his interpretations of the geological formations he examined during the voyage on the uniformitarian theory.

His rapid acceptance of this theory is particularly strange as he later commented in his diary that 'everything betrays marks of extreme violence'. Similarly, having experienced an earthquake in Chile, he was particularly impressed by the enormous changes that could occur in a short time. However, in his publications he tended to play down earlier observations which conflicted with uniformitarianism.

Darwin was vigorous, and during the *Beagle* expedition displayed remarkable endurance, on one occasion walking fifteen miles on a hot day without food or water. He did, however, suffer considerably from seasickness on the voyage, and the illness he experienced during most of the rest of his life seems to have started at this time. Various biographers have attributed this ill-health to eye-strain, glandular disturbances, heart trouble, and the bite of an insect in South America; but in recent times it has become generally accepted that it was mental rather than physical. It seems more than a coincidence that it began in 1837 when he started the work which culminated, after much procrastination, in *The Origin of Species* twenty-two years later. It was perhaps most likely due to a combination of fear of hostile criticism, a desire for honour, and the psychological tension between the logic of his theory and his lingering religious convictions. His wife was very religious, and although they lived in harmony this was a difference between them.[14] From 1842 he passed his time at Down, Kent, as a country gentleman, devoting himself unremittingly, in spite of his ill-health, to his estate and to science. His second major book *The Descent of Man* was published in 1871. This derives the human race from a hairy quadrumanous animal belonging to the great anthropoid group, and related to the progenitors of the orangutan, chimpanzee, and gorilla. He died in 1882 and was buried in Westminster Abbey.

He is mainly remembered as the great leader of evolutionary biology. Though not himself the originator of the evolution hypothesis, nor even the first to apply the conception to particular plants and animals, he was undoubtedly the first thinker to win it a wide acceptance among biological experts. By adding to the crude evolutionism of Erasmus Darwin, Lamarck and others, his own idea of natural selection, he supplied the process with a convincing mechanism. This raised it at once from an interesting hypothesis to a veritable theory. His success was aided by his kindliness, honesty of purpose, devotion to truth and attachment to his friends, which made him as remarkable on the moral and emotional as on the intellectual side of his nature.

When considering the contributions of Lyell and Darwin, however, it is important to notice a point which applies to both — a tendency to make sweeping generalizations from rather limited data even in the face of contradictory evidence.

Concerning Lyell, Stephen Jay Gould, Professor of Geology at Harvard University, a prominent evolutionist, has commented:

'Charles Lyell was a lawyer by profession, and his book is one of the most brilliant briefs ever published by an advocate. . . . Lyell relied on two bits of cunning to establish his uniformitarian views as the only geology. First he set up a straw man to demolish . . . . The geological record does seem to require catastrophes: rocks are fractured and contorted; whole faunas are wiped out. To circumvent this literal appearance he argued for the imperfection of the record, claiming that we should interpolate into it what we cannot see. The catastrophists were the hard-nosed empiricists of their day, not the blinded theological apologists.

'Secondly, Lyell's uniformity is a hodgepodge of claims. One is a methodological statement that must be accepted by any scientist, catastrophist and uniformitarian alike. Other claims are substantive notions that have since been tested and abandoned. Lyell gave them a common name . . . and tried to slip the substantive claim (uniformitarianism) by with an argument that the methodological proposition (the need for careful analysis) had to be accepted.'[15]

Darwin is vulnerable to similar charges. First, he argues that the absence of 'missing links' between fossils are due to the imperfection of the record. Secondly, his rapid acceptance of Lyell's uniformitarianism conflicts with his observations. Then, having experienced the earthquake in Chile, he was particularly impressed by the enormous changes that could occur in a short time.

2.5 THE PUBLICATION OF *ORIGIN* AND ITS AFTERMATH

The publication of *The Origin of Species* was uncertain until the last moment. John Murray, the publisher, was induced by Lyell to go ahead with it, but retained serious doubts both of its scientific value and of its commercial viability. Darwin was himself very uncertain of its success and gave Murray complete freedom to withdraw from publishing the book, saying ' . . . though I shall be a little disappointed, I shall in no way be injured'.[16] When correcting the proofs, Darwin rewrote so much of it that he offered to pay Murray for the heavy costs of the amendments.

It finally appeared on 24 November 1959. The 1,250 copies printed sold out on the day of publication. This is not, however, as impressive as it sounds since they had all been taken up by dealers and book agents at Murray's annual sale a few days before.

The theory of evolution proposed by the book challenged the Bible account of origins in a way that no previous scientific theory had done. It was soon popularized by writers such as Charles Lyell, Herbert Spencer, Roderick Murchison, and Thomas Huxley. Huxley's nine-member 'X' Club assisted the process through its influence in appointing men to key university posts. In Germany the evolution message was spread by Ernst Haeckel and in America by Asa Gray.[17]

The critical point in its general acceptance is regarded as having come at the debate between Thomas Huxley and Bishop Samuel Wilberforce at the British Association for the Advancement of Science in Oxford in 1860. According to one account, Wilberforce finished his speech by enquiring of Huxley whether it was 'through his grandfather or his grandmother that he claimed his descent from a monkey?' Huxley murmured to Sir Benjamin Brodie sitting next to him, 'The Lord hath delivered him into mine hands', but refused to speak until the crowd was calling for him. Once on his feet he defended Darwin's views, but took advantage of the bishop's distasteful jibe by adding that if the choice was between an ape for a grandfather or man who misused his eloquence to introduce ridicule into a grave scientific discussion then he unhesitatingly affirmed his 'preference for the ape'.[18]

The exact words of both speakers are now uncertain but their effect is not. The encounter came to be viewed as a critical confrontation, where the Church had appeared to disadvantage and science had earned the right to lecture it.

Nevertheless, it was not unquestioned. Writers such as Cuvier, Linnaeus, and Richard Owen had always been sceptical of trans-specific evolution, and this scepticism continued in spite of its strong advocacy by Huxley, Herbert Spencer, and others. Also, the undesirable moral implications of the theory had been perceived from the very beginning.

Adam Sedgwick wrote to Darwin:

'There is a moral or metaphysical part of nature as well as the physical. A man who denies this is deep in the mire of folly. 'Tis the crown and glory of organic science that it *does*, through *final cause*, link material and moral. . . .'

Sedgwick believed that once science ceased to attribute the laws of nature to the will of God, but rather set them up as independent causes, then all sense of divine plan would be lost. There was a necessary link between natural laws and divine power. He continued:

'You have ignored this link; and, if I do not mistake your meaning, you have done your best in one or two pregnant cases to break it. Were it possible (which, thank God, it is not) to break it, humanity, in my mind, would suffer a damage that might brutalize it and sink the human race into a lower grade of degradation than any into which it has fallen since written records tell us of its history'.[19]

In the light of some of the events of the twentieth century, these words sound prophetic.

Sedgwick's fears were shared by Thomas Carlyle[20] and by some members of the Brethren Movement and the Free Evangelicals. These groups, among others, saw it as counter to biblical faith, though they were prepared to countenance the idea of an old earth by accepting the Gap Theory.[21]

2.6 CONDITIONS IN VICTORIAN BRITAIN FAVOURING THE ACCEPTANCE OF DARWINISM

Victorian Britain proved to be fertile soil for the widespread acceptance of Darwinism within about twenty years. There were a number of reasons for this. The intellectual climate was favourable. People accepted that most phenomena had natural causes, and Darwin's explanations, apparently supported by a mass of new and fascinating evidence, appeared scientific. The theory supplied a missing key to biology, which had been relatively backward in relation to other sciences. Social conditions were also favourable. The long peace following the Napoleonic wars had made for general optimism. This encouraged a belief in the inevitability of upward progress, even if it was gradual and spasmodic. The success of the free-market economy seemed to support the idea of natural selection. Also important was a relatively prosperous and independent scientific community with opportunities and inclination for worldwide travel and investigation.

Darwinian theory also had some backing from religious sources. The attack on the Bible from the Higher Critical angle had converted many Churches to the idea that religion had evolved from primitive origins. There was some popular condemnation of what appeared to be Christian prejudice against science. Wilberforce's stance at the British Association debate was seen as unscientific. Disbelief in evolution became associated with theological prejudice. This was probably helped by the comforting belief that a sinful act was not now something wicked and blameworthy, but a relic of animal ancestry.

2.7 MENDEL'S IMPACT ON THE THEORY

Gregor Mendel (1822–84) was an Austrian priest, subsequently becoming an abbot, who conducted numerous cross-breeding experiments on pea plants. He discovered that various characteristics (height, colour, etc.) appeared in first and second generation plants in accordance with simple mathematical proportions. Although the exact mathematics of these proportions has since been challenged, the general relationship has not.

But from the point of view of the evolution question, his other discovery is the most important. This was that although two parents pass on a variety of characteristics to their offspring, these characteristics cannot go beyond the limit of what was in the original genes. No amount of breeding can produce species with completely new characteristics. The heritable characters are stable and constant. Although they can skip one or more generations and then reappear, when they do they are just the same as they were before.

Darwin believed that evolution came about through continual small differences between individuals, the best of which were preserved by natural selection. Mendel's results confine this possibility within the limits of discrete groups. This was acknowledged by geneticists, and led to their proposing another mechanism. This relies on the fact that a *very* small proportion of offspring is noticeably different from the parents. These are called mutants. Their appearance is due to significant alterations of the genes of the parents. Although badly damaged cells are aborted, slightly damaged cells may live but possess some abnormality or disfigurement. It is these mutants which evolutionists claim may occasionally, under changing environmental conditions, be better adapted than the parents and thus propagate successfully. With further mutations, it is presumed that a new species will appear. This has so changed the basis of Darwin's theory that it is now called Neo-Darwinism. The possibility that such mutations can explain evolution is considered further in chapter 9.

2.8 SUMMARY

It is impossible to understand the impact of the theory of evolution on our society without considering its intellectual origins. It represents a culmination of a long history of thought. Its roots can be traced to the classical dichotomy between Greek science and Hebrew religion. Throughout history there has been a persistent urge to find a unitary philosophy which synthesized these two, but a continuing inability to achieve it. Attempts at synthesis were made by such thinkers as Philo, Augustine, and Aquinas. The first twelve centuries of the Christian era were characterized by the wide acceptance of Augustine's theological system which, while considering science to be the handmaid of theology, in fact discouraged the observation of nature.

The Renaissance was in part a reaction against this, and the subsequent developments of Western science have established and maintained its separation from theology. This separation was one of the factors facilitating the acceptance of the evolution theory by marginalizing theological objections.

The evolution theory represented a culmination of the work of a line of scientists among whom Buffon, Lamarck, Cuvier, Malthus, and Lyell are notable. Darwin's *Origin* appeared in 1859. It faced considerable criticism at first but won general acceptance through the advocacy of writers such as Herbert Spencer and Thomas Huxley, and through the generally favourable intellectual and social conditions in Victorian Britain, perhaps the most advanced society of its day.

The theory had to be modified in the light of Mendel's discovery of the genetic limits to heritable change within a population. It is now widely held in the form of Neo-Darwinism. This believes in evolutionary change through the natural selection of living forms possessing favourable mutations.

REFERENCES

[1] Singer 1966, page 133. [2] Tenney 1975, vol. 4, page 775. [3] John 1:3. [4] John 1:14. [5] Clark 1972a, pages 16, 17. [6] Gilbert 1980, pages 36-38. [7] Bowden 1982, page 10. [8] King-Hele 1977. [9] 1798. [10] 1875, 1898: Introduction. [11] 1892, pages 317, 318, quoted by Whitcomb and Morris 1974, page 96. [12] page 214. [13] Barlow 1958, page 58. [14] Davidheiser 1969, page 66. [15] 1975. [16] quoted by Bowden 1982, page 56. [17] Bowden 1982, pages 112-116. [18] quoted by Blackmore and Page 1989, page 103. [19] quoted from Blackmore and Page 1989, pages 109, 110. [20] Clark 1972b, page 96. [21] Bowden 1982, page 114.

CHAPTER 3

PHILOSOPHICAL PROBLEMS WITH EVOLUTION THEORY

3.1 SCIENTIFIC CREATIONISM: IS IT SCIENCE?

Since the theory of evolution has been widely accepted, creationism has often been condemned as unscientific. A useful way of considering whether this is so is to review the 'Arkansas trial' which centred around the definition of the phrase 'scientific creationism'.

In the 1970s creationists had participated in debates with prominent evolutionists on many university campuses, and a few became politically active in sponsoring legislation in numerous American states that would require public schools to teach creation along with evolution in science classes, if either view is taught. The State of Arkansas passed such a bill (Act 590) in 1981.

A teacher brought a legal action against the State of Arkansas because it prevented him from teaching evolution in the class-room without also teaching scientific creation (McLean vs Arkansas). He charged that the latter was not scientific because it prejudged the results of science by importing religious dogma. Against this, the defence maintained that it was as scientific as evolution.

According to Section 4 of the Arkansas law, scientific creationism includes the following beliefs:

1. Sudden creation of the universe, energy, and life from nothing.

2. Insufficiency of mutation and natural selection to explain the occurrence of living forms.

3. Changes of species only ocurring within fixed limits.

4. Separate ancestry for man and apes.

5. Explanation of geology by catastrophism including a world-wide flood.

6. Relatively recent inception of the earth and living kinds.

In his judgement on the case, Judge Overton opined that for educational purposes creationism should *not* be given equal consideration with evolution because the former was religious teaching under the guise of science, and not amenable to the Popperian test of falsifiability. It was therefore a breach of the US Constitution.

He supported this view by identifying five properties requisite for scientific knowledge, which scientific creationism did not fulfil:

1. It is guided by natural law.
2. It has to be explanatory by reference to natural law.
3. It is testable against the empirical world.
4. Its conclusions are tentative (that is, are not necessarily the final word).
5. It is falsifiable.

This judgement was arguably unjust to creationism. It *does* fulfil these criteria, certainly as well as does evolutionism. The first two conditions require only law-likeness and explanatory ability. These characterize creationism as much as evolutionism. All the last three criteria (testability, revisability and falsifiability) can be met merely by a creationist saying, 'I will abandon my views if we find a living specimen of a species intermediate between apes and man.' The real question is not whether scientific creationism is scientific but whether the existing evidence provides stronger arguments for evolutionary theory than for creationism.[1]

To make a scientific decision, the two theories should be tested against each other. Gish[2] suggests that such a test could involve three steps:

1. Present creation and evolution in the form of models,
2. Make predictions based on each model,
3. Compare actual scientific evidence with these predictions.

Fossils are the key, specifically the presence or absence of 'missing links'. Their non-existence is probably decisive because the evolutionary model would require an inconceivably great number of them.

3.2 PRIMARY AND SECONDARY CAUSES

One of the main features commending the evolution theory is that it is seen as being capable of giving a complete explanation of the world in a way that creationism cannot. After the Big Bang, the evolution to modern humans is seen as a continuous natural process, at no point requiring the intervention of the supernatural. Although natural causes clearly cannot explain the origin of the universe, it is thought that they can explain such events as the origin of life and its subdivision into major forms.

But this view cannot be sustained. All these changes are dramatic contrasts with anything that could have preceded them. They must be regarded *origin events* which cannot be explained by the routine operation of natural laws. Secondary causes are not enough. Matter must have had a primary cause, and this must have been under conditions in which the known laws of physics were not valid, and as a product of forces which we cannot discover. The spontaneous generation of life on Earth is so obviously unlikely that it has sometimes been suggested that it must have come from outer space. But even if true, this would merely push the argument back one stage. The incoming life must have started somewhere. The same difficulty occurs when trying to explain the origins of the main subdivisions of the plant and animal kingdoms. The evidence is strongly against these having happened without the intervention of outside intelligence. A belief in uniformitarianism actually makes origin events more difficult rather than easier to explain. This is because the more regular have events been, the more singular and contrasting must origins have been. Origin events are singularities and therefore are not amenable to methods of study which apply to regularities. They must be approached through *origin science*, not *operation science*.

This confusion of origin with operation followed from the discoveries of Galileo, Kepler, and Newton, which generally established a mechanical view of causation of natural phenomena. These scientists had confined their explanations of the motions of the planets around the sun to secondary causes, but as time passed these explanations came increasingly to be extended to include those of primary causes, such as that originating the universe. The role of primary causation of the various origin events was therefore gradually squeezed out of the scientific study of the past. As time passed, the astronomers discovered more and more secondary causes and continually reduced the place of primary causes. Hutton, Lyell, and others did the same thing for geology, and Darwin for biology. The key principles of this secondary causality were uniformity, continuity, and secondary causality. The legitimate search for secondary causes in operation science was inappropriately applied to origin science.

Believers in the divine origin of the universe, however, undermined their own case by appealing to the supernatural to explain anomalies in its operation, because when natural explanations were found the objection looked absurd. This happened, for instance, when science revealed the true explanations of phenomena such as meteors and earthquakes.

The necessity for invoking primary causes to explain origins argues strongly for creationism. Just as the earlier scientific advances, by explaining astronomical phenomena in terms of secondary causes opened the way to a decline of creationism, so today's emphasis on a cataclysmic origin to the universe may open the way for its resurgence. As the emphasis on secondary causes which started with astronomy was extended to geology and biology, a renewed emphasis on astronomical catastrophism could encourage primary cause explanations in these latter sciences also.[3]

3.3 THE ARGUMENT FROM ENTROPY

The first law of thermodynamics states that although energy can be converted from one form to another, the total amount remains unchanged. Energy is neither being created nor destroyed at the present time.

The second law states that although the total amount of energy in any closed mechanical system remains unchanged, there is always a tendency for it to become less available for future work. Put another way, where energy conversions are accomplishing work the entropy (that is, the non-availability of the energy) increases. This applies to all geological, physical, and biological systems. They tend towards increasing disorder and disorganization.

These two laws are accepted by physicists as perhaps the most secure generalizations from experience that exist. One can apply them to any concrete situation in the confidence that nature will not let one down. It is not too much to state that they provide the foundation for modern science and technology.

Certain consequences follow. First, if energy cannot be added or subtracted, it must originally have been created. This requires an external cause — a creator. Secondly, the entropy law contradicts the central evolutionary affirmation that life forms can evolve upwards towards increasing complexity. The biological evidence is at least as strongly indicative of degeneration and diminution in the size of living things as it is of their refinement and enlargement.

Some evolutionists have sought to refute the obvious challenge of the law of entropy by contending that it applies only to closed systems, whereas the Earth is an open system since it interacts with the Sun, Moon, and other bodies in space, receiving and emitting energy and matter. It forms, however, a small part of an infinitely large closed system to the which the entropy law applies. There is no evidence of a source *within* this large closed system which could or did provide the information needed to effect the upward evolution of life forms. It needed an external source which transcended the thermodynamic laws.

It is also contended that within a universe proceeding towards entropy there must be local inversions towards greater complexity, which could explain evolutionary processes. It is hard to find any instance of this which does not owe its increased complication to prior information. An example sometimes quoted is the crystallization of minerals, where order appears to emerge from disorder. But this is not a spontaneous movement using new information. The crystallization process is purely chemical and consists in the repetition of a simple pattern which has been predetermined by the arrangement of atoms in the mineral's molecule. It contrasts sharply with the biological reproduction of DNA or proteins where the repeating unit is highly complex and stores much information in its structure.

3.4 SUMMARY

There are three significant philosophic problems which affect the creation/evolution debate: a. is creationism scientific? b. are origins amenable to study by conventional scientific methods? and c. can evolutionism be harmonized with themodynamic laws?

Although the Arkansas trial rejected the idea that creationism was as scientific as evolutionism, an examination of the two views shows that they largely meet the same criteria.

There are some primary events in Earth's history which are not amenable to explanation by secondary causes. These include the origin of matter, the origin of life, and the separation of the main branches of the plant and animal kingdoms. These demand an approach to study which considers the fundamentals of primary causation. The concept that living things have evolved from simple to complex cannot be reconciled with the law of entropy which teaches the inevitability of deterioration in any closed thermodynamic system. The Earth forms a minute part of such a system and the entropy law applies to the whole. There is no evidence of a source of information within it that can explain an upward evolution of living things.

REFERENCES
[1] Laudan 1988. [2] 1988. [3] Geisler and Anderson 1987, page 120.

PART II

THE SCIENTIFIC CASE FOR CREATIONISM

CHAPTER 4

ASTRONOMICAL ARGUMENTS FOR THE GENESIS RECORD

4.1 THE ORIGIN OF THE UNIVERSE

Astronomy has always been important in the study of origins. When we look up at the heavens we cannot help asking 'How did it all start, When? Where? Why?' These questions have exercised philosophers and scientists for thousands of years. The Bible gives definite, but not exhaustive, instruction about them. Modern astronomy has answered many questions. Every answered question opens the door to at least two more. Most data can be seen to accord with the biblical explanation of origins. But there are a number of issues where disagreement remains.

Although the idea has recently come under increasing fire, most scientists believe that the universe began with the Big Bang. It is thought that all matter was first concentrated in an intensely hot super-dense core. This was a mix of strongly interacting elementary particles composed mainly of mesons, protons, and neutrons with a smaller proportion of photons and the lighter-weight muons, electrinos and neutrinos. At the near-instantaneous origin of time, there was an annihilation of heavier elementary particles into gamma radiation resulting in a huge fireball. The light-weight particles annihilated each other, continuing the fireball. The fireball stage ended as radiation decoupled from matter. Quasars and clusters of galaxies condensed. Finally, galaxies and stars formed, and are still forming today.[1]

The fragments of the explosion formed astral bodies whose character depended on their size. In order of increasing magnitude these are: brown dwarfs, white dwarfs, neutron stars, and black holes.

As White[2] has pointed out, this scenario, although it helps explain some of the observed phenomena, suffers from a number of scientific difficulties which make it untenable.

1. If the original super-dense mass was of the size hypothesized, it would collapse rather than explode because the force of gravity would be so great that even photons could not escape. It would become a black hole. That this did not happen calls the whole idea of the original mass into question.

2. One of the implications of the Big Bang is that galaxies should be moving away from each other at velocities proportional to the distances separating them. This was apparently supported by Edwin Hubble's discovery in 1924 that when the light from distant galaxies was studied spectroscopically, the absorption lines of the elements were not seen at their usual wave length but were shifted towards the red end of the spectrum, a sort of Doppler shift of light. This is analogous to the 'Doppler' effect which lowers the pitch of a receding sound like a siren in proportion to its rate of movement away from us. Light behaves in the same way as sound. If it is moving away from us the pitch of the light drops, just like the sound of the siren, and betrays a red shift. Hubble and others claimed that the amount of this 'red shift' was a. directly proportional to the velocity with which the galaxies were receding, and b. that the more distant the galaxy, the greater the observed 'red shift', that is, the greater its velocity.

However, the 'red shift' may be due to other things than the recession of galaxies. It could be due either to the mutual collisions of photons and the depletion of their energy when acting over long distances[3] or to a decrease in the speed of light.[4]

3. Quasars, faint objects with very large red shifts, appear to be very far from the Earth. Their brightness can, however, be seen to change within the space of a day. They must therefore be less than one light-day across. But if they were as far away as the red shift indicates, it is impossible for an object of such size to radiate energy at so great a rate. Therefore, they must be much closer than the

red shift indicates. But if this is so, the red shift cannot be a reliable indicator of distance. Since some quasars have been observed with as many as five red shifts it is impossible to know which of these can be used in order to calculate distance. Finally, radio telescopes show that some quasars appear to expand at two or three times the speed of light. But the Theory of Relativity tells us that nothing can exceed the speed of light, if the quasars are actually at the distances indicated by their red shifts. Therefore the red shift again appears an unreliable guide to distance and therefore to the question of whether and how much the universe is expanding.[5]

4. The Big Bang theory would indicate that the chemical composition of stars should change considerably with time as they evolve from one type to another. But the spectra of a variety of stars of widely different supposed ages shows their atmospheric composition to be relatively similar and to resemble that of the Sun.

'Bo' stars are, according to the evolutionary scheme, thought to have formed only a few million years ago. On the other hand, red giant stars and extra-galactic nebulae are thought to be among the oldest objects in the universe and hence seven or more billion years old. Other stars are intermediate between these. All, however, have similar chemical compositions. This shows that the interstellar matter of which they are composed can hardly have changed at all since their formation. There is a serious lack of evidence for chemical evolution. For instance, the sun, a very young 'Bo' star, *Tau Scorpii*, planetary nebulae, a giant red *Epsilon Virginis*, and many other 'normal' stars all have the same chemical composition, within the limits of observational error. This is significant because the alleged ages of these objects cover the whole history of the Milky Way (our galaxy). The most reasonable explanation is that all were formed at the same time a few thousand years ago, since when there has been no time for differences in chemical composition to take place.[6]

4.2 THE INHOMOGENEITY OF THE UNIVERSE

The standard Big Bang scenario includes an inflationary phase at a very early epoch in the existence of the universe. At that time the universe expanded very rapidly and the foundation for the subsequent formation of stars and galaxies was laid. However, for galaxies to form, the universe must have possessed some degree of inhomogeneity. Small inhomogenities became the nuclei around which galaxies later formed.

Today's background radiation in the universe is 2.8 degrees Kelvin, known as '3 K radiation'. If it is the residue of the Big Bang from that early period, it must also show such inhomogeneities. This is not observed. The 3 K radiation is very homogeneous at all scales.

This poses a serious problem for the Big Bang theory.

4.3 THE ORIGIN OF THE SOLAR SYSTEM

When we turn to the smaller scale of our own solar system, we find other evidence to show that it is relatively young, with an age measured in thousands rather than millions of years.

The solar system consists of the Sun and the nine planets which revolve around it: Mercury, Venus, Earth, Mars, Jupiter, Saturn, Uranus, Neptune, and Pluto. There are also smaller bodies called asteroids, mainly between the orbits of Mars and Jupiter, meteoroids (small particles of rock and dust), and comets.

Various theories have been proposed for the formation of the planets. The *nebular hypothesis* of Kant and Laplace pictured a hot rotating disc of gas from which the planets were formed when gaseous rings were detached by centrifugal force from the main body of the sun during the early stages of its contraction. This theory was abandoned by the end of the nineteenth century when it was shown that such gaseous rings could never condense into planets and even if they did they could not have retained 98% of the angular momentum of the solar system which the planets do today.

The Laplacian theory was followed by various *encounter* or *planetesimal* theories which postulated the near approach of another star to our Sun to draw out and distribute the material of the planets. But these too were largely abandoned as inadequate by about 1940.

Beginning in 1944 a number of authors attempted to avoid the difficulties of the planetesimal theories by returning to a form of nebular hypothesis, whereby the Sun and its planets condensed out of interstellar clouds of gas and dust, which were rotating in eddies.

There are so many difficulties with this hypothesis that it cannot be sustained. They are as follows:

1. Before any condensation of gas and dust could occur, the nebula would have dispersed into outer space. Before gravitational attraction could become significant, the particles would have to be as big as the Moon. The theory also assumes that particles would stick together as they collide, but this does not occur in dust storms or any other known situation.

2. It is difficult to conceive that the rotating eddies could have survived long enough to get the condensation of the building material for the planets under way before they would have dispersed or fallen into the Sun.

3. There is no obvious reason why this process, if it has once started, would not end in the formation of one large body rather than our planetary system. The Sun already makes up 99.8% of the mass of the solar system. What preserved the other 0.2% from the same fate?

4. These theories cannot explain why the Sun with over 99% of the mass of the solar system has only 2% of its angular momentum (spin). Although astronomers do have explanations of how the proto-sun lost its angular momentum, the conditions under which this might have occurred are highly speculative. It is equally difficult to explain why the converse applies between the planets and their moons, most of the angular momentum in each planet-moon system being in the planet.

5. Some planets and some of their moons have motions

which are extremely hard to harmonize with hypotheses that they came out of the Sun or that they were formed from an original rotating mass. Uranus and Venus have retrograde rotations in relation to the direction of their orbits, and no less than eleven of the thirty-two satellites also do so, as shown in Table 4.1. It has been suggested that such retrograde motions are due to the bodies having been accidentally captured from elsewhere, but the large number with this characteristic argues against this.

TABLE 4.1 **Number of moons in the solar system with retrograde orbits in comparison with the total number.**

SATELLITE	NO OF MOONS	MOONS WITH RETROGRADE ORBITS
Earth	1	nil
Mars	2	nil
Jupiter	12	outer 4
Saturn	9	outer 1
Uranus	5	all 5
Neptune	2	inner 1

6. The current theories are not able to explain comets. These cannot be aged in millions of years. This is because the vaporized matter in their tails is lost at a rate which would end the life of all short-period comets in less than about 10,000 years, and all known comets in less than say 100,000 years. It has been proposed, in order to explain the presence of comets, that there was a cloud of numerous long-term comets orbiting the solar system effectively in 'cold storage' in outer space, but this is only speculation for which there is no evidence.[7]

7. The composition of the planets is substantially different from the Sun and other stars and so must have had a different origin. Only about 1% of the Sun's mass consists of any elements except hydrogen and helium. On Earth and the other planets these elements are minor constituents. One suggested explanation is that the effects of

sunlight removed these two gases from the planets, but this is entirely speculative and does not explain why any remains in them at all. The Big Bang theory claims that all elements were built up in the first few minutes, and the fleeing matter thereafter formed stars, planets and galaxies. The process of building the elements must have been by neutron capture. But a serious problem with this is the absence of any stable atom of mass 5 or of mass 8. It is not clear how the build-up of elements could have got past these gaps. The process could not go beyond helium 4, and even if it spanned this gap it would be stopped again at mass 8. In short, if neutron capture were the only process by which elements could be built, starting with hydrogen, the build-up would get no further than helium.[8]

4.4 METEORIC DUST

Another indication for a young Earth and Moon is the amount of meteoric dust that falls onto their surfaces. In the Earth's atmosphere there are about 28.6 million tons of this material, half of which settles to the Earth's surface and is replaced from outer space each year.[9] If the Earth were four and a half thousand million years old, this would give a layer 16.5 metres thick on its surface, and much in the oceans. It would be recognizable because it contains about 2.5% of nickel. Amounts of nickel on Earth, in the ocean or on the ocean floor are, however, much lower than this model would require. The oceans, for instance, only contain some 9,000 years' accumulation at this rate.[10]

The argument that any dust falling would have been dispersed and thus lost from the calculations cannot apply to the Moon where there is no wind or moving water. Far from there being 16.5 metres of dust on its surface, there was less than 2.5 centimetres even in the low lying 'mare' in which Neil Armstrong landed, where some gravity accumulation might have been expected.

More fundamentally, in the hypothesized five-billion-year time span, all dust in the solar system should long ago have disappeared into the Sun, whose gravity causes particles in space to slow down and fall into it. This sweeping effect would at present rates have cleared the whole solar system of dust as far as Pluto in two-and-a-half million years.[11]

4.5 A CHANGE IN THE SPEED OF LIGHT?

The calculation of distances of objects in space is based on an assumed constant speed of light (c). This constancy over time is fundamental to astronomical measurements and to many atomic constants. Any change would cause 'light years' to represent different distances at different times.

Norman and Setterfield have recently presented a strong case that the speed of light has decreased. One hundred and sixty-three measurements by sixteen different methods over 300 years appear to show a decay from 307,600 ± 5400 km/s in 1675 to 299,792.458 ± about .004 km/s in 1975. They claim that this decrease is not explainable by experimental error and is real. The rate of decrease appears not to have been constant but to have diminished from the first observation until it tapered off to a constant in about 1960.[12] If the post-1675 trend is extrapolated backwards in time beyond that date, c could have been very much higher in the past. To find a scientific explanation for these anomalies, Setterfield programmed a computer to search for the best curve to fit the data. It gave a curve in which the speed of light increased backwards in time and approached infinity in about 4,000 BC, a suggestive date in view of Ussher's biblical chronology.

Other physical constants depend on the speed of light and must change if it does. Every one of those tested by Setterfield showed the trend which would be predicted if c were decreasing.

If confirmed, this theory would have wide-ranging implications. Radioactive decay rates are a function of the speed of light. If c was greater in the past, decay products would be produced more rapidly, exaggerating the age shown by decay measurements. It is sometimes said that the universe must be old because of the time required for the light we now see to travel to us from distant galaxies. A faster speed of light would automatically reduce the validity of this view.

A much increased speed of light in the past would have caused the oldest stars at the centre of galaxies to experience much higher rates of radioactivity. This would have made the more massive stars explode as supernovas and the smaller ones become red giants. Most of the emitted energy would have been in the form of X-rays which, when shifted ten million times lower in frequency as c decreased, would account for today's 3 K background radiation, which is conventionally explained as being a residue from the Big Bang.

Superluminals are composed of material in space doing the apparently impossible by moving at many times the speed of light. If c was much greater in the past, these would represent events which occurred when light was much faster which we are only now seeing because of their distance.

The concept of the expanding universe, because it is based on the 'red shift', also supports the idea of a decay in the speed of light. Light moves in waves. The distance between the crest or trough of any wave to the midpoint is called the amplitude. The equations demand that, for a decay in c, the amplitude energy increases. This means that the crests must heighten and the troughs deepen as c decays. However, for energy to be conserved with light in transit, the wave amplitudes must grow at the expense of the wave length. Energy is therefore taken from the wave length which gets longer or redder since longer wave lengths have less energy. As c decays, therefore, a red shift will occur in light from distant objects. The further away those objects are, the more c has decayed and the greater will be the resultant red shift. Therefore, far from indicating an expanding universe, the red shift can give evidence for slowing c and slowing atomic processes.[13]

These studies had some confirmation from other workers. In 1984 van Flandern showed that the atomic clock was slowing down relative to astronomical time. Troitskii of the Radiophysical Research Institute, Gorky, concluded that light was initially up to 10^{10} times its present value and that radioactive decay rates are affected. He independently suggested that c decay accounts for the red shift, the even distribution of the relict background radiation and of superluminal speed in quasars.[14]

If verified, a change in the speed of light also has implications for the fossil record. Any increase in c would also increase what are called 'transport constants' which affect such properties as viscosity, diffusion, osmosis, and the speed of ions and electrons. This would affect many living things.

A larger value of c would increase the efficiency of plant growth helping to explain its luxuriance in parts of the fossil record and therefore the vast deposits of hydrocarbons which resulted from this. The leaves of plants would not have needed to be so large to trap the sun's energy. It is interesting that many fossil plants, especially in Carboniferous rocks, have very few leaves, or needle-like ones.

Lower viscosities and higher diffusion would have made breathing and blood flow easier in animals and humans, thus increasing oxygen intake and reducing the strain on the heart. This could have far-reaching effects on digestive and brain activity and might help explain the large body size of some fossil creatures and insects and the longevity of the biblical patriarchs.[15]

There have, however, been strong criticisms of the reliability of Norman and Setterfield's assumptions and calculations. Aardsma[16] claimed that their data have margins of error too great for firm conclusions and that they rely too much on the earliest measurements by Roemer in 1675 and Cassini in 1693 and 1736 where possible errors of interpretation are greatest. He also points out that a change in the speed of light by the amounts proposed would have strongly affected radiocarbon dating of ancient objects of known age. The radiocarbon dates, for instance, of an Egyptian funerary ship at 1845–31 BC, and the Dead Sea Scrolls at 135 BC–AD 68 agree with archaeological data. If the decay of c has been at the rates suggested by Norman and Setterfield, the former would have been dated at about AD 600, the latter at about AD 800. Holt[17] argued that the consistency of pulsar signals is against the idea that c has changed. Most criticism has centred on the unreliability of the authors' statistical analyses and of the risk of extrapolating data from 300 years over several thousand. For instance, Humphreys[18] questioned the reliability of the data from the earliest observations and the statistical methods used. Reeves[19] questioned both the assumptions and the methods, and Brown[20] the reliability of the calculations.

Setterfield[21] replied to these criticisms, pointing out that Troitskii[22] independently agreed with his conclusions and claimed an initial value of c was of the order of 10,000 million times its current value. He also pointed to logical flaws in Holt's argument from pulsars and mathematical mistakes in that by Brown.

There must remain, however, some doubt about the statistical rigour of Norman and Setterfield's analysis and a discrepancy between a radiocarbon dating based on the presumption of a constant speed of light, which agrees with archaeology, and one based on the speed-change idea which does not.

4.6 SUMMARY

The origin of the universe has of recent years generally been ascribed to a Big Bang, partly on evidence from the red shift that it appears to be expanding. A composite mass of matter of requisite size would, however, have been more likely to collapse than to explode in a bang. Evidence for a possible change in the speed of light and for the relative proximity quasars calls into question the validity of the red shift as an indicator of distance and movement. The absence of chemical evolution in stars argues against their being very old.

There is no satisfactory evolutionary explanation for the origin of the solar system. Current theories depend on either a mass of gas which contracts into sun and planets, or on the extraction of material from the proto-sun by a near-passing star. It is not possible to harmonize either of these ideas with a. the far-flung arrangement of the planets, b. the large proportion of the angular momentum of the solar system that they contain, c. the reverse rotations of some planets and the reverse orbits of some moons, and d. the differences in chemical composition between the Sun and planets. There is too little dust on the Earth or the Moon for their hypothesized multi-million-year ages.

There is some debated evidence for a change in the speed of light. This, if verified, would have wide implications for the origin and age of the universe and solar system.

REFERENCES

[1] Slusher 1974. [2] 1978. [3] Kofahl and Segraves 1975, page 153. [4] Norman and Setterfield 1987, pages 57, 58. [5] White 1978, page 62. [6] Slusher 1974; White 1978, page 68. [7] White 1985, pages 80, 81. [8] Fowler 1956. [9] Whitcomb and Morris 1974, pages 379, 380; Andrews 1982, pages 117, 118. [10] Morris 1976, page 153. [11] White 1978, pages 58, 59. [12] Setterfield 1983, Norman and Setterfield 1987, pages 11-29; Bowden 1988. [13] Norman and Setterfield 1987, page 85. [14] 1987, quoted by Bowden 1988. [15] Bowden 1991, pages 146, 147. [16] 1988. [17] 1988. [18] 1988. [19] 1992. [20] 1988b. [21] 1989. [22] 1987.

CHAPTER 5

THE ORIGIN OF LIFE

5.1 SPONTANEOUS GENERATION

The origin of life is, with the origin of the universe and the origins of the major classes of living things, one of the three fundamental questions which evolution sets out to answer.

The Earth is thought to be about 4,500 million years old. The earliest fossil algae are found in rocks said to be about 3,500 million years old. It is generally believed that life began spontaneously during this 1,000 million-year interval by chemical action on non-living matter. However, organic materials are being found in increasingly early rocks, so the time available for the origin of life is tending to be reduced. It would have required the presence of a 'primeval soup' containing the basic organic elements.

Since it is impossible to reproduce the conditions that existed on the primeval Earth, this topic can only be studied by proposing mechanisms which can be tested for feasibility in part by laboratory experiments and by computer simulation.

Laboratory experiments have shown that it is possible to synthesize simple organic molecules. It is done by heating carbon dioxide (CO_2), methane (CH_4), ammonia (NH_3) and hydrogen (H_2) in the presence of water and energizing the process by electrical discharges or ultraviolet radiation. This process formed products such as hydrogen cyanide (HCN) and formaldehyde (H_2CO) which, in aqueous solution, generated the four major classes of small organic molecules found in cells: amino acids, nucleotides, sugars, and fatty acids. The first two associated to form large polymers, the most important being polypeptides and polynucleotides. The former are proteins, the latter are ribonucleic acids (RNA) and deoxyribonucleic acids (DNA). According to the evolutionary model some of the polymers of RNA must have been able to direct their own replication.

At least two more steps would be needed before the formation of the first cell:

1. the development of mechanisms by which an RNA molecule could direct the synthesis of a protein.

2. the assembling of a membrane to enclose the self-replicating mixture of RNA and protein molecules.

At a later stage DNA could have taken the place of RNA as the material involved in heredity.

Then, it is believed, about 1.5 billion years ago the small simple cells called *procaryotes* (including bacteria) gave rise to the more complex *eucaryotic cells*, which have separate nuclei and cytoplasm such as are found in plants and higher animals.

Procaryotes have existed alongside eucaryotes ever since. In fact, study of the molecular biology of mitochondria which are responsible for oxidative phosphorylation (the production of chemical energy for the cell to use) strongly suggests that they originated as procaryotic cells which infected eucaryotes and developed a symbiotic relationship with them.

It is assumed that the eucaryotic cells were able to express their hereditary information in many different ways and that they could function co-operatively as a single organism. They generated multicellular organisms whose cell types were differentiated into internal and external cells, nerve cells, muscle cells, and connective cells.

The same fundamental strategies are thought to have developed an increasing number of specialized cell types and different methods of co-ordination between them. Most notable in higher animals are the vetebrate immune system which can produce myriads of different protein antibodies, and the nervous system which in higher animals can modify itself through nerve cells altering their connections.[1] Immune systems and nervous systems are very special because they are capable of much adaptation to the environment within an individual rather than evolving over generations.

Today research into the origins of life centres around three approaches:

a. Speculations about feasible mechanisms which could explain the sequence outlined above,

b. Reproduction of small parts of the mechanisms in the laboratory,

c. Computer simulations of the possible processes of natural selection.

It is virtually impossible to believe that processes of this complexity could have occurred by chance. All the laboratory experiments quoted above were under highly controlled conditions, which are extremely unlikely to have occurred together in nature. Polymerization of amino acids and/or DNA molecules, for instance, would have required either anhydrous conditions or special catalytic molecules. There is no evidence that either existed.

The gap between the 'primeval soup' (assuming it ever existed) and the simplest living cell is immense. A cell has enormous complexity. Its origin by natural inorganic processes would have involved an inconceivably unlikely feat of self-organization. And it would have needed to occur in the brief period of viability of the first proto-cell.

The spontaneous generation of life would have required all the following components simultaneously at the start so that they could work interactively:

a. DNA (deoxyribonucleic acid), the 'double helix'.

b. Four nitrogenous bases in abundance: adenine, guanine, cytosine, and thiamine.

c. DNA polymerase: enzymes which make and copy DNA.

d. Ribonucleoside phosphates, for the 'backbone' of the strands of DNA.

e. RNA polymerase, which copies DNA to RNA.

f. A supply of amino acids.

g. Aminoacyl-RNA polymerase ribozomes: a complex molecular structure which, in combination with transfer

RNA, reads gene codes in RNA and translates them into protein molecules.

In addition the following would probably be necessary:

h. a cell membrane

i. a constant supply of energy.

The chances of these occurring in combination by random processes are negligible. So far scientists have been able to synthesize only a, b, d, and f above under laboratory conditions.

The mere citing of these characteristics of living things indicates the enormous gap between organic and non-organic materials. The simplest living cell in its overall chemical plan is the same as that of all other living beings. There is no hint that any biological groups are transitional in character. At a molecular level each class is unique, isolated, and unlinked by intermediates; no organism is ancestral, primitive, or advanced compared to its relatives. Nothing in our knowledge can lead us to believe that primeval matter had or could develop the properties of living things.

A final consideration concerns the atmosphere surrounding the hypothesized primeval soup. It is thought that an essential condition for the generation of life by the processes described above is that it would have been chemically reducing (that is, with no free oxygen). This is because oxygen would quickly have oxidized any organic molecules formed. Also, had ozone (O_3) been abundant in the atmosphere it would have shielded the Earth from the ultraviolet rays which are thought to have provided the energy for the process.[2]

The evidence is against there having been a reducing atmosphere. The Earth's crustal rock is highly oxygenated. Ultraviolet light would have caused the rapid production of free oxygen from water vapour, leading to the escape of the hydrogen from the Earth's gravity. Even if a reducing atmosphere did exist, it is more than doubtful that life could have begun. There is no evidence today that plant life can arise from anaerobic photosynthesis.

All this points to the fact that the quantum leap from non-life to life would require not only the presence of material components, energy, and time in the right proportions in the right ambient atmosphere, but also the input of intelligent design. We cannot place the chemicals of life in a mixer, add unintelligent and undirected energy, and obtain life. Know-how (information, concept, logos) must always be added.

5.2 FIRST DEVELOPMENT OF LIFE

If for the moment we accept the evolutionary assumption that life could have occurred spontaneously, we must also accept that once formed it would continue to develop and multiply. This is by no means tenable.

Any development of life beyond the first cell would have required an abundance of oxygen a. to build further living cells and b. to provide an ozone layer to filter out the destructive ultraviolet radiation from the Sun. The absence of such screening would probably have had a lethal effect on any living organisms. No life could exist on Earth today without it.

Such oxygen could only have come from plants. It is not possible to see how they could have given off oxygen quickly enough to prevent the ultraviolet rays from sterilizing any living matter that had developed. Our present supply of green plants would require 5,000 years to double the present level of atmospheric oxygen.

Further, any early evolution of life could only have been possible if all the stages worked without a hitch. A failure at any one stage would have precluded any further stage. No such step-wise progress could have worked without outside control and information. Complex systems cannot be approached gradually through functional intermediates because of the necessity of perfect co-adaptation of their components as a condition of function.[3]

Finally, living creatures have two further levels of complexity which effectively rule out the possibility of chance development:

1. They all incorporate near-miraculous capabilities of reproduction and self-repair.

2. The human mind can be conceptually creative. Humans can, for instance, breed plant and animal species and construct machines which can do tasks far beyond their own capacities. This creativity holds the potential for maintaining a pace of improvements from generation to generation.

5.3 SUMMARY

Evolutionary theory depends on the possibility that life was generated on Earth by spontaneous chemical action between 3,500 and 4,500 million years ago in a primeval soup under a chemically reducing atmosphere. Simple compounds thus formed then gave rise to organic molecules which ultimately formed proteins, membranes, and cells. These in turn led to the development of specialized cell types and systems for co-ordinating them.

Modern research concentrates on laboratory testing and computer simulation of mechanisms which could have formed parts of this sequence.

It is virtually impossible to see how processes of this complexity could have occurred by chance. The existence of the primeval soup is purely speculative and the evidence is against any original atmosphere having been chemically reducing. The complexity of a single cell is so great that the chances against it having formed randomly are astronomical. Still less is it possible that once formed, it could have lived and multiplied. To reproduce, it would have immediately required oxygen to build further cells and an ozone layer to protect it from destructive ultraviolet radiation. If the initial atmosphere was oxygen free, this would not have been possible. Any evolutionary progress thereafter would have needed living creatures to evolve from one form to another without a hitch. All would have to have transmitted a capacity for self-repair and reproduction. The process must also have allowed humans to evolve a capacity for creativity. The chances against this sequence of events happening by natural processes without intelligent design are so great as to amount to impossibility.

REFERENCES
[1] Alberts et al. 1983. [2] Zimmerman 1971. [3] Denton 1985, page 270.

CHAPTER 6

GEOLOGICAL ARGUMENTS FOR A YOUNG EARTH

6.1 GEOLOGY AND EVOLUTION

Geology was the first science to adopt the uniformitarian view of Earth processes. Since the publication of Lyell's *Principles of Geology* in 1830, scientists have generally accepted that the Earth is very old and that the land surface has been continually modified by the same processes that operate today and at approximately the present rates. The time has been so long that the appearance of the land has been completely transformed from its original state. This process of transformation has, it is believed, accompanied the evolution of life from simple beginnings around 3.5 billion years ago to the developed forms we see today.

This view is clearly at variance with the Scriptural teaching of a relatively young Earth whose surface modifications are due to a single cataclysmic and universal flood.

6.2 THE GEOLOGICAL COLUMN

Rocks are of three types: igneous, sedimentary and metamorphic. Igneous rocks have solidified from molten magma at some time in the past. They can be subdivided into volcanics which have solidified at the surface and plutonics which have solidified at some depth in the Earth's crust. Sedimentary rocks have been laid down as sequences of strata by the action of wind and water. Their chronological sequence is determined by their order of superposition and by their fossil content. Metamorphic rocks represent the product of the other two types which have been deformed by the intense crustal pressures which accompany mountain building. Fossils seldom occur in igneous rocks, and are often deformed in metamorphic rocks.

Matching strata and fossils between different areas enables scientists to work out a consecutive sequence of events and construct a geological column. World-wide correlation of such columns has given the generalized scheme shown on Figure 6.1.

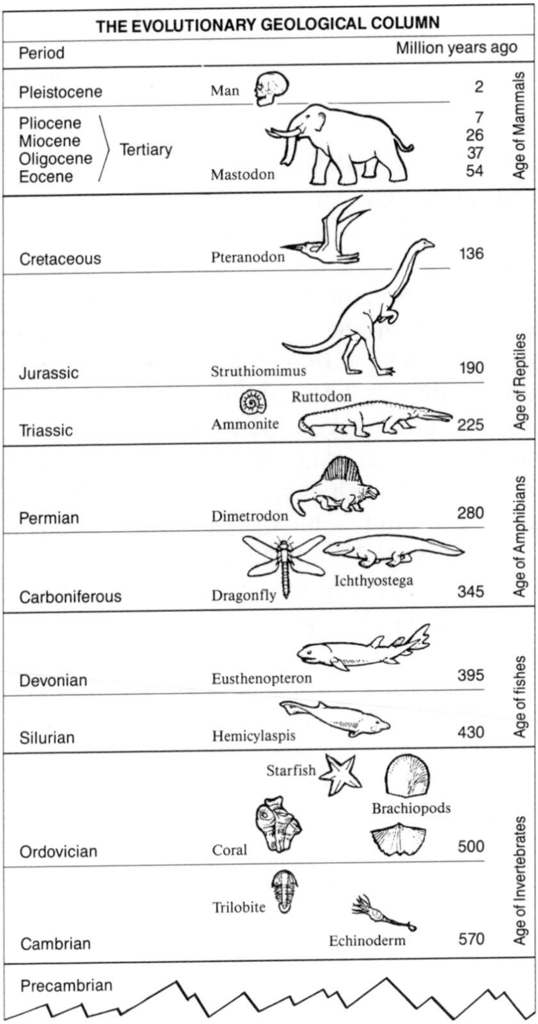

THE EVOLUTIONARY GEOLOGICAL COLUMN		
Period		Million years ago

FIGURE 6.1. Source: Baker 1976, page 7.

Rocks are dated approximately by their assumed rates of deposition, their included fossils, and more exactly by the degree of decomposition of contained radioactive materials.

The geological record provides abundant evidence that past Earth processes were substantially different from those of today. This applies both to rates of erosion on land and deposition in the sea. Noah's flood must have involved both.

6.3 VOLCANIC CRUSTAL ACCRETION

The outflow of lava on to the Earth's surface currently adds about 0.8 cubic kilometres of material a year. At this rate volcanoes would have ejected the total volume of the continents in three billion years. The present volume of volcanic material in the crust is much less than this. It could have accumulated in about 500 million years. In fact, the outflow rate has been atypically low since AD 1500, and so the actual time required would have been much less than this. It indicates that the Earth's age must be considerably shorter than the hypothesized 4.5 billion years.

Volcanoes also add water to the Earth's surface. This is called 'juvenile water' and 4.2 cubic kilometres is added annually to the oceans from this source. The latter contain about 1,312 million cubic kilometres of water (1,414 million cubic kilometres if all the water in the Earth's crust and atmosphere, ice, rivers, lakes, etc., is added). This 1,312 million cubic kilometres could all have been added in 312 million years by volcanic action alone, making this an absolute maximum figure for the age of the Earth. Its actual age must be lower than this to the extent that some water must have come from non-volcanic sources. This again argues for a much younger Earth than current theory allows.

6.4 SALT IN THE OCEANS

One compelling reason that the Earth cannot be millions of years old is the relatively small amount of salt in the oceans. It is revealing to compute the time that would be required to add their current contents. White[1] lists seventy-six calculations made by different writers, with conclusions ranging from a few thousand to 500 million years.

A typical estimate was that the oceans contain about 10,800 parts per million of sodium and 19,600 ppm of chlorine. The oceans are continually fed by rivers, which add about 34,100 cubic kilometres of water to them annually. River water is estimated on average to contain 8.5 ppm sodium and 8.3 ppm chlorine.

The sodium added per year will then total:
$8.5 \times 10^{-6} \times 34,100 = 0.290$ cubic kilometres per year.

The chlorine added per year will total:
$8.3 \times 10^{-6} \times 34,100 = 0.283$ cubic kilometres per year.

Let us make the simplifying assumption that none of this annually added salt is lost through evaporation or precipitation.

The oceans currently contain:
$10,800/10^6 \times 1,312 \times 10^6 = 14.17 \times 10^6$ cubic kilometres of sodium, and

$19,600/10^6 \times 1,312 \times 10^6 = 25.72 \times 10^6$ cubic kilometres of chlorine.

Therefore, to accumulate the present oceanic content of sodium would have required $14.17 \times 10^6/0.290 = 49$ million years, and to accumulate the present oceanic content of chlorine would have required $25.72 \times 10^6/0.283 = 91$ million years. The maximum age of the ocean as determined by its sodium content is thus about 49 million years, and as determined by its chlorine content is about 92 million years.[2] And this does not allow for any of these elements present in the primordial oceans, which would further shorten the calculated times. Since both marine biologists and oceanographers believe that ocean salinity has always been about as it is now, the arguments for young oceans are reinforced.[3]

The normal evolutionary answer is to contend that ocean

salinity is relatively low because the elements are continually being removed and recycled. But this cannot be sufficient explanation for the vast amount of recycling that would be necessary to explain the low figures. Salt loss cannot be due to normal chemical precipitation because the oceans are not supersaturated with either of these elements. Assuming an age of the Earth of 4.5 billion years, we would have to assume that almost 99 per cent of all sodium and 98 per cent of all chlorine ever added to the seas had been removed from them in sediments, rock salt beds, or fossils. Although some recycling clearly occurs, it is inconceivable that it has happened to this extent.

The conclusion must be that the oceans are youthful.

6.5 EVIDENCES FOR RAPID NATURAL PROCESSES

The erosion of rocks depends on their cohesion and the external stresses applied to them. In general their rate of destruction increases with temperature and moisture because these provide the environment for chemical and biological weathering. The transportation and removal of rock debris depends on the forces of wind and water. Even today these forces can be extremely destructive during hurricanes and violent rainstorms, especially in the tropics. They can effect changes in the landscape in a few hours which normally take decades or centuries. Forty-eight hours of rain in the catchment of Bijou Creek, Colorado, for instance, laid down 4 metres of apparently stratified sediments in two days.[4]

The new island of Surtsey off the coast of Iceland, was formed by an eruption on the sea bed from November 1963 to June 1967. Within months, sandy beaches, cliffs, and channels had formed in the lava. The island now supports considerable vegetation and gives the impression of much greater age than it has.[5]

Stalactites often hang from the roofs of caves and stalagmites build up in columns from the floors. Since they are caused by the evaporation and dripping of lime-charged water, they are assumed to form very slowly. But this assumption is not always valid. If the percolating water is abundant, its lime content high, and evaporation quick, quite large features can appear relatively rapidly and growth rates of tens of cubic centimetres a year have been recorded. Stalactites, for instance, often occur in man-made tunnels that are only a few years old, and they already occur on Surtsey. A 150-centimetre stalactite on the Lincoln Memorial in Washington took only forty-five years to form, and a bat has been found entombed in a stalagmite.[6] The presence of these features does not therefore necessarily indicate that their surroundings are very old.

6.6 TURBIDITES

Turbidites are rocks formed by deposition from turbid water. They are often conglomerates but can be sandstones or shales. They generally grade upwards from coarse materials at the bottom to fine at the top. They are frequently associated with the slumping of river-borne materials which have attained considerable depth in estuaries or inshore situations, and are both thick and widespread in the stratigraphic record. They can be deposited rapidly, up to 60 metres an hour, and in wide layers, locally up to 200 metres thick. They may be far more widespread than had previously been thought and may even account for 30% of all sediments.[7]

One outstanding example of submarine slumping was during the 'Grand Banks Earthquake' at 3 pm on 18 November 1929. It destroyed the world's busiest submarine cable, connecting Europe with North America. This consisted of thirteen parallel strands lying on the continental shelf off the southern coasts of Newfoundland and Nova Scotia. The eight higher cables were snapped instantly, the other five then broke in order in a north-south direction in two hours. At the same time a sea-floor area of 100,000 square kilometres was covered with silt to a depth of 60 centimetres. The cutting of these cables appears to have been due to a suspended mass of turbidites spreading rapidly downslope of the southern end of Nova Scotia, breaking the strands one by one. Laboratory experiments of such processes have demonstrated their efficacy.[8] The event shows that submarine action can be very destructive and can lead to extensive deposition in the space of hours.

Turbidites are often separated by quiescent deposits such as limestones, shales and fine sandstones. Although these apparently require conditions of slow deposition, much faster rates occur when rapidly-moving water is abruptly slowed or the chemistry is altered so as to flocculate and agglomerate smaller particles into larger units. Raising water temperature or increasing carbon dioxide content of the water will accelerate carbonate deposition by increasing the numbers of sea creatures whose hard parts include it.

6.7 SEABED SEDIMENTATION AMOUNT

A comparison of the amount of present sea-floor sediments with their calculated rate of accumulation shows that the process must have been much shorter than the supposed age of the Earth.

Although their locations have moved, the total area of ocean basins is not thought to have changed greatly since their original formation. Deep-sea drilling and seismic surveys have shown that the average thickness of deep ocean sediments is only about 700 metres. Although greater thicknesses are found on continental shelves, the best estimate for the average thickness of sediments over the entire ocean floor would certainly not be more than 900 metres. The area of world oceans is 360.9 million square kilometres, giving 325 million cubic kilometres of sediment present on the ocean floor. Assuming a bulk density of 2.3 grams per cubic centimetre, this would give a total weight of ocean floor sediment of about 748 million billion tonnes.

The present continents are estimated to have a volume of about 126.6 million cubic kilometres above sea level and a mass of about 291 million billion tonnes. If they were eroded to sea level and the debris deposited on the ocean floor, this mass would be about 40% of the mass of sediment present in today's ocean. So it would take only the erosion of two-and-a-half times our present continental mass to produce today's ocean floor sediments.

The best estimate from river data is that 19.9 billion tonnes of suspended sediment enter the ocean every year. Rivers add about 4.5 billion tonnes of dissolved chemical substances annually. Glaciers are currently breaking into the sea and floating off as icebergs. When the ice melts, entrapped solids are dropped to the ocean floor, adding another 2.2 billion tonnes. The water added to the ocean from submerged volcanoes contains dissolved chemicals. This is estimated to add 0.46 billion tonnes. Windblown dust adds a further 0.06 billion. The total of these annual additions is 27.12 billion tonnes. We must subtract from this the small amount, about 0.28 billion tonnes, of salts removed from the ocean and deposited on the land by evaporation and wind action. This leaves a total of about 26.8 billion tonnes of solids added to the oceans annually.

To determine the time required to erode all the existing continents into the ocean, we divide their volume, 291 million billion cubic kilometres, by 26.8 billion. This gives 11 million years. If we adopt the evolutionary view that the continents have been in existence for around 1 billion years, this means that they would have been reduced to sea level by erosion at the present rate at least ninety times. This is grossly at variance with the evidence of geology which recognizes only about four major cycles of erosion and deposition of continental scale, none of which completely levelled pre-existing mountains.

Looked at another way, one billion years of ocean-floor deposition at a rate of 26.8 billion tonnes per year would give 26.8 billion billion tonnes, equivalent to 11.7 million cubic kilometres. If the area of the oceans is 360.9 million square kilometres, one billion years would allow the ocean floors to be buried to a depth of 32.4 kilometres. The actual depth of ocean floor sediment, 900 metres, could therefore be laid down in 3% of this time. Alternatively, we can say that dividing the 748 million billion tonnes of present ocean-floor sediment by their annual increment of 26.8 billion tonnes would give only 28 million years to deposit the 900 metres now found. This is only 3% of the assumed history of sedimentation of 1 billion years or more.

Even allowing for the recycling of sediments, these facts clearly argue either that erosion rates must have been orders of magnitude less in the past, or much more reasonably, the Earth must be very much younger than current theory allows.[9]

6.8 SEABED SEDIMENTATION RATES

There is also evidence for a young Earth from the rate of accumulation of ocean-floor sediments. This rate varies considerably with climate, tectonism, and the organic productivity of the ocean. Parker[10] gives a range between 0.01 and 2 centimetres per thousand years, but West[11] quotes one as high as 9cm per thousand years. The wide difference between these figures underlines the difficulty of making any generally reliable time estimates from the thickness of ocean-floor sediments. Using the extreme figures above, the present average of 900 metres could have required anything between 10 million and 900 million years.

The rate of accumulation was probably much greater in the past, which would shorten the hypothesized age. There are a number of indications for this.

First, there are evidences that there are too many disturbances to the ocean floor to permit gradual undisturbed accumulation, and which suggest that processes can be relatively rapid. Some areas have recent deposits of *freshwater* diatoms, some have layers of coarse deposits such as sands immediately below the surface, and some have ripple marks.[12]

Secondly, the rate of accumulation of organic materials on the ocean floor indicates a shorter chronology. Forty-seven % of the detritus is carbonatic, 15% siliceous, and 38% clay. The rate of carbonate accumulation is therefore a controlling factor. This is of biogenic origin and mainly consists of foraminifera and coccoliths (globular shells less than one millimetre in diameter). The rate therefore depends on a. the supply of biogenic material, b. the rate this is dissolved, and c. its subsequent diagenetic alteration.

The supply of biogenic material depends on the availability of calcium carbonate from near-surface zooplankton. This depends on its rate of production which in turn depends on the sunlight in the photoic zone (the top 100 metres of the ocean) and on the amount of available nutrients. Thus the supply of biogenic material to the ooze ultimately depends on the food chain near to the surface.[13]

There is some evidence that this food chain was more productive in the past. Three nutrients: silicon, phosphorus, and nitrogen, determine the rate of growth of zooplankton. These are now seriously depleted in the ocean's surface layer due to biological activity and to their flux into deeper water by sinking foraminifera and coccolith shells. However, the water below the thermocline (the intermediate layer of water between the relatively disturbed upper layer and the relatively stagnant lower layer) is overloaded with these nutrients, mostly as a result of the dissolution of the zooplankton cells. Accordingly, areas of high biological activity are mainly confined to areas of oceanic upwelling, where the nutrients are transported from the deeper ocean to the surface layer.[14]

Conditions would have been much more favourable for the production of zooplankton at the end of the Flood and in the early post-Flood period for three main reasons. First, there would have been much more mixing, bringing nutrients to the surface. This would enable sunlight, which would have been at least as strong then as now, to act on and multiply the organisms. Secondly, the higher rainfall would generate more river runoff and add more nutrients to the sea. Thirdly, the warmer water would increase biological reproduction rates. Once deposited, the ooze suffers relatively little oxidation or other diagenetic alteration which could indicate its age. Thus the depth of biogenic sediments now observed on the ocean floor could have been formed in a much shorter time than current estimates would suggest. Roth[15] estimates that under ideal conditions and assuming no dissolution, it could be produced in less than 1,000-2,000 years.

6.9 INDICATIONS OF PAST MARINE CONDITIONS

Evidences for the marine origin of sediments derive from their manner of deposition and their fossils. The vast majority of sedimentary strata show such evidences. Some are hundreds of metres thick and highly fossiliferous. These have no analogies with any sediments forming today.

Recent research has tended to increase rather than decrease the proportion of sediments that are assigned a marine origin. For instance, a number of sedimentary rocks hitherto ascribed to wind deposition are now thought to have formed under water. Fossil sand dunes are diagnosed from the following features: a. current bedding, b. 'frosted' grain surfaces, c. a large proportion of 'millet-sized' grains about $\frac{1}{2}$ millimetre in diameter, and d. the presence of numerous wind-shaped pebbles called 'dreikanter'. All but the last of these are characteristic of submarine dunes formed on shallow shelf areas as well as of wind-formed surface dunes. Some sedimentary strata between the Carboniferous and the Cretaceous also show fossil tracks of amphibians and reptiles most reasonably explained by underwater formation followed by rapid burial. This includes the (Permian) Coconino Sandstone and the (Jurassic) Navajo Sandstone of the Grand Canyon area, both formerly thought to be wind-laid but now ascribed to shallow marine conditions.[16]

Pre-Ice-Age fossils generally testify to rather uniform warm conditions over the world, even near the poles. Miocene rocks in Iceland and Spitzbergen have European vegetation. There is very little indication of glaciation before the Pleistocene Ice-Age.

Glaciations in a number of areas have been reported as occurring in the geological record, mainly in Precambrian[17] and Permian rocks. The main evidence for them is the occurrence of tillites, striations, erratics, and varves.

Tillites are hardened tills, which are non-sorted aggregations of gravel, sand, and some boulders, in a clay matrix. Striations are longitudinal scratches, presumably made by rocks carried in the overlying ice sheet. Erratics are large rock fragments transported by moving ice away from their places of origin. They differ from exotic blocks in that the latter have not been transported by ice, but it is sometimes difficult to distinguish the two. Varves are thin alternating light and dark laminar beds representing coarser and finer particles respectively. They are thought to represent annual fluctuations of flow resulting from freezing and melting.

Specialists have debated whether or not such features are glacial.[18] Although Harland contends for this explanation in some Precambrian rocks, he admits it is still debated. Uncertainty is not surprising since it is much more difficult to recognize 'ancient' glaciations than Pleistocene ones. They are not related to obviously glaciated landscapes, nor in locations where the previous climates are known to be cold.[19]

Other explanations are possible and in some cases have been shown to be correct. The two most obvious characteristics of tillites are absence of stratification and lack of size sorting. These can be caused by subaqueous currents and sliding which, together with rafting, can also account for exotic rocks appearing as erratics. Striations can be made by any flowing of floating heavy masses across an exposed rock surface. Varves are not necessarily annual and freeze-melt related but can be due to more frequent fluctuations of water flow and sediment load.

The presumed Permian glaciations cover wide areas of Africa, Australia, India, and South America, and smaller tracts in North America and Europe. In the first three they extend down to sea level and are locally very thick, up to 3,000 metres in Australia. In India and Southern Africa the direction of movement was radially from the equator, in Australia from south to north. Their faunal distributions show that their locations lay equatorward of latitude 40 degrees. Thus the materials were deposited where it is unlikely to have been cold enough for any glaciation, still less one that could have moved great thicknesses of material. Also, the apparently glacial layers have intercalations of warmer deposits.

Further evidence that apparently glacial sequences have a marine origin comes from Permian sequences in northern Mexico and south-western United States. In the latter they are a great complex of coral reef structures. Since corals are only active in tropical and subtropical waters, a combination with glacial features is intrinsically unlikely. In Mexico they are boulder beds and volcanic rocks. The boulder beds were originally considered to be tillites but are now recognized probably to be submarine slide deposits that accumulated in a stagnant basin adjacent to active volcanoes fringed with growing reefs. Submarine slide deposits are much more abundant in the stratigraphic record than are tillites, and stratigraphers are becoming increasingly alert to their significance.[20]

Vegetable remains including whole trees are often oriented within beds in ways indicating suspension in directional currents.[21] Some are sorted in a manner indicating past floating. Fossil trees are occasionally found in an upright, diagonal, or upside-down state surrounded by horizontal deposits. These are sometimes called 'polystrate trees'. One example is a complete 20-metre fossil tree trunk at Craigleath Quarry, Edinburgh, discovered in 1830. This is inclined at about 30 degrees from the horizontal, cutting diagonally across sandy layers, indicating very rapid burial.[22] Keane reports a fossilized tree trunk which projects through two or more coal seams at Swansea Heads, New South Wales.[23] Ritland[24] shows a photograph of another example which can be best explained by supposing that the tree floated in an upright position to its present location where it was quickly covered with sediments. Similar examples from near St. Etienne (France) and near Essen-Kupferdreh (Germany) are illustrated by Bowden.[25] Erect petrified stumps are found in Yellowstone Park and the Fossil Grove in Victoria Park, Glasgow.

The mechanism appears to be that the trees are uprooted and moved in silt-laden water whose flow can be generated by volcanic action. Many will remain upright and retain this position when deposited surrounded by sediments. Others will lie horizontally or obliquely. This process, repeated rapidly and episodically will lead to the formation of considerable thicknesses of strata containing tree trunks which may then become petrified. That deposition and destruction can be extremely rapid is evidenced by the effects of the Mount St. Helens eruption in 1980. Tree stumps were transported and deposited in new locations, some upright and some diagonal.[26]

6.10 THE WIDE EXTENT OF SOME DEPOSITS

The wide extent of some deposits is also indicative of a marine rather than a fluvial (river-borne) origin. The Shinarump Conglomerate is a water-laid sediment about 30 metres thick which can be recognized over an area of over 250,000 square kilometres in Utah, Colorado, Arizona, and New Mexico. The material is coarse and so must have been deposited from rapidly-moving water. No river could have spread deposits this widely. The most reasonable explanation would be a great catastrophe like a flood. A number of other deposits in the same area show a comparably wide spread. The Chinle Formation covers 450,000 square kilometres, covering much the same area as the Shinarump but extending also into California and Nevada. The Dakota Formation spreads even wider going north as far as the Black Hills of South Dakota, and the Morrison Formation wider still to include a tract of more than a million square kilometres from Texas to Canada. These deposits are commonly ascribed to local floods, but no local flood could have carried so much material and laid it so uniformly over so wide an area.

6.11 THE ORIGIN OF COAL

Coal formation has been traditionally ascribed to the slow burial of peat deposits on land. But a more likely origin is rafting and burial under flood conditions.

In-situ deposition rather than flood transport is apparently supported by the evidence of *Stigmaria*. These are root-like fossils that project out under the coal seams into the underclay, and have been interpreted as the roots of trees which formerly grew in the peat bog. But other explanations are possible. They may have been transported along with the plants and deposited with them. Alternatively, they may be rhizomes of different plants which were able to develop under water in close association with the trees without being a part of them.[27]

The underclays have been considered to be the soils in which the vegetation grew. Their relation to the coal, however, indicates that they were formed before the coal was deposited. They have a similar mineralogy throughout and lack the indications of a soil profile. This suggests that they were essentially unchanged since their deposition.

Brown coals, such as the German lignites, often show a delicate preservation of plants, animals, and insects. These are sometimes in fresh condition, the chlorophyll still green and insects beautifully preserved.[28] This shows that they must have been entombed in an aseptic medium suddenly and completely because they would otherwise have decayed or changed in colour within a few hours.

The thicknesses of coal seams are too great for them to be derived from terrestrial peat. A seam 10 metres thick would, for instance, require 100 metres of peat. This is nowhere to be found on earth. In the Permo-Carboniferous of India, the Barakar Series of the Damuda Series, overlying the Talchir Boulder Bed, includes numerous coal seams, some up to 30 metres thick.[29] Some coal beds in

Australia are even thicker — up to 240 metres, impossibly thick for an accumulation of peat.[30] Also, coal seams often cover a wider geographical area than could reasonably have been occupied by vegetated swamps. Drift accumulation under flood conditions seems the only reasonable explanation.

Furthermore, marine fossils often accompany coal. An example is the small tubeworm *Spirorbis*, which secretes a calcareous tube for body protection, and attaches to suitable substrates such as corals, mollusks, bryozoans, other invertebrates, or Sargassum weed. Spirorbis is abundant in the fossil record from Ordovician to Recent, and is a frequent constituent of Carboniferous coal measures, attached to the plant debris and mixed into coal seams. It is also ubiquitous in modern oceans. But no member of the family *Surpulidae*, to which it belongs, is found in a fresh water habitat. Its reproduction by means of a trochophore larva is unknown in freshwater invertebrates. Its presence in coal is therefore strong evidence for a marine origin.[31]

6.12 CHERT

Chert, of which flint is a type, is a concretion of silica found in limestone and chalk, often distributed in bands. There are three main theories of its origin:

1. Replacement of non-chert rock by migrating silica-bearing water.

2. Secretion by small organisms.

3. Direct precipitation by sea water at the same time as the formation of the surrounding rock.

The problem with explanation one is the thickness and areal extent of chert deposits and the rhythmic nature of the beds in which it occurs. They are seldom distributed in clear relation to movements of underground water as they should be if this was the transporting medium. Explanation two is unsatisfactory because of the lack of traces of any organism which could have precipitated the silica. When fossil silica-secreting organisms are found, they are usually in such a perfect state of preservation that the surrounding microcrystalline chert could not be made from them. A few cherts may, however, be due to this.

In support of explanation three is the fact that no chert appears to be forming today. The Flood could have provided the precipitating conditions. If the water was highly saturated with silicates, conditions would have been right for the flocculation and deposition of silica.[32]

6.13 FOSSIL PRESERVATION

An indication for rapid marine deposition is the remarkable concentration and preservation of many fossils. Some sea creatures appear to have been suddenly overwhelmed in vast masses and buried uninjured. This is visible in many marine geological deposits.

The outstanding example is that of the fish fossils in Devonian strata. Devonian fish fossils give the impression that a disaster must have suddenly destroyed and buried vast shoals of fish, piling them one above another without damage to their skeletons, and with every fin erect and intact. Some specimens even retain their colouring. Dead fish quickly lose colour and their fins droop. Scavengers and predators damage or tear the body apart. Even if transported by water for only a short distance, fish disintegrate and their bones scatter. But the fossil record shows that some perished in the midst of their activities, such as feeding or giving birth. Their death may have been violent. Deep and shallow water mollusks are often found mixed together.

Speaking of a level platform of strata within the Devonian Old Red Sandstone in Scotland, Miller wrote:

'At this period of our history some terrible catastrophe involved in sudden destruction the fish of an area at least a hundred miles from boundary to boundary, perhaps much more. The same platform in Orkney as at Cromarty is strewed thick with remains which exhibit unequivocally the marks of violent death. The figures are contorted, contracted, curved; the tail in many instances is bent round the head; the spines stick out; the fins are spread to the full, as in fishes that die in convulsions. . . . The attitudes of all the ichthyolites on this platform (that is, the stratum) are attitudes of fear, anger, and pain. The remains, too, appear to have suffered nothing from the after effects of predaceous fish; none such seem to have survived. The record is one of destruction at once widely spread, and total so far as it extended. There are proofs that, whatever may have been the cause of the catastrophe, it must have taken place in a sea unusually still. The scales, when scattered by some slight undulation, are scattered by the distance of only a few inches and still exhibit their enamel entire and their peculiar fineness of edge. . . . Destruction must have come in the calm, and it must have been of a kind by which the calm was nothing disturbed.'[33]

The cause of this destruction in still water is unclear but a sudden change of temperature due to volcanic action from the Earth's interior during the Noachic deluge could provide an explanation.

In some Carboniferous sediments a mixture of corals and crinoids suggests cataclysmic destruction, and similar features occur in Cretaceous rocks. A 4-metre skeleton of a fish encloses a well-preserved 2-metre fish that the larger fish must have swallowed just before its death. Ichthyosaurs (dophin-shaped marine reptiles) have also been found with remains of prey in their stomachs.[34]

Sudden destruction can also be seen in land fossils. Some are remarkably unchanged from their living state in a way which suggests instant submergence in an anaerobic environment. Fossil insects have the contents of their stomachs intact.[35] Microscopic protozoa retain their delicate flagellae. Land creatures are also sometimes preserved in mid-activity. Two kinds of Triassic reptile often have their skeleton curled up with the head near the tail, a sleep-like posture. Many other reptiles appear in walking or paddling positions.

Some vulnerable substances have escaped decomposition through rapid burial. The turtle-like backs and cores of the horns of some dinosaurs consisted of keratin, a protein substance that decays in a few years even underground. Carbon deposits from it have been found where these would have been on the skeletons, indicating that burial by sediment was so rapid that soil bacteria could not achieve its full decomposition. Chitin (the hard substance of insect bodies) which normally decomposes rapidly under bacterial attack, still exists in fossil Eurypterids (giant scorpions) in Ordovician clay deposits. Even jellyfish, which would dry quickly on exposure to air, have left imprints.

The general picture given by all these instances is of creatures being suddenly overwhelmed in a way that remarkably preserved them. Burial by a flood seems by far the most reasonable explanation.

6.14 CALCAREOUS SEDIMENTS

It is sometimes stated that the great thicknesses of calcareous sediments of largely organic origin in many parts of the world argue against the possibility of rapid deposition. Such deposition, however, is not inconsistent with the character of the biblical Flood. The molten rock which would have poured out of the earth's upper mantle would have been both very hot and strongly alkaline. This would have raised both the temperature and the pH of the oceans to levels which would have accelerated the precipitation of lime and dolomite. Cook[36] maintains that a pH rise from 7-9 would account for all the chemical precipitates in the Flood waters.

6.15 CORAL REEFS

It is sometimes objected that the formation and burial of coral reefs is inconsistent with the short bibical chronology. However, the total mass of material in a reef is a function not only of time but also of numbers of corals. A new reef established in Krakatoa after the eruption of 1883 grew at the rate of four centimetres a year. This rate of growth could certainly account for most of the coral reef depths found around the world during the few thousand years since the Deluge. Ladd[37] states:

'Many colonies of reef corals are round and with little or no wear between perfect boulders. When such boulders are transported, an appreciable percentage of them will come to rest in "a position of growth", whether they be moved a mile across a reef flat or a mile down a seaward talus slope. Even elongated or slab-like colonies may end their journey right side up.'

Reefs formed in the warm antediluvian seas, therefore, when eroded and redeposited, could give the appearance of ancient reefs of great extent.[38]

6.16 MAGNETIC FIELD AND THE AGE OF THE EARTH

Two French scientists, Drs. E. and O. Thelier, measured the iron magnetization in bricks made in France in AD200, 1463, and 1933. The results indicated that since 1463 the Earth's magnetic field (or 'dipole moment') had diminished by 18% and since 200 by 35%. Barnes[39] has confirmed that measurements of the Earth's magnetic field since 1835 show that it has been steadily decreasing since then. Continuing decrease has been confirmed by satellite observations[40]. It is expected to decay exponentially because it is produced by the internal circulation of liquids in the Earth's core. This must flow against resistance and so generate heat. The process must decay because of this heat loss, and the indication is that such decay is continual and must have started not more than a few thousand years ago.[41]

This decay has a half-life of 1,400 years, and so its overall value will double every 1,400 years back into the past. The magnetic field could therefore have been many times as strong only a few thousand years ago, and values beyond about 10,000 years would exceed a reasonable estimate for any planet like the Earth. Beyond 20,000 years they would have been quite astronomical. Barnes suggested 10,000 years as about the upper limit for the age of the Earth since when there has been a dissipation of magnetic field as the electrical energy of the core is gradually being changed into heat energy.[42]

Against this, Strangway[43] has contended that evidence preserved in rocks indicates that there have been frequent reversals of the magnetic field and changes in its strength which have extended over long periods of geologic time.

Against this it should be said:

a. The data for paleomagnetic reversals are from individual sites subject to strong local influences. Some rocks can be magnetized by lightning and some by stress (magnetostriction).[44] It is thus not feasible to extrapolate the magnetic record of a suite of rocks or an archaeological site to determine the Earth's overall magnetic strength.

b. Variations in polarity can occur over short distances. A Silurian stratum that had been rapidly deposited had both normal and reversed polarity at various positions along its length. At another site, normal and reversed polarity have been found in the same stratum, sometimes in close association. This could not be due to a reversal of the Earth's magnetic field as all samples would have been affected.[45]

c. Some rocks show a rapid polarity change. Humphreys[46] reports an instance of this occurring in a few weeks in a basalt.

6.17 SUMMARY

Geology was the first science to adopt the uniformitarian view of Earth processes. The geological column shows about five major episodes of tectonic upheaval followed by a similar number of quiescent phases of sedimentation. Although the uniformitarian view would accord this process many millions of years, there are a number of reasons why a history of only a few thousand years punctuated by one universal deluge is more credible.

Arguments for a relatively young Earth are based on the rate of ejection of lava and water from the Earth's interior, the rate of accumulation of salt in the sea, the high proportion of turbidites among sedimentary rocks, the shallowness of ocean floor deposits, and the relatively rapid rate at which they can accumulate.

Indications for diluvial action are the ubiquity of marine deposits, the wide geographical extent of some beds, and in some characteristics of coal and chert beds. That diluvial burial can be rapid is shown by the perfect preservation of many fossils. Coral beds could be rapidly incorporated in sediments by submarine transportation, and calcareous rocks such as limestone and chalk could form in seas with rapidly raised temperature and pH levels.

The rate of decay of the Earth's magnetic field and evidence that polarity reversals are both rapid and local argue against the idea of an old Earth.

REFERENCES

[1] 1978, pages 128, 129. [2] Whitcomb and Morris 1974, pages 385-387. [3] Fox 1952, page 28; Hutchinson 1957. [4] McKee 1967. [5] Thorarinsson 1966, pages 37-39. [6] Whitcomb 1974, page 134. [7] Geoscience Research Institute 1990. [8] ibid. [9] Calculations adapted from Nevins 1975, 1990. [10] 1980, page 263. [11] 1972, page 188. [12] Whitcomb and Morris 1974, pages 409-412. [13] Oard 1990, page 183. [14] ibid, page 183. [15] 1985. [16] Brand 1976, pages 4-7. [17] Harland 1964. [18] For example, Schwarzbach 1964, page 81; Harland 1964, pages 119, 120. [19] Schwarzbach 1964, pages 81, 82. [20] Newell 1957. [21] Coffin 1983a, pages 123, 124. [22] Garton 1991. [23] 1991, Figure 9 following page 79. [24] 1970, page 100. [25] 1991, page 7. [26] Coffin 1983b, pages 126, 148-151, 170, 171. [27] Whitcomb and Morris 1974, pages 164, 165. [28] Coffin 1983a, pages 37, 38, 229. [29] Morris 1974, page 109. [30] Coffin 1983a, page 47. [31] Coffin 1971. [32] Nevins 1973. [33] 1870, page 237, parentheses added. [34] Wheeler 1978, page 13. [35] Coffin 1983a, page 37. [36] 1971. [37] 1957, page 35. [38] Whitcomb and Morris 1974, pages 408, 409. [39] 1983, pages 32-34. [40] Barnes 1981. [41] Barnes 1983. [42] quoted by Gish 1975. [43] 1970, pages 100-117, quoted by Young 1982, page 120. [44] Bowden 1991, page 36. [45] ibid, page 136. [46] 1990.

CHAPTER 7

THE FOSSIL SEQUENCE

7.1 PRINCIPLES OF CORRELATION

We can trace the history of the Earth by correlating the sequences of sediments between different areas. Their fossils show a rough progression of life forms from primitive beginnings in the lowest Precambrian rocks to the wider spectrum of modern life in the uppermost strata. The stages are marked by major disturbances in the sequence of erosion and deposition. These can be correlated with changes in the prominence of particular groups of flora and fauna. The main features of this fossil sequence are shown on Figure 6.1, page 73.

The lowest Palaeozoic sediments mainly contain bottom-dwelling marine creatures. Fish become dominant in the Devonian and terrestrial plant remains in the Carboniferous. Reptiles, some far larger than any creatures living today, dominate the Mesozoic. Mammals appear in the late Mesozoic but become increasingly important in the Tertiary. Human remains and artifacts become prominent only in the Quaternary, although there is some evidence for them in the preceding Pliocene.

It is assumed that this sequence represents the evolution of life over millions of years. But there are a number of indications against this.

7.2 CIRCULAR REASONING

First, this view suffers from circular reasoning. The assumption of fossil evolution is used to classify and date rock strata, while at the same time the sequence of strata is used as the main argument for fossil evolution. The two views can support each other but neither provides an independent check of the other. The belief in their reliability has been strengthened by the use of radiometric dating, which appears to date rocks in the millions of years demanded by evolutionary theory, although the sedimentary column does not clearly support this.

7.3 PARACONFORMITIES

Paraconformities are junctions between apparently continuous sedimentary sequences where there is considerable time lapse between those above and below the junction, but where there is weathering or erosion of the lower strata before the upper were deposited. The gap may be thought to be long, often millions of years, simply because the fossils above the gap are conceived to be much later than those below it.

The creationist explanation is that there is no time gap, that deposition was continuous, and that the fossils, although different, do not represent an evolutionary sequence, but are contemporaneous.

Paraconformities are relatively common, and the strata of almost any period can be found resting apparently conformably on those of any other period.

Price[1] quoted the following examples:

1. Cretaceous over Devonian at Lake Athabasca, Canada.
2. Lower Cretaceous over Lower Carboniferous at Banff, Alberta.
3. Mid-Devonian over mid-Silurian at Bear Grass Quarries, Louisville, Kentucky and Newsom, Tennessee.
4. Mid-Devonian over Upper Silurian at Buffalo, New York.
5. Lower Carboniferous Chattanooga shales over lower Silurian in eastern Tennessee.
6. Upper Carboniferous over Lower Ordovician in northeastern China.
7. Pleistocene over Permian on the Dwina, northern Russia.
8. Lower Pennsylvanian (Carboniferous) over Ordovician at Bolivar, Missouri.

It is worth examining one specific example: the Grand

TABLE 7.1.

THE GEOLOGICAL SEQUENCE IN THE GRAND CANYON
(in the neighbourhood of the South Rim).

CENOZOIC (70 million years) and MESOZOIC (155 million years)
Sediments of these periods are missing from the immediate vicinity of the canyon, from which they appear to have been removed by erosion. Where they occur echelonned back in Colorado and Utah they are stratigraphically continuous with the underlying Permian rocks and reach a peak at Brian Head. They appear to have been laid down in rapid succession.[2]

MIDDLE and UPPER PERMIAN (30 million years):
Kaibab marine limestone (white) (100m)
Toroweap sandstone and limestone (80-100m)
Coconino sandstone (100-115m)
Hermit shale (100m)

LOWER PERMIAN (c15 million years) or PENNSYLVANIAN (c45 million years)
Supai red sandstone and shale (the thickest bed-280m), a continental deposit possibly formed by Genesis wind.

UPPER and MIDDLE MISSISSIPPIAN (c30 million years)
Missing.

LOWER MISSISSIPPIAN (c15 million years)
Redwall limestone (170m)

DEVONIAN (c50 million years)
Temple Butte Limestone (50m)

ORDOVICIAN, SILURIAN and part of DEVONIAN (c100 million years)
These are missing. There is generally no unconformity between Cambrian and Devonian. Sometimes the Mississippian Redwall immediately overlies Muav without apparent unconformity or stratigraphic break, and sometimes the two are interstratified.

CAMBRIAN (c70 million years)
Muav limestone (30m)
Bright Angel shale (150-200m)
Tapeats sandstone (70m).

PRECAMBRIAN (up to 1,000 million years). (The Inner Gorge is cut into this).
Vishnu schist (metamorphic) intruded with granites. In some places this is tilted and truncated with the Cambrian resting unconformably on it.[3]

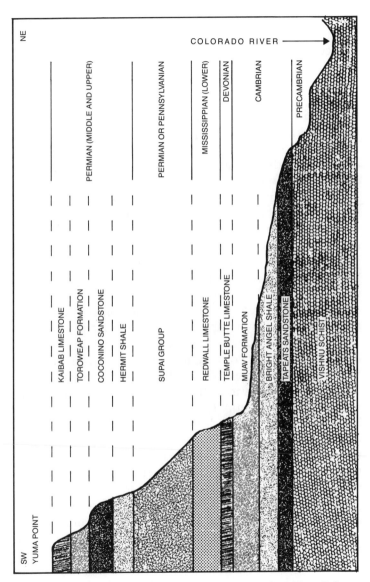

FIGURE 7.1. Geological cross section of the Grand Canyon from Yuma Point to the Colorado River. Note the apparent time gap above the Cambrian and above the Lower Mississippian.

Source: Judge 1969 and Grand Canyon Natural History Association 1976.

Canyon of the Colorado River in western USA (Figure 7.1).

Ascending the canyon we find a continuous sequence of deposits from Precambrian to Permian but with some significant gaps. These are shown on Table 7.1.

The essential point shown on the table that challenges the validity of dating the deposits by the fossil record is the two vast notional time gaps: a. between the Cambrian and the Devonian, and b. between the Lower Mississippian and the overlying Supai formation which is variously designated Lower Permian or Pennsylvanian.

The Devonian appears to overlie the Cambrian without a break despite the supposed lapse of 100 million years between them. Indeed, it is said that 'you can put your thumb on the Devonian and your little finger on the Cambrian in almost any place in Arizona'.[4] The only evidence for a time lapse is the presumed evolutionary gap between the fossils on each side of the paraconformity.

Secondly, the Redwall Limestone, the Supai Group, and the Hermit Shale are apparently a continuous sequence. The Redwall is Lower Mississippian (equivalent to the lower part of the Lower Carboniferous of Britain). The Supai has sometimes been called Lower Permian[5] and sometimes Pennsylvanian (equivalent to the Upper Carboniferous of Britain).[6] The Hermit Shale is mid-Permian. Either way the accepted chronology is suspect. If the Supai is Permian there is a 40-million-year gap between it and the underlying Lower Mississippian due to the absence of the Middle and Upper Mississippian and the Pennsylvanian. If the Supai is Pennsylvanian, there is still a notional gap below it of about 15 million years due to the absence of the Middle and Upper Mississippian, and another gap of similar length above it due to the absence of the Lower Permian.

It seems more reasonable to conclude that the whole sequence was laid down continuously in a fairly short time and that all the fossils were contemporaneous.

Further evidence that the fossils are not an evolutionary

sequence is that all the rocks from the Precambrian upwards contain pollen and spores from spruce, hemlock, and fir.[7]

7.4 OVERTURNED STRATA

There are some situations where older rocks overlie younger without apparent unconformity or disturbance. These situations are assumed to be due to overthrusting, because they appear to invert the evolutionary fossil sequence.

The evidence for overthrusting is normally fairly clear where it exists. There is a disturbed zone near the actual thrust plane. There are shearing and slickensides (shiny crack surfaces) on the actual cleavage surfaces. Rocks are metamorphosed and develop schistosity. This is where minerals are drawn out into streaky or wavy lines parallel to the direction of thrust. Along the actual thrust plane the original character of the rocks is normally almost completely effaced. In detail, one can find gouging indicated by rock powder, ground rock (mylonite), and tectonic breccia (conglomerate including rock fragments set in a matrix).[8]

One example of overthrust is in the Santa Rita Mountains south of Tucson, Arizona. Here the Permian is pushed northwards for about half a mile. There is a 1-metre-thick gouge layer of rock powder or mylonite, ground fine by the differential movement of two rock plates.

Overthrusts of more than a small fraction of a kilometre, however, are intrinsically unlikely. This is because the strain would normally be relieved by a succession of limited ruptures and the development of imbricated (piled in echelon) structures rather than by a smooth movement of a large mobile block over a passive underlying block.[9]

An extensive bibliography of presumed overthrusts, mainly but not entirely, in the United States, has been compiled by Lammerts.[10] Some are in the following places:

In the Glarus overthrust in Switzerland (Lochseite) near

Schwanden, Jurassic rocks (claimed as 180 million years old) overlie Eocene (60 million years old). It is suggested that there has been a 34 kilometre overthrust, but there is no evidence for unconformity.

In the Franklin Mountains near El Paso, Texas, Upper Ordovician limestone (450 million years old) overlies Lower Cretaceous strata (130 million years) without evidence of thrusting.

Heart Mountain and Sheep Mountain, Wyoming, are capped by Palaeozoic limestones overlying Eocene rocks, which in turn overlie Jurassic.[11]

In Glacier National Park (southern Alberta and Montana) and for 800 kilometres along the Rockies there is an area of several thousand square miles, where Precambrian limestones (>600 million years old), Cambrian, and other Palaeozoic sediments cap Cretaceous shales (100 million years old) containing dinosaur fossils without unconformity. This is known as the Lewis overthrust, and is especially clear in the isolated mass of Chief Mountain, Montana. The inversion of the usual fossil order is explained by hypothesizing a vast overthrust from the west sliding rocks eastwards over a distance of 50 to 100 kilometres. But the evidence for resulting metamorphism is lacking.[12]

On Empire Mountain in Pine County, Arizona, Permian rocks (>200 million years) overlie Cretaceous (c100 million years old). The Permian fits into deep grooves eroded in the underlying Cretaceous material. No projections are planed off, and there are no brecciation, gouge, or slickensides. In places the contact resembles a meshing of gears, inconceivable if one had pushed over the other.[13]

The obvious explanation in all these cases is that the concept of fossil evolution is at fault and the rocks were laid down originally in the order in which they now occur.

7.5 SUMMARY

The fossil sequence is generally regarded as an evidence of relatively slow evolution. This view suffers, however, from a number of difficulties. There is a danger of circular reasoning in using presumed fossil evolution to data rock strata at the same time as quoting the sequence of strata as an evidence of fossil evolution.

Sometimes the evolution theory leads to overriding of obvious stratigraphic evidence. This is seen in some paraconformities and presumed overthrusts. Many apparently continuous sedimentary sequences contain a sudden change in fossil assemblage. This change is interpreted as a long gap in the sedimentation record because of the assumed evolutionary gap between the fossils above and below. But it is more logical to see the deposition as unbroken and the change of fossils as due to a contemporaneous change in fossil population rather than to an evolutionary time gap.

Similarly, there are many situations where strata containing apparently 'older' fossils overlie strata containing 'younger' ones. This is often interpreted, on fossil evidence, as due to tectonic overthrust of older over younger rocks. However, the stratigraphic sequence appears continuous and shows no sign of such overthrusting.

In all these cases, the most obvious explanation is that deposition was continuous and the fossils both above and below the apparent break were contemporaneous.

REFERENCES
[1] 1926, pages 90-104. [2] Clark 1971a. [3] ibid. [4] Burdick 1974, page 50. [5] Judge 1969, page 680; Burdick 1974, page 27. [6] Grand Canyon Natural History Association 1976. [7] Burdick 1974, pages 66-74. [8] Peach and Horne 1884; Geikie 1885, pages 506, 512. [9] Lawson 1928. [10] 1984-1987. [11] Whitcomb and Morris 1974 pp 181-184. [12] ibid., pages 185-188. [13] Gish 1975.

CHAPTER 8

DATING METHODS

8.1 GENERAL PRINCIPLES OF RADIOMETRIC DATING

Geochronology is the science of measuring the age of rocks by analysing the radioactive materials they contain. Most rocks contain isotopes of radioactive 'parent' elements, which decompose to give 'daughter' products. The rate of decomposition is quoted in terms of the 'half-life' of the isotope, that is, the time required for half of any given sample to change from parent to daughter through decay. If the sample still mainly consists of the parent isotope, it is old, if mainly of the daughter, it is young. The exact ratio between the two is therefore seen as an accurate index of the time that has elapsed since decomposition began. The method mainly applies to igneous rocks because of the low radioactivity of sediments and the difficulty of knowing the conditions of emplacement of radioactive materials in them.

To determine the age of a rock from its contained radioactive materials, the geochronologist must know three things: a. the relative amounts of parent isotope and daughter products at the time of the formation of the rock, b. the rate at which the daughter is formed from the parent, and c. the relative amounts of parent isotopes and daughter products in the sample.

It is generally possible to measure c., but a. and b. present serious difficulties. Even if the present rate of radioactive decomposition can be determined, it is necessary to assume that it has been constant in the past. The geochronologist has to make an initial assumption about the relative proportions of parent and daughter isotopes at the time the rock was formed. This can never be more than a guess and it is unlikely that the original rock contained only the parent isotope and none of the daughter. In the potassium-argon method, for instance, argon is usually present at the start.

The specific methods involve the decay of uranium and thorium to lead, potassium to argon, rubidium to strontium, and radiocarbon to ordinary carbon.

8.2 RADIOACTIVE DECAY METHODS INVOLVING LEAD

Lead has four isotopes: ^{204}Pb, ^{206}Pb, ^{207}Pb, and ^{208}Pb. The last three, together with helium, sometimes occur as products of the radioactive decay of uranium and thorium, by the following decomposition processes, each proceeding through a number of intermediate stages:

^{238}U>^{206}Pb, emitting 8 alpha and 6 beta particles

^{235}U>^{207}Pb, emitting 7 alpha and 4 beta particles

^{232}Th>^{208}Pb, emitting 6 alpha and 4 beta particles

Alpha particles are the nuclei of helium atoms and so ^{4}He is a product of all the decompositions.

Measurements of age from these different isotope changes, however, give consistently different results from the same samples and so must be corrected by multiplying by the following factors:

^{238}U>^{206}Pb   1.12

^{235}U>^{207}Pb   1.18

^{232}Th>^{208}Pb 1.00

Calculations of age based on these processes are open to a number of serious objections:

1. Measurements are difficult and subject to error, partly because the minerals tested normally have much lead and only a little uranium or thorium.

2. It is difficult to ensure that the samples have not been contaminated by chemical change since their formation. Leaching of both uranium and lead is common.[1]

3. It is difficult to know how much of the daughter isotopes were present when the rock was formed. The evidence is that a substantial amount was always there. Volcanic rocks, in particular, often contain much more lead than can ever have been generated from the radioactive

substances present in them. Holmes[2] quotes the example of the Giant's Causeway in Antrim. The amount of radiogenic lead is 300-400 times as much as could have been generated in the hypothesized lapse since the Tertiary (up to 65 million years ago) when they were formed. Even if this material had existed for as much as 1,600 million years, he says, the accumulated radiogenic lead could not have amounted to more than one eighth of the lead present. Also, recently formed lavas contain radiogenic lead when they first cool and the minerals crystallize.[3]

The same difficulty applies to helium, the other decomposition product. It is unknown how much there was in the original rocks. It can diffuse from the point of formation, especially in coarse materials and where it is trapped under great pressure.

Furthermore, there is much too little helium in the earth and atmosphere to account for the amount of apparently radiogenic lead. 1.2–3.6 million years would be typical calculations for the age of the Earth based on this consideration alone. There is no evidence that this low amount can be explained by helium diffusing into outer space because it cannot attain the escape velocity needed. On the contrary, there is even a strong possibility that helium-4 is actually *entering* the atmosphere in significant amounts from cosmic rays.[4]

4. In radiometric dating it is always assumed that radioactive decay rates are constant, but White[5] quotes examples where this is not so. For instance, the rate of decay of beryllium-7 is affected, albeit only slightly, by pressure.[6] Also, Setterfield's theory of changes in the speed of light, if verified, would affect all radioactive decay rates.

5. Sometimes different values are obtained from the same rock. A study on contemporaneous Hawaiian basalts gave seven ages ranging from zero to 3,340,000 years.[7]

6. Different methods of measuring the same rock can give widely different results. For example: The same Upper Tertiary basalt in Nigeria gave the following ages:[8]

Conventional geology: 2-26 million years

Fission tracks:	<30 million years
Potassium-argon:	95 million years
Uranium-helium:	750 million years

Clementson[9] tested the internal consistency of the ^{238}U> ^{206}Pb method. He assumed that no ^{206}Pb was present when the rock crystallized. He created a theoretical time scale by computing the amounts of these and all intervening isotopes that should be present after different lapses of time. He then compared these computations with actual values published about recent volcanic rocks from the Azores, Tristan da Cunha, and Vesuvius. Although these rocks are known to be only a few hundred years old, the values obtained for them by this method ranged from 100 million to 10,500 million years.

7. Uranium-lead calculations are also distorted by the phenomenon of neutron flux, illustrated on Figure 8.1. The different 'vertical' reactions give different results for age. If ^{232}Th–^{208}Pb is taken as the standard clock, ^{238}U–^{206}Pb gives a 12% longer age, and ^{235}U–^{207}Pb an 18% longer age. ^{207}Pb, when isolated, continues to decompose to ^{206}Pb and this gives a 35% greater age. The crucial question is: why should these clocks give substantially different ages?

Chemical differentiation could account for some of it because uranium is more easily leached out of radioactive

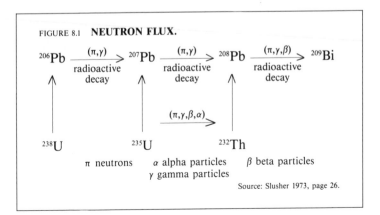

FIGURE 8.1 **NEUTRON FLUX.**

Source: Slusher 1973, page 26.

minerals than is thorium, but this does not explain every one.

Cook[10] has suggested that the reason is that ^{206}Pb is being converted to ^{207}Pb and ^{207}Pb to ^{208}Pb by adding neutrons and beta and gamma particles as shown by the horizontal arrows on Figure 8.1.

He explains it this way. The age determined by the ratio ^{238}U–^{206}Pb is less than that by ^{235}U–^{207}Pb because neutron bombardment converts more ^{206}Pb to ^{207}Pb than ^{207}Pb to ^{208}Pb. Two instances support this:

a. a uranium ore from Shinokolobwe, Katanga, had an age calculated from radiometric dating at 600 million years. It lacked both ^{204}Pb and ^{232}Th but contained some ^{208}Pb. Where did this come from?

The absence of ^{204}Pb shows that there is no 'common lead'. There is an assumption that lead which has never been contaminated by radiogenic lead from the decay of uranium and thorium has the following proportions of the different isotopes: ^{204}Pb 1; ^{206}Pb 18.5; ^{207}Pb 15.7; and ^{208}Pb 38. This is known as common lead. Any deviation from these proportions is assumed to represent a radio-active decay contribution.

All the Shinokolobwe lead must therefore be radiogenic. Its ^{208}Pb must therefore have come from ^{207}Pb.[11] This reduces the alleged age from 600 million years to nearly zero.

The absence of ^{232}Th shows that the ^{208}Pb cannot have come from this source. It must therefore have come from the ^{207}Pb. Cook applied a correction factor to the age calculation to account for the neutron and gamma re-actions producing ^{208}Pb. This reduced the calculated age to nearly zero.

b. A similar calculation on an ore from Martin Lake in the Canadian Shield reduced the alleged age from 1.7 billion years to nearly zero.

Almost all large uranium mines have such anomalous conditions. The neutron and gamma reactions apparently change the ^{207}Pb–^{206}Pb ratio rapidly, causing radioactive decay measurements to give a large apparent age. In fact, the indication is that the rocks are too young to have produced appreciable decay products. Cook[12] suggests that literally all of the so-called radiogenic isotopes of lead found in U-Th systems anywhere can be accounted for by this process alone.[13]

Even at the low level of neutron flux in a massive ore body, this process would be ample to upset completely the uranium-lead-thorium time clocks and give 'billion-year-old' minerals in a few thousand years.[14]

There is evidence that the abundance of xenon-131 found in lunar samples can be explained by the transmutation of barium-130 under neutron bombardment.[15]

As an analogy, there are two isotopes of nitrogen: ^{14}N and ^{15}N. Their ratio in the atmosphere is 1:269, but in radioactive materials in the earth it is 1:162. The only way this larger proportion can have arisen is through this same process — neutron flux. If neutron reactions can produce such a large change in the $^{14}N/^{15}N$ ratio, it is reasonable to infer that it could change the $^{206}Pb/^{207}Pb$ ratio by a large amount also.

8.3 PLEOCHROIC HALOES

The discovery of the significance of pleochroic haloes in dating the Earth is largely due to the American scientist Robert Gentry, whose book *Creation's Tiny Mystery* was published in 1986.

Igneous rocks contain microspherical haloes caused by the damage trails of alpha particles spreading in a sunburst pattern from a decaying radioactive atom at the centre. Typically, haloes are microscopically small, something like 2% of a millimetre. They are widespread in the Precambrian of Canada, in Sweden, Japan, the United States, and India.

Gentry conducted three separate experiments.

First, he analysed haloes from Precambrian granites in deep boreholes. Some of these haloes were formed by the decomposition of polonium isotopes with extremely short half-lives. These were the following:

^{210}Po   138.4 days
^{214}Po   164 microseconds
^{218}Po   3 minutes

Conventional geological theory would consider it impossible for polonium to be a component of these primordial rocks because their half-lives are so short that there would not be time to emplace them in the rock before the halo developed. For this reason, the original worker, Henderson, had assumed that the polonium isotopes must have been secondary products from the decay of uranium. Gentry showed that this could not be so for two reasons. First, uranium was absent from the rocks in which the haloes were found, and secondly, the polonium halo radiocentres contained a composition of the chemical element lead which was different from any previously known. This new type of lead, greatly enriched in the isotope ^{206}Pb, could not be accounted for by uranium decay; yet it was exactly what would be expected from the decay of polonium.[16] The most reasonable explanation is that the original material was polonium and that the rocks containing its haloes were created instantaneously.

Secondly, Gentry discovered haloes in coalified wood, all from the decomposition of ^{210}Po whose half-life is 138 days. Neither of the other two polonium isotopes (^{214}Po and ^{218}Po) found in the Precambrian granites was present in the wood. Thus one can assume that the ^{210}Po atoms survived long enough to be captured from an infiltrating uranium solution before they decayed away, while the other Po isotopes decayed away before they had time to accumulate in the tiny polonium sites. Nature had provided the most favourable conditions for reproducing polonium haloes, namely a highly mobile and abundant uranium supply. Yet even under these conditions only one type of polonium halo had formed.

This incidentally casts further light on the granite haloes considered above. If only the longest-lived of the three polonium isotopes could penetrate the relatively porous woody material under these favourable conditions, it seems impossible that the haloes in granite could have been due to penetration by a solution, and argues that they must have existed *in situ* at the time the rock was formed.

To return to the wood haloes. They were elliptical, clearly due to the compression of the wood after the haloes were formed. But there were sites with *both* an elliptical and a spherical halo, the first from ^{210}Po, the second from ^{210}Pb (with a half-life of 22 years). This shows that the compression of the wood occurred in more than 138 days (after the polonium halo had formed), but in less than 22 years (before the lead halo had time to form). This strongly suggests conditions of rapid deposition such as one would find in a flood.

The same combination of circular and elliptical haloes occurs in no less than three separated deposits within the Colorado Plateau: Triassic, Jurassic, and Eocene. Were these haloes formed on three occasions millions of years apart or on one occasion only? Let us test these two possibilities.

The basic ingredients for the formation of the haloes were: 1. water, 2. wood fragments in a gel-like condition (implying that they must have been living only shortly before), 3. a rich uranium concentration near to the wood, and 4. a compression event occurring after the uranium solution entered the wood, but prior to its becoming compressed and coalified. The percolating water must previously have traversed a uranium deposit. There is evidence that the uranium in all three deposits came from the same source.

The evolutionary scenario requires this complex sequence of events to have occurred three times, separated by periods of approximately 10 and 50 million years respectively, and each time to have occurred just at the moment when the wood was in a gel-like state. This seems most unlikely. It is far more reasonable to suppose that the same uranium-rich solution infiltrated all the samples at about the same time, and that all the sediments from Triassic to Eocene were deposited in rapid sequence.

Thirdly, while looking for disposal sites for nuclear waste, Gentry took samples of zircon at five different depths from 960 to 4,310 metres from Precambrian granites in New Mexico. These made it possible to see how well these zircons resisted leakage under the increasing temperatures, from 105 degrees Celsius near the top to 313 degrees Celsius at the bottom. The zircons contained both uranium and thorium, which are held relatively tightly in its lattice. Their daughter lead, however, migrates slowly at surface temperatures, but increasingly rapidly at higher temperatures. If the granites in New Mexico are over a billion and half years old as current geology teaches, there would be time for considerable lead to be lost from the deepest (highest temperature) section of the drill hole. In fact the lead should steadily diminish with increasing depth (due to steadily increasing temperatures). However, if the Earth is only several thousand years old, only negligible lead loss is to be expected and the amount of lead should be about the same at all depths. This provided a clear test of the relative credibility of creationist and uniformitarian views. The answer was definitive. Virtually no lead was lost from any sample. This is exceptionally strong evidence that the presumed 1.5-billion-year-age of these granites is drastically in error.[17]

Because of the evidence for a young Earth derived from the haloes, Gentry decided to analyse the microscopic-sized zircons from the same five depths for their content of helium, the other radiogenic decay product of uranium and thorium. Being a gas, helium diffuses far more easily than lead, and can migrate out of minerals such as zircon at room temperatures. Because of this continual loss, scientists have generally given up using the helium content to estimate the radiometric age of zircons found at or near the Earth's surface. Thus, according to the uniformitarian model, it would be senseless to attempt to measure the helium content of zircons taken from deep granite cores.

The results showed a helium retention of about 58% in zircons from 960m depth (105 degrees C), about 27% in zircons from 2,170m (151 degrees C) and a phenomenal 17% retention of helium even at 2,900m (197 degrees C). This test had only been done because of the surprising results from lead. It reinforces doubts about the whole uniformitarian chronology and incidentally shows that creation-based science does possess predictive capabilities which can be scientifically tested.[18]

8.4 THE POTASSIUM-ARGON METHOD

Potassium 40 (^{40}K) decomposes either to calcium 40 (^{40}Ca) or to argon 40 (^{40}Ar) by losing beta particles which consist of one neutrino and one electron. The two processes have different half-lives which are difficult to measure.

First, the decay of ^{40}K to ^{40}Ar tends to give somewhat different results from the same rocks as does the U/Pb method, against which it must be calibrated to determine how much potassium becomes calcium and how much becomes argon. Normally these values are 89% and 11% respectively but can vary from 88% to 92% calcium and from 8% to 12% argon. This dependence on calibration means that it is not independent of the U/Pb methods and its accuracy is conditioned by theirs.

In the earth, argon has two main isotopes: ^{40}Ar and ^{36}Ar, but the only radioactive decay product is ^{40}Ar, and rocks contain almost no ^{36}Ar. In measuring the argon in rocks, it is assumed the original rock contained the same ^{40}Ar/^{36}Ar ratio as the general ratio in the modern world. It follows that any deviation from this ratio is due to radiogenic argon, and the amount of deviation is an index of the age of the rock.

The weakness of this theory is the lack of evidence for assuming that the overall ^{40}Ar/^{36}Ar ratio in the earth has always been constant. Whitelaw[19] argues that it is false because ^{36}Ar is produced by cosmic rays and the ^{40}Ar/^{36}Ar has decreased through time to its present value of

295.5:1. Using this modern value as a baseline will therefore underestimate the original $^{40}Ar/^{36}Ar$ ratios in rock samples and hence overestimate their ages.

Some of the same difficulties surround the K-Ar method as the U-Pb method. Potassium is a highly reactive element most of whose compounds are soluble and easily leached. It is also difficult to determine the amount of radiogenic ^{40}Ar. First, it is indistinguishable from non-radiogenic ^{40}Ar. Secondly, it is highly mobile and diffuses from mineral to mineral with great ease and can enter rocks from the air. Thirdly, there is far too much argon in the Earth for more than a small percentage of it to have been formed by radioactive decay. The actual amount in K-bearing minerals is hard to measure because they vary in their capacity to trap it, notably in relation to their grain size. The mobility of both these elements and calcium makes it particularly difficult to ensure that samples have suffered no chemical change since their formation.

Non-radiogenic argon was probably present at the formation of the rocks containing radiogenic potassium. The evidence is that many inherit it from their magmas. Lavas from the ocean floor near Hawaii, for instance, known to be only 200 years old, gave a radiometric age of 22 million years.[20]

8.5 THE RUBIDIUM-STRONTIUM METHOD

Rubidium, a trace element which is chemically similar to potassium, is naturally radioactive. Twenty-eight % of rubidium atoms are in the rubidium-87 (^{87}Rb) form. It decays without intermediates to strontium-87 (^{87}Sr) which is a common, stable isotope of strontium. The half-life of ^{87}Rb is 48.8 billion years, and so this decay reaction is considered appropriate for measuring rocks of great apparent age.

The favoured method of age determination is the 'whole-rock isochron method', which analyses rocks containing a suite of minerals each with a different rubidium/

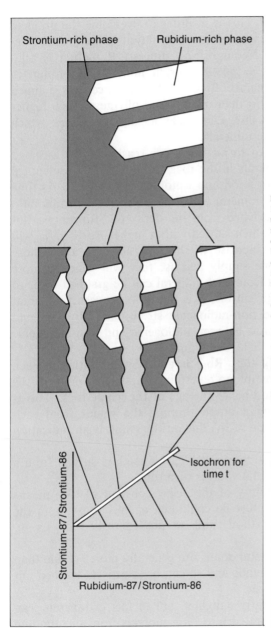

Strontium-rich phase   Rubidium-rich phase

Strontium-87 / Strontium-86

Rubidium-87 / Strontium-86

Isochron for time t

FIGURE 8.2
Diagram to illustrate the whole-rock rubidium-strontium dating method. It is based on the evolution of the $^{87}Sr/^{86}Sr$ ratios in time t as a result of rubidium decay in variously rubidium-enriched parts of a crystalline rock body. At the date of formation of the rock, the $^{87}Sr/^{86}Sr$ ratios of each part of the body (the separate columns in the middle diagram) are assumed to be exactly the same. However, as time passes, each part will gain ^{87}Sr at a rate proportional to the amount of rubidium it started with, and the time since its formation.

If the rock is not disturbed by geological processes, a graph of the rubidium/strontium ratios of the different parts will form a straight line, whose angle of slope is therefore claimed to indicate the age of the rock.

Source: Eicher 1968, page 127.

strontium ratio.[21] This is in order to overcome the problem of determining the amount of strontium present at the beginning of the decomposition process. Rubidium is relatively abundant in potassium-rich minerals, strontium in calcium-rich minerals. Ilmenite, for instance, has a much higher Rb/Sr ratio than olivine, and olivine a much higher one than plagioclase. One seeks ideally for a rock which contains all these minerals.

At their time of formation it can reasonably be assumed that all the minerals in the rock to be tested have identical ratios of the two strontium isotopes: ^{87}Sr and ^{86}Sr. As time progresses, each mineral will show an increase in this ratio as the ^{87}Sr is enriched from the decay of ^{87}Rb atoms. But those minerals which started with a higher Rb/Sr ratio will show a greater increase in the $^{87}Sr/^{86}Sr$ ratio than those with a lower one simply because they will generate more ^{87}Sr. The values from each mineral can be graphed so as to show the change: on one axis the ratio between the parent isotope and the non-radiogenic strontium ($^{87}Rb/^{86}Sr$) and the other the ratio between radiogenic and non-radiogenic strontium ($^{87}Sr/^{86}Sr$). (See Figure 8.2.)

By comparing the $^{87}Rb/^{87}Sr$ and $^{87}Sr/^{86}Sr$ ratios in each mineral, it is possible to determine the starting point of the decay process and hence the age of the whole rock. This is done by drawing a graph through the values from each mineral. The *slope* of the line on the graph is an indication of the age.[22]

Although apparently reliable, this method suffers from a number of potential sources of error.[23]

1. The uncertainty of the decay constant of ^{87}Rb means that the results must be calibrated against those from the uranium/lead method, and so are controlled by its reliability.

2. Rubidium compounds are generally more soluble than strontium compounds and so can be selectively leached out of an Rb-Sr system.

3. ^{87}Sr, apparently daughter, but in fact extraneous, can easily be incorporated into ^{87}Rb minerals from surrounding

rocks, giving the appearance that radioactive decay has occurred when none has.

4. ^{87}Sr can be formed by the same neutron capture process from ^{86}Sr that can form ^{208}Pb from ^{207}Pb.

5. There is no valid way of determining the initial content of the daughter isotope ^{87}Sr. This is at least ten times as abundant on Earth as it should be if it was all formed from ^{87}Rb over 5 billion years. Most must therefore be non-radiogenic.

6. The method underestimates the possibilities of diffusion of ^{87}Sr after it has been generated by radioactive decay. It can easily migrate from into or out of the mineral being tested through natural ion exchange.[24]

7. The assumption that $^{87}Sr/^{86}Sr$ ratios for all closely associated minerals are identical at zero age lies at the heart of the method, but is questionable both because of the differential mobility of the two isotopes, and because the isotopic ratio varies widely in nature.[25]

8. Any rock containing two or more minerals with different initial $^{87}Sr/^{86}Sr$ ratios will automatically give a false 'isochron', possibly of several hundred million years, even at zero age. It can also give different ages for rocks supposed to be of the same age. Brooks et al.,[26] lists twenty-two rock samples assigned to the Tertiary period (65 million years old or less according to uniformitarian theory), for which the rubidium-strontium method gave ages ranging from 70 million to 3,340 million years. Austin[27] quotes an instance where a surface basalt flow from the Grand Canyon area gave greater age values than did deeply buried Precambrian lavas nearby.

Therefore, the slope of the line graphed in this method may have nothing to do with age but may be simply the result of natural isotope variations in the rock.[28]

8.6 RADIOCARBON DATING

The basis of radiocarbon dating is that neutrons, produced as secondary particles in the atmosphere by cosmic rays, are captured by nitrogen nuclei to form the radioactive isotope of carbon with mass 14 (^{14}C). This ^{14}C mainly becomes attached to oxygen to make carbon dioxide. Both this and the normal isotope of carbon of mass 12 (^{12}C) are ingested interchangeably by plants and animals until they die. The ^{14}C atoms in the dead organisms will then slowly decay to the normal ^{12}C form. Therefore by knowing the ^{14}C/^{12}C ratio of the plant or animal at death, the ratio today, and the rate of decay of ^{14}C, it should be possible to calculate the amount of time since death.

A ^{14}C half-life of 5,568 years is used in most ^{14}C dating work, rather than the more recent and accurate value of 5,730 years. This is in order to avoid confusion in comparing recent determinations with the many older ones when 5,568 was generally accepted. (The conversion factor of 1.03 does not cause much confusion in dating calculations.) Any calculation beyond say 30,000 years will only have a tiny part of the sample left, and the weakness of its radioactivity makes it almost useless beyond 10,000 years. The method's originator, Dr. Libby, conceded that it was probably risky to use it beyond about 5,000 years,[29] and it is probable that dates longer ago than 2,000-3,000 years are suspect.[30] It therefore applies only to materials of historic or very late prehistoric age, where its conclusions seldom conflict with biblical chronology.

There are a number of reasons for its unreliability over periods longer than about 4,000 years.

1. Carbon is a constituent of all fossils and living things, and is an outstandingly mobile element. It migrates and reacts so readily that it is hard to find any fossils which have been free of chemical change since their formation. Living things can also exchange it with their surroundings, and this can alter the ^{14}C/^{12}C ratio to the extent that living mollusks, for example, have shown a radiocarbon age of up to 2,300 years.[31]

2. Some radioactive carbon has been discovered in supposedly ancient rocks, giving them ages of only a few thousand years. Some was found, for instance, in tree remains in a supposedly 'ancient' rock of unspecified age.

This calls into question either the reliability of the decay rate of ^{14}C or the age of the material.[32]

3. The decay rate of carbon-14 may not be constant.[33]

4. When radiocarbon dating began, it was assumed that the rates of atmospheric ^{14}C production and decay had reached a balance, so that the ^{14}C/^{12}C ratio at the time of an organism's death would be the same as in today's atmosphere. There is, however, considerable evidence against this.

The present rate of ^{14}C production in the atmosphere exceeds its rate of decay by about 25%, and equilibrium would require about 30,000 years to attain. This imbalance, if calculated backwards to a time of nil ^{14}C gives an age of the atmosphere of about 10,500 years.[34] Even if one accepts Johnson's contention[35] that the production excess is nearer 20% than 25%, it does not alter the main conclusion that the atmosphere is only a few thousand years old.

Furthermore, it is thought that the Earth's magnetic field deflects a large proportion of the incoming cosmic ray particles so that they do not interact with the atmosphere, and hence do not form ^{14}C. This effect would have been much greater in the past when the magnetic field was stronger. It has been reliably estimated that if the present magnetic field were to disappear the ^{14}C production rate would double. On the other hand an elevenfold increase in magnetic field would reduce the rate to one fourth of the present value and a hundredfold increase would bring it to near zero.[36]

5. There is a strong indication in Scripture that the pre-Flood Earth was surrounded by a water-vapour canopy. This appears from the separation of atmospheric from terrestrial waters,[37] the fact that the Earth was mist-watered,[38] and that rain was apparently unknown until the time of the Flood. Such a water-vapour canopy would have inhibited the formation of ^{14}C because the atmosphere, and hence the nitrogen in it, would have been protected from cosmic ray bombardment. The water-vapour canopy would also have inhibited atmospheric mixing, so that any ^{14}C

that did form would be slow to diffuse from the upper atmosphere. The Flood saw the end of this canopy, and so the formation of ^{14}C would have sharply increased. Hence, tracing the history of ^{14}C in the atmosphere would be a valuable approach to determining the date of the Flood.[39]

6. The Bible suggestion that the pre-Flood Earth had luxuriant vegetation and abundant animal life seems to be confirmed by the Earth's great reserves of limestone, coal, and oil. This indicates a world very rich in carbon dioxide. Also, significant carbon-14 had not had time to form. This means that the $^{14}C/^{12}C$ ratio must have been low and would therefore give a deceptively high appearance of age.

A combination of the three conditions listed under 3, 4, and 5 above: high early magnetic field, abundant water vapour, and abundant non-radiogenic carbon in the early atmosphere, would have meant relatively low ^{14}C levels. The effect would be greatly to exaggerate the apparent age of radiocarbon samples measured today.

7. If radiocarbon formation had always been at current rates, it should give ages of organic material in sediments increasing in linear relationship with depth. The available data on ^{14}C age profiles, however, indicates that this relationship is non-linear in a direction that suggests that the $^{14}C/^{12}C$ ratio was less in the past than it is now. It also suggests that the total range of ^{14}C dates for plant and animal remains can be accommodated within a time span of 5,000 years.[40]

There is a final consideration which underlines the necessity for caution in interpreting the scientific data. A low radiocarbon value from a fossil thought to be more than a few thousand years old would be amenable to two opposite interpretations. A uniformitarian would conclude that it is old because much of its ^{14}C has decomposed. A creationist would maintain that it was emplaced before appreciable ^{14}C was available in the atmosphere, and therefore it dated from shortly after the Flood. The difference could be determined not by the facts but by the bias of the observer.

8.7 THERMOLUMINESCENCE AND ELECTRON SPIN RADIANCE

Thermoluminescence is a method for dating pottery and minerals thought to be valid up to about one million years of age. It depends on the fact that alpha, beta, gamma, and cosmic rays affecting a crystal generate free electrons that move around the crystal lattice. A free electron is eventually captured by an irregularity in the crystal lattice that is deficient in a negative ion, and the electron is 'trapped'. Heating gradually releases the trapped electrons which then recombine with thermoluminescence centres and in so doing emit light. The light can be measured as the sample is heated to 500 degrees Celsius. This gives a measure of the total amount of radiation received by the sample since its origin, and hence of its age.

The method is especially useful for dating pottery because its manufacture includes firing which expels all previous luminescence and thus 'sets the clock to zero'. Electrons trapped after this will accumulate and indicate the time since this firing.

There are a number of sources of unreliability. The free electrons mainly come from potassium, thorium, and uranium either in the specimen or its surroundings. Their concentration and therefore the amount of electrons they generate can vary widely. Results may also be affected by earlier heating, moisture content, grinding of the sample and external beta rays affecting the outer 2 millimetres which has to be removed. Also, if the speed of light was greater in the past, the resulting accelerated radioactivity would have generated more electrons and exaggerated the apparent age of samples.

Electron spin radiance is a related method. It resembles thermoluminescence except that the trapped electrons are measured not by heating but by resonating in a magnetic field. As the strength of the magnetic field is varied, certain electrons resonate and the absorption of the magnetic field is increased. At particular frequencies, the amount of absorption of the magnetic field gives a measure of the number of trapped electrons that are resonating and hence of the age of the sample.

This method suffers from the same problems as thermoluminescence and has given from one site dates which can vary by more than 100%.[41] Both this and thermoluminescence must still be regarded as somewhat experimental methods.

8.8 DENDROCHRONOLOGY

Dendrochronology is historical research through tree rings which are alternations of 'densewood' and 'sparsewood'. Since the 1950s this method has been used to determine climatic conditions at specific dates in the past. Every tree adds a ring for each year of growth. The size of the ring indicates the amount of the growth and hence the rainfall of that year. Rings vary in absolute width between trees but the relative widths of every year are reliably the same for all types. No sequence of years is remotely likely to be repeated. Therefore it is possible to match any sample core of wood with others that overlap it in date, pushing the series farther and farther back into prehistory as more samples are analysed.

Most information has come from trees in California. The large conifer *Sequoia gigantea* can live for up to 3,000 years. Evidence also comes from bristlecone pines (*Pinus aristata*) growing at altitudes of around 3,000 metres in the White Mountains. Since these endure chronic drought, they are a super-sensitive rain gauge. They are even longer-lived than sequoias, the oldest living today reportedly being more than 4,900 years. There appears to be no evidence of more than one generation. This would accord with the idea that the present generation began immediately after the Flood.

Dendrochronology has provided an independent check on radiocarbon dating. Radiocarbon analysis of tree rings of known age indicates that the amount of radiocarbon in the atmosphere has only been constant for about the last 3,500 years. Before this, error mounts rapidly until there is a 700 year discrepancy between the two methods in the millenium before 1500 BC.[42]

There are a number of reasons why dating by dendrochronology may not be completely reliable. First, it is not always certain that the alternation between densewood and sparsewood represents annual cycles. Factors promoting growth may fluctuate within as well as between years, depending on the local environment. Lammerts[43] has shown that an extra growth ring can develop in bristlecone pines as a result of a period of summer drought. Secondly, boundaries between rings may not always be sharp enough to identify. Densewoods can be up to 10–15 cells in thickness, but they can also be as narrow as one cell. Thirdly, about 5% or more of the annual rings may be 'missing' along a given radius or core that spans many centuries, although they can generally be found by scanning through as little as 10cm of circuit.

Fourthly, it is sometimes difficult to check new samples against a master chronology because the rings show little variation from year to year. There are not enough marker rings for cross-checking purposes. This has often compelled the dendrochronologist to resort to radiocarbon dating in order to determine the 'age' of a wood sample, say from a bristlecone pine, before attempting to match it with the master chronology. Hence the method is partially dependent on radiocarbon dating, the inaccuracies of which have been described. This runs the risk of adding the inaccuracies of one method to those of another.[44]

8.9 SUMMARY

The main method of dating rocks is by measuring the relative proportions of two atomic isotopes in rock samples, when it is assumed that one has been derived from the other by radioactive decomposition at a known rate. The main measurements used for millions of years are uranium-lead, potassium-argon, and rubidium-strontium, for durations of up to about 60,000 years, radiocarbon and for periods of a few thousand years, dendrochronology.

All are subject to severe limitations and can give rise to large errors. These are sufficient to undermine any apparent evidence they give against biblical chronology. The uranium-lead methods depend on unprovable assumptions about the original ratio of parent to daughter isotopes, can vary widely between different measurements of the same rock, and are vulnerable to sample contamination including alterations of the parent-daughter isotope ratios by neutron flux. Pleochroic haloes argue for a fairly recent instantaneous creation of the Earth and a relatively rapid deposition of all strata from Triassic to Eocene.

The potassium-argon method suffers from some of the same problems. The Earth's original content of argon and the original ratio of its two isotopes cannot be known, since non-radiogenic and radiogenic argon are indistinguishable. Both potassium and argon are highly mobile elements and vulnerable to both secondary gain or loss.

Rubidium-strontium decay chronology is rendered questionable by the impossibility of knowing the original $^{87}Rb/^{87}Sr$ ratio in any rock, the uncertainty about the decay constant of ^{87}Rb, the difficulty of avoiding sample contamination, and the possibility of neutron flux.

Radiocarbon deals with periods notionally up to about 60,000 years BP, but cannot be claimed as accurate over anything like this duration. It is vulnerable to error through the high chemical mobility of carbon and possible variations in the decay rate of ^{14}C. It also depends on the constancy of the rates of production and decay of atmospheric ^{14}C over recent millenia, especially in view of the changes which could be associated with a great flood.

Thermoluminescence and electron spin radiance are relatively new and still experimental methods whose reliability is largely unproved. Dendrochronology covers relatively recent time which does not conflict with biblical chronology.

REFERENCES
[1] Acrey 1971. [2] 1936. [3] Clementson 1970. [4] Cook 1957. [5] 1985, pages 69-71. [6] Hensley et al., 1973. [7] Evernden et al., 1964. [8] White 1985, page 74. [9] 1970. [10] 1966, page 62. [11] Cook 1960, pages

54-60; Morris 1976, page 142. [12] 1966. [13] ibid., pages 53, 54. [14] Slusher 1973, page 29. [15] ibid., page 47. [16] Gentry 1971, pages 22-24. [17] ibid., pages 163, 164, 258, 259. [18] ibid., pages 263, 264. [19] 1970a, 1970b. [20] Morris 1974, page 147. [21] Miller 1984. [22] Miller 1984. [23] Morris 1974, pages 148, 149. [24] Slusher 1973. [25] Andrews 1982, pages 118-123. [26] 1976. [27] 1992. [28] Slusher 1974. [29] 1963. [30] Morris 1974, page 162. [31] ibid., page 162. [32] Andrews 1982, pages 118-123. [33] Anderson 1971. [34] Cook 1966. [35] 1988, pages 74, 75. [36] Brown 1979. [37] Genesis 1:6-8. [38] Genesis 2:6. [39] White 1978, page 138. [40] Brown 1988a. [41] Bowden 1991, pages 131-133. [42] Johnson 1973, page 21. [43] 1983. [44] White 1978, page 142.

CHAPTER 9

BIOLOGICAL DIFFICULTIES WITH THE EVOLUTIONARY VIEW

9.1 MICRO-EVOLUTION

Creationists accept micro-evolution but reject macro-evolution. Evolutionists accept both. Micro-evolution can be seen in common domestic animals such as cats and dogs, each of which despite wide variations forms a recognizable interfertile unit. Some micro-evolutionary variations are due to environmental adaptation.

An example of this are the finches in the Galapagos Islands, first noted by Charles Darwin during the voyage of the *Beagle*. These finches vary from island to island and are officially classified into four genera and fourteen species. Their variations seem to be due to differences in natural selection between the different islands. Nevertheless, all the birds remain finches within the same gene pool. The variations between them are in fact no greater than within a single species, such as the (American) song sparrow.

Another well-known example is the research done by H. B. D. Kettlewell in the early 1950s into the Peppered Moth (*Biston betularia*), an inhabitant of British woodlands. Its normal wing colour is speckled grey-brown, but some melanic individuals, which are completely black, occur by chance in the population. Kettlewell[1] bred these melanic moths and marked them and some normal types. He released equal numbers of both in two areas: a polluted wood in the Midlands and an unpolluted forest in the south of England. When he recovered the moths he found that in the polluted area about twice as many melanic as normal moths had survived; in the unpolluted area about twice as many normal as melanic. The explanation appeared to be in the differences between the two habitats. The polluted woods had blackened tree trunks which camouflaged the melanic moths, but revealed the normal moths to bird predators. The lichen-covered trees of the unpolluted wood had the opposite effect, camouflaging the normal but showing up the melanic[2]. Kettlewell saw this as due to selective predation so that, after generations have passed, a different coloured moth will be dominant in each wood. The results are, however, less conclusive than Kettlewell thought. The distribution of the peppered moths may be due more to differential breeding and migration than to selective predation.[3] Thus even an apparently obvious case for micro-evolution by natural selection can be questionable.

Micro-evolutionary changes are sometimes claimed to be macro-evolutionary. One example is the *Micraster* genus of echinoids in the English Upper Chalk. It has been contended that the fossils of this genus change from a narrow cuneiform to a more oval shape between the bottom and top of the strata, whose deposition is thought to have taken over 20 million years. Ward[4] shows, however, that these changes are hardly as great as the variations between races of mankind living today. Likewise Smith's study[5] of Lake Turkana showed that certain snails and bivalves (freshwater mollusks) changed substantially when the lake was isolated from other waters, but such changes stopped when the isolation ended. There is no evidence that such changes transgress the limits of micro-evolution.

The lesser black-backed gull and the herring gull in Britain and Scandinavia behave as separate species without hybridizing but are linked by a series of forms encircling the Arctic. Their present situation probably results from two branches of the original gene pool migrating around the Earth in opposite directions, so that each was substantially changed before they met again. But they all remain gulls and differ less than do some breeds of dog.

9.2 MUTATIONS

Mutations are sudden heritable changes in living species. The basic evolutionary argument is that favourable mutations give an advantage in natural selection so that forms possessing them multiply more easily, and ultimately become dominant, in a population. A continuation of this process will, it is claimed, lead to macro-evolution. But there are a number of reasons why this cannot be so:

1. It is estimated that over 99% of mutations are harmful and over 90% are lethal to the organisms which contain them. Tests have shown, for instance, that mutations in roses are mainly harmful,[6] and that tricotyledonous tomatoes are less vigorous than the dicotyledonous type.[7]

2. Macro-evolution requires not one but a multitude of simultaneous changes in an organism. None could survive unless there was also a perfect coadaptation of its new components as they developed. This would be a precondition of effective function.

3. Not all mutations are heritable, and there is no evidence that the genetic code will induce them always to continue in the same direction in which they begin. Some work in reverse, transforming back to greater, rather than lesser, resemblance to ancestors.

4. Mutational changes tend to be very slow, so that many generations of selection in a given direction would be needed to effect substantial change.

5. Mutational changes have definite limits which they cannot transgress. This has been demonstrated, for instance, in the planned breeding of tallest and shortest beans together for many generations. They ultimately reached a limit determined by the variability of the racial type, beyond which no amount of selection could change them further.

9.3 THE PRESUMED MACRO-EVOLUTIONARY SEQUENCE

The general progression of life forms from the evolutionary point of view is envisaged as follows:[8]

1. First cell, a protozoan similar to amoeba.

2. More advanced protozoan, with a flagellum similar to Euglena.

3. Multicellular group of flagellates, such as Volvox.

4. Specialized flagellates such as seaweeds or sponges.

5. Creatures with a mouth, such as jellyfish.

6. Worms. These were the first creatures to have organs. There were three basic types: flat, round, and segmented, with the flatworm first on the scene. Segmented worms developed a circulatory system. Shells and skin appeared.

7. Mollusks and arthropods developed from worms. Eyes and gills developed. Mollusks gave rise to those with eyes such as octopus. Arthropods developed jointed legs.

8. Earliest chordate, the lancelet.

9. Jawless fish, with improved brains, then, following an upheaval about 300 million years ago:

10. Plants develop from seaweeds.

11. First land animal, probably the scorpion; gills changed for lungs, then centipedes, millipedes, and small crawling insects developed. Some mollusks moved to land but they were not so successful as the arthropods and fewer descendants are found today.

12. Amphibians developed from fish.

13. Reptiles developed from amphibians.

14. Mammals and birds developed from reptiles.

15. A small insect-eating mammal, similar to the tree shrew became the first primate.

16. Monkey family and humans developed from primates.

This list clearly includes very large jumps not only between categories but within them. To substantiate any claim that the changes evolved naturally, it is necessary to find, or at least credibly hypothesize, missing links between all the stages. In the early days the absence of these was ascribed to a very inadequate knowledge of the world's rocks and it was confidently expected that the gaps would be filled. This has not happened. Cuffey[9] suggested a list of several hundred intermediate forms, but these were largely speculative and some have since been abandoned. The gaps are actually greater than in Darwin's time since many examples of suggested transitions have been abandoned since then.

9.4 THE ABSENCE OF MISSING LINKS

There are no 'missing links'. There are wide gaps between the major kinds of life. Such links must have existed if evolution is a fact. Fossil material is now so abundant and the record so complete that these gaps cannot be explained by scarcity of material. The deficiencies are real. They will never be filled.

Especially destructive of the evolution theory are the abrupt appearances of 'advanced' fossils. The most outstanding example is the sudden flush of forms in Cambrian rocks. They contrast strongly with all Precambrian rocks which have only the very simplest forms of multicellular life, and these mainly in the uppermost part of the sequence. Some patterning in rocks hitherto thought to be due to fossils seems to be of non-biological origin. Almost all Precambrian fossils in Canada are probably non-biological.[10] By contrast, Cambrian rocks contain representatives of every modern phylum except two,[11] and one of these, the vertebrates, appears in the Silurian.

Nor are Cambrian fossils the simplest or least complex representatives of their groups. The abundant trilobites, for instance, can be up to 45 cm long, have compound eyes and belong to the same group as crayfish, and lobsters. They are abundant in the lower Palaeozoic and became extinct at the end of that period.

On the other hand, Cambrian rocks do not contain many fossils of the simplest organisms. For instance, protozoa, which are thought to have been among the earliest forms of life, only appear after the Cambrian, which contains an abundance of more advanced fossils.

Sudden appearances of different types of life are not confined to the Cambrian. Fishes appear in the Devonian, turtles and tortoises in the Triassic, and ungulates in the Tertiary.

Darwin, in the first edition of *Origin*, foresaw the difficulty for the evolution theory posed by such sudden appearances when he said, 'If it could be demonstrated that any complex organ existed, which could not possibly have been formed by numerous, successive slight modifications, my theory would absolutely break down'.[12]

Gould[13], a leading evolutionist, also conceded that 'the absence of fossil evidence for intermediary stages for major transitions in organic design, indeed our inability, even in our imagination, to construct functional intermediates in many cases, has been a persistent and nagging problem for gradualistic accounts of evolution'. He further admitted the uselessness of anything short of perfection in every stage of evolutionary development by asking: 'Of what possible use to a reptile is 2% of a wing?'

To avoid the obvious conclusion he suggested that evolution may have operated by a twofold mechanism: preadaptation and self-multiplication. Organisms may first have preadapted to a role by considerable hidden internal adaptation before actually showing functional change in their physical make-up. Such change could, he claims, have begun with small mutations which were self-multiplying. But these suggestions are merely speculative. There is no evidence for them.

9.5 LARGE UNBRIDGED GAPS

Numerous lines of evidence show that micro-evolution within kinds cannot lead to macro-evolution between kinds. Some evolutionary steps are so large that it is inconceivable that any process of natural selection acting on random mutations could ever make them.

FISH TO AMPHIBIA. The transition from fish to amphibia is supposed to have taken 30 million years or so. The evolutionary contention is that the amphibian *Ichthyostega* evolved from rhipidistrian crossopterygian fish such as

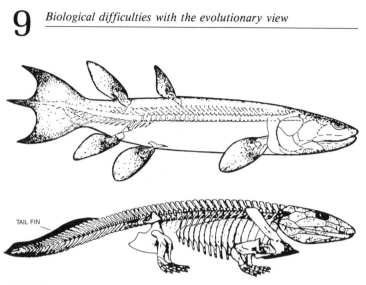

FIGURE 9.1

Reconstructions of a crossopterygian fish, *Eusthenopteron* (above) and his supposed ichthyostegid amphibian descendant (below).

Upper diagram from Gregory and Raven (1941), figure 10 facing page 296: Lower diagram from Benton (1990), figure 3.4 page 52, reproduced by permission of Chapman and Hall.

Eusthenopteron since they have similar bones and musculature. But, as Figure 9.1 shows, the gap is still very wide. The crossopterygian fish have fins designed for water. The pelvic bones are small and loosely embedded in muscle with no attachment to the vertical column. None is needed. The fins do not support the weight of the body.

Ichtyostega, by contrast, has the basic amphibian feet and legs, with a large bone firmly anchored to the vertical column and no trace of fins.[14] Also, the two groups have quite differently shaped heads and tails, the amphibian having its eye position further back and higher, and having a bony tail extending its vertebrae.

REPTILES TO MAMMALS. All mammals have a single bone, the dentary, on each side of the lower jaw, and three auditory ossicles or earbones — the malleus, incus, and stapes. Some fossil reptiles have fewer and smaller bones of the lower jaw than do living reptiles. Every reptile, living or fossil, however, has at least four bones in the lower jaw and only one auditory ossicle, the stapes.

There are no transitional forms. 'How would it be possible for any intermediate creature to chew while his jaw was being unhinged and rearticulated, or how would he hear while dragging two of his jawbones up to his ear?'[15]

FLIGHT. Even more inexplicable is an evolutionary origin of flight. Indeed, it is a critical test case. Almost every structure in a non-flying animal would require modification. Flight is supposed to have evolved four times separately and independently — in insects, birds, mammals (bats), and reptiles (pterosaurs, now extinct). In each case it is supposed to have required many millions of years, and almost innumerable transitional forms would have been involved. Yet none has been found. Birds' bodies are built for flight from the start. Nearly all their larger bones are adapted for lightness by being hollow with very little marrow.

Feathers are sometimes said to have originated from the fraying of scales, but the gap between the two is very large. Feathers are constructed of a unique system of quills carrying interlocking barbs and barbules, not remotely similar to the scales of a reptile. A half-developed feather would be worse than useless. It would be impossible for an impervious reptile scale to turn into an impervious feather without passing through a frayed scale intermediate which would be weak, easily deformed, and still quite permeable to air. The stiff, impervious property of the feather which makes it so beautiful an adaptation to flight, depends basically on such a highly involved and unique system of co-adapted components that it seems impossible that any transitional feather-like structure could possess even to a slight degree the crucial properties.[16]

Birds' lungs are fundamentally different from those of other vertebrates. In most of the latter, air comes in and out of the lungs through the same passage. In birds, it has continuous circulation through the lungs.

Just as the feather cannot function as an organ of flight

until the hooks and barbules are co-adapted to fit together perfectly, so the avian lung cannot function as an organ of respiration until the circulatory system can work in a perfectly integrated manner. The slightest malfunction would lead to death within minutes.[17]

Archaeopteryx is sometimes quoted as a transitional form between reptiles and birds, but cannot fill the gap. It was a true bird. It had wings, was completely feathered, and flew. It is similar in size and structure to a living bird species: the hoatzin of Amazon Valley woods and swamps.[18] Any claim it might have to be a missing link is finally refuted by the finding of another bird species in the same deposit in which Archaeopteryx occurs (Upper Jurassic).[19]

9.6 GAPS BETWEEN SIMILAR CREATURES

Can smaller gaps between recognizably similar animals in comparable environments be bridged by evolutionary processes? The answer is likewise almost certainly no.

ELECTRIC EELS. Electric eels and some fishes destroy or paralyse their prey with electric shocks. Such a capability could not be developed if its possessor needed it to survive. How could an ancestral electric eel have lived while the electrical parts were being developed? How could it have known when starting the complex process of generating electricity that it would succeed, and not only succeed but generate a current strong enough? Half measures would have been worse than useless. There is no evidence that electricity in any existing species is nascent.

HORSE SERIES. The horse series has often been cited as an example of evolution. No other sequence is nearly so easy to sustain as evidence. But any evolution that occurred is strictly between very similar forms, and contains unbridged gaps. There are five hypothetical stages representing the geological periods from Eocene to Pleistocene. The fossils show an increase in size, but there are a number of objections to the view that it is an evolutionary series. They include the following:

1. There are substantial differences between the different stages without evidence for transition between them. Most of the morphological characteristics of the feet, skull, and teeth, which are traditionally supposed to have exhibited an almost perfect sequence of change throughout the Tertiary period, progress from one stable adaptive level to another by a sequence of short step-like transitions.

2. The most famous of all the equid trends, the gradual reduction of the side toes, cannot be traced as a sequence. The Eocene horses had padded dog-like feet with four functional toes in front and three behind. The early Oligocene and all subsequent horses are without a functional front toe and concentrate weight on the middle 'toe'.[20]

3. *Eohippus* is Eocene and Miocene, but its bones are often to be found at the surface, and the only reason for calling these strata Eocene is that 'Eohippus' fossils have been found in them!

4. The fossils are represented as showing an increase in size from Eocene to the present day. However, horses with as wide a range of sizes exist today.[21]

5. *Eohippus* and the modern horse both have eighteen pairs of ribs, but of the supposed intermediate forms, one (*Orohippus*) had fifteen, and another (*Pliohippus*) had nineteen.

6. *Eohippus* has a skeleton very similar to the present day *Hyrax*, (a small ungulate of rodent-like appearance somewhat resembling a large guinea pig). Some scientists believe that *Eohippus* has no connection with modern horses, but is simply a variant form of *Hyrax*.

7. The horse sequence, if indeed it shows genetic change at all, is an example of micro- rather than of macro-evolution. The very fact that it is the most convincing sequence available argues strongly against the whole evolutionary theory. The period from Eocene to Recent is considered to have taken around 60 million years. If it took this time to effect the relatively minor changes in the horse, it must have taken at least, say, ten times this to develop a

new biological order and at least ten times again to develop a new class. This would total 6 billion years — an order of magnitude longer than the 600 million currently allotted to the evolution of life since the Cambrian. And this is only for the generation of a new class.

9.7 CREATURES WITHOUT A CONNECTION TO ANCESTRAL FORMS

There are a number of examples of members of the animal kingdom with highly distinctive physical characteristics for which there is no evidence of evolutionary ancestry.

ELEPHANTS. The lineage of elephants is thought to date back 55 million years to the Eocene. However, even the earliest supposed ancestor, the *Palaeomastodon*, had a completely formed trunk essentially the same as that of modern elephants. *Palaeomastodon* is assumed to have descended from a proboscidean ancestor, but no half-trunked intermediate form is found.[22]

GIRAFFES. Darwin wrote in *Origins*:

' . . . with the nascent giraffe, the individuals which were the highest browsers, and were able during dearths to reach even an inch above the others will often have been preserved; . . . These will have intercrossed and left offspring inheriting the same bodily peculiarities, whilst the individuals, less favoured in the same respects, will have been the most likely to perish . . . . By this process long-continued, . . . it seems to me almost certain that an ordinary hoofed quadruped might be converted into a giraffe'.[23]

We now know that acquired characteristics cannot be inherited and there is no fossil evidence that giraffes have evolved from short-necked ancestors.

There are further reasons why the giraffe's neck cannot have evolved. Because its head is a long way from its body, the giraffe requires an extra large heart to pump the blood to its head to avoid brain damage. But it also has to lower its head to drink and the very power of the heart would then risk causing an excessive blood flow to the brain. There are three ways in which it avoids this danger. First, it spreads its front legs apart, thus lowering the heart and reducing the blood pressure somewhat. Secondly, the jugular veins have a series of valves to stop blood rushing to the brain when it lowers its head and flowing back too fast when it raises its head again. Thirdly, to protect it from excessive blood flow from the carotid artery, the giraffe has a net of spongy tissue at the base of the brain which 'soaks up' any excess blood. Thus the giraffe can raise and lower its head without suffering any ill effects.

These features indicate design and cannot be explained by evolution. The giraffe could never have survived unless all developed *simultaneously*. Without an extra-large heart it would have died of brain damage through lack of blood. Without the valves and spongy tissue it could not have survived its first drink.

WHALES. Whales differ widely from the land mammals from which they are thought to have descended. None of the following changes can be explained in the absence of any missing links: a. that hind limbs became tail flukes, b. that pelvic bones were reduced c. that forelimbs became paddles, d. that suckling developed underwater, e. that all the accompanying musculature changes occurred, and f. that the sieve (baleen) developed in the whale's mouth.

BOMBARDIER BEETLE. The bombardier beetle (*Brachinus sp.*) is a creature that defends itself by paralysing an enemy with a jet of noxious fluid. It has two glands which produce a liquid mixture, two connected storage chambers, two combustion chambers and two external tubes which can be aimed like flexible guns at an attacker.

The stored liquid is an explosive-reaction mixture of 10% hydroquinone and 23% hydrogen peroxide held in a special chamber. The beetle adds an inhibitor which prevents the explosion. When an enemy approaches, it squirts the solution into the twin combustion-tubes and adds an anti-inhibitor to set off an explosion aimed at the enemy.

The existence of this beetle is quite destructive to the theory of evolution. By what possible process of natural selection could a creature evolve these characteristics? It could not survive the process of developing the explosive chemicals without first having the inhibitor. It would be pointless to develop the inhibitor without knowing beforehand both that it would have the chemicals and that it would be able to develop the anti-inhibitor. If it started to develop the counter-inhibitor first, what guarantee would it have that it could subsequently develop the inhibitor and the chemicals? Without such a guarantee, why should it bother to try? None of these could be used without the chamber and the explosion tubes, but how could it develop these without knowing it could manage the chemical processes? And so on. There is no way that an evolutionary process could operate at all, let alone operate without destroying the beetle. Its very existence presupposes an external designer.[24]

9.8 BEHAVIOURAL CHANGES REQUIRING EXTERNAL INFORMATION

There are many instances where life depends not so much on a physical change as on a behavioural adaptation for which no evolutionary explanation is feasible.

BUTTERFLIES. Butterflies live on nectar concealed deep in the pockets of flowers. To reach their food they must unroll their tongues and thrust them far down into these recesses. How could they survive during the long period when the development of this long tongue was taking place?[25]

YUCCA AND THE PRONUBA MOTH. The pollination of yucca, sometimes called the 'Spanish bayonet', by the pronuba moth in Mexico and the south-western United States is an outstanding example of symbiosis. There are several species of both plants and moths, and each species of the one has its own species of the other. The yucca flower is cup-shaped, about 5cm long, and droops downwards. Buds open at nightfall and give a strong fragrance.

The female pronuba moth has special tentacles covered with stiff bristles, clearly designed to collect pollen. She is attracted by the scent of the yucca flowers, enters one, goes to the top of the stamen, and scrapes together a big load of pollen from the anthers. This she works into a ball, sometimes three times as large as her own head. She carries this in her jaws and tentacles to the flower of another yucca plant.

The stigma inside the flower of this second plant is hollow and inaccessible to wind or other insects so that ordinary pollination is impossible. She enters it by going backwards to the interior of the flower, pierces a hole with her egg-laying needle, and lays her eggs among the seed cells in the bulbous ovary.

As soon as she has done this she performs a most surprising act. Crawling back down the long hanging style she finds the tubular stigma at the lower end and proceeds to pack it full of the pollen remaining in her mouth. Provision has now been made both for her offspring and for the reproduction of the yucca.

The eggs are ready to hatch when the seeds are about ripe, so when the larvae (caterpillars) emerge they have an ample supply of food at hand. They eat their fill of seeds, grow and cut a hole in the pod, lowering themselves to the ground by spinning a silken thread. The mother moth never eats; all she does is lay eggs, pollinate the yucca plant and then die.

A remarkable part of the whole business is that the yucca ovary contains about 200 ovules, each of which, fertilized by the pollen packed into the stigmas, is capable of developing into a seed. The larvae eat only about 20% of the seeds in the pod, which allows an abundance to mature and the plant to continue.

Thus the mother moth has 'planned' ahead and deliberately bred the plants so that her offspring will have a supply of food when they are born.

But this is not the end of the story. There are years in which the yucca plants in a given locality do not flower. If the moths which in those years are in the chrysalis stage were to emerge, they would find no flowers, and there would be no new generation of moths. But in these years the moths remain dormant in the chrysalis. When the flowers do appear, the moths are able to emerge and use them.

The yucca could not produce seeds without the moth. How does the moth know enough to pack the stigma full of pollen? Instinct? Yes, but instinct is merely an inherited action pattern. Before the pattern can be inherited it must be formed. But how could yucca plants mature seeds while waiting for the moths to learn the process and set a pattern? How could the yucca survive while the moths were learning? How could the chrysalis know when the yucca will flower? This all points to intelligent design.[26]

BEES. Some bees in the hive are nurses whose task is to feed the queen bee and the larvae. The milk for this purpose is formed by special glands in the nurse bee's head. Other bees have a different chemical laboratory which turns honey into beeswax. These chemical factories are unfailing. The hidden secret is in the minute genes of the bee. It is quite impossible for evolution to explain the purposeful co-ordination in the production of bee-milk and beeswax, and the maintenance of the correct proportion of each type. The failure of either would upset the whole colony and quickly lead to its extinction. But the productions do not fail. That is the mystery, inexplicable without prior design.

9.9 EVIDENCES OF ADVANCED SOPHISTICATION OF FORM

There are numerous examples of living forms of such complexity and sophistication that to achieve them by random evolution seems inconceivable.

SPIDER'S WEB. Every species of spider makes its own kind of web. When a baby spider spins its first web, even if it has never seen a web before, it makes one just like its forbears but on a smaller scale.[27]

Skills which are instinctive are not preceded by inferior skills. Every ant, bee, and spider fulfils its life purpose with exactitude. There are no bunglers or semi-skilled workers.[28]

EYES. Most creatures have eyes. It is a wonderful organ but only if it is all there. It could not have developed from single small changes because a very large number would have had to occur simultaneously not only to the eye but to its surrounding structures. There is no evidence for transitional forms.

A necessary part of the evolutionary view must be that there was a time when eyes were unknown. It then must be supposed that a piece of pigment or a freckle appeared on the skin of an animal that had no eyes. This piece of pigment or freckle must then have converged the rays of the sun upon that spot and when the little animal felt the heat on that spot it turned the spot to the sun to get more heat. The increased heat irritated the skin so that a nerve came there, and out of the nerve came the eye. The mere recitation of this scenario shows how intensely speculative must be any theory that the eye evolved.

Sylvia Baker[29] graphically describes a university seminar about the eye which led her to the same conclusion:

'We began . . . to discuss how that marvellous organ might have evolved. For an hour we argued round and round in circles. Its evolution was clearly impossible. All the specialized and complex cells that make up our eyes are supposed to have evolved because of advantageous mutations in some more simple cells that were there before. But what use is a hole in the front of the eye to allow light to pass through if there are no cells at the back of the eye to receive the light? What use is a lens forming an image if there is no nervous system to interpret that image? How could a visual nervous system have evolved before there was an eye to give it information?

'We discussed the problem from every possible angle, but in the end had to admit that we had no idea how this might have happened. I then said that since we had found it impossible to describe how the eye had evolved, the honest and scientific thing was to admit the possibility that it had *not* evolved. My words were followed by a shocked silence. The lecturer leading the seminar then said that he refused to enter into any controversy, while the others in the group began to mock me for believing in God. I had not mentioned God! I had simply been trying to view the problem in an objective and scientific way.'

THE HUMAN BRAIN. The human brain consists of about ten thousand million nerve cells. Each nerve cell puts out somewhere in the region of 10,000 to 100,000 connecting fibres by which it makes contact with other nerve cells in the brain. Altogether the total number of connections in the brain approaches 10^{15} or ten thousand million million. Numbers of this order are of course completely beyond comprehension. Imagine an area the size of the whole European Community (one million square miles) covered in forest trees containing 10,000 trees per square mile. If each tree contained 100,000 leaves, the total number of leaves in the forest would be 10^{15}, equivalent to the number of connections in the human brain! Surely it is inconceivable that such an amazing organization could be achieved by chance processes?

But even this is not all. Each of the brain's constituent nerve cells is both perfect and immensely complex, infinitely more so than a modern city. If the evolution of the whole brain by random processes is inconceivable, so also must be that of each individual cell that composes it.[30]

9.10 USE INHERITANCE

It has sometimes been argued that descendants can inherit physical attributes developed by their parents in their lifetimes. This is known as use inheritance. If it were true it might explain how over a number of generations a family of basketball players, for instance, would develop long arms, or a family of skiers strong ankles. By extension this could be used to explain the giraffe's neck or the elephant's trunk. But there is no evidence that it is true.

Unless it is already in the parents' genetic code, a descendant cannot inherit characteristics they acquired in their lifetimes. A possible resemblance to use inheritance can be due to a recessive gene, retained in a population, which favourable circumstances bring out at a later date. But the gene must have been there to begin with. A tendency to certain diseases is often heritable, but this is due not to characteristics acquired in the parents' lifetimes. It results from psychological and physical characteristics in the family background.

9.11 HOMOLOGY

Homology, also called convergence, is the situation wherein different creatures have body parts with similar structures, but which may have different functions.

Darwin asked, for instance:

'What can be more curious than that the hand of a man, formed for grasping, that of a mole for digging, the leg of the horse, the paddle of the porpoise, and the wing of the bat should all be constructed on the same pattern, and should all include the same bones in the same relative positions?'[31]

He contended that such examples are evidence of common ancestry modified by natural selection.

But this view cannot be sustained. First, homologous structures are often not specified by homologous genes and do not follow homologous patterns of embryological development, which would be required if they had common ancestry. To take an example: the vertebrate alimentary canal appears to be homologous. It is, however, formed from quite different embryological sites in different vertebrate classes. It is formed from the *roof of the embryonic gut cavity* in sharks, from the *floor* of the lamprey, from *roof and floor* in frogs, and from the *lower layer of the embryonic disc* (the blastoderm) in birds and reptiles. Another example is vertebrate forelimbs which develop from quite different segments of the body trunk in newts, lizards, and humans.[32]

Biological difficulties with the evolutionary view

The seeds of conifers (gymnosperms) and of flowering plants (angiosperms) provide a botanical example. They are generally considered to be homologous. Each seed consists of an enclosed egg cell or ovule plus a food store (the endosperm) which surrounds the ovule and supplies nourishment to the growing embryo after fertilization. Yet the way in which the ovule and endosperm are formed profoundly differs between the two groups.[33]

The concept that evolution explains homology is perhaps even more strongly damaged by the discovery that apparently homologous structures are specified by quite different genes in different species. Almost every gene that has been studied in higher organisms affects more than one organ system, a multiple effect which is known as pleiotropy. For instance, a mutation in one gene of the domestic chicken causes abnormalities in a number of organs, some such as air sacs and downy feathers which are unique to birds and others, such as lungs and kidney, which occur in many other vertebrate classes. The more physical characters the gene controls, the more inconceivable it becomes a mutation in the gene can effect *advantageous* changes in all these characters simultaneously. If the evolution of, say, the chicken's feathers was due to a particular gene, and the same gene also controlled its air sac, lungs and kidney, evolution would require that the changes to all four were both simultanenous and advantageous to the chicken. Therefore, pleiotropy argues against the idea that homologous organs in different creatures indicate an origin from the same gene pool.[34]

The evolutionary interpretation of homology is further clouded by the fact that there are many cases of apparent homology which cannot be due to descent from a common ancestor. An obvious example is that forelimbs and hindlimbs of all terrestrial vertebrates have the same pentadactyl design, yet it would be absurd to suggest that one evolved from the other or that both evolved from a common source. The fact that humans have five fingers and five toes in no way argues that fingers evolved from toes or vice versa.[35]

Homologies appear to owe their origin to an accordance of design in meeting similar practical needs without necessarily involving genetic relationships.

9.12 VESTIGIAL STRUCTURES

Vestigial structures are those parts of the bodies of animals which seem to have no current purpose but to be hangovers from an earlier stage in the evolutionary pathway. This view was early advocated by Ernst Haeckel, professor of Zoology at Jena from 1862 to 1909. He taught that creatures in their embryonic state 'relive' the sequence of forms through which they have evolved. This is known as the Embryological Recapitulation Theory or Haeckel's Biogenetic Law.

The human womb, it is suggested, reproduces the conditions of primeval seas. The human embryo recapitulates earlier evolutionary forms, displaying in order the features of marine organisms, amphibians, reptiles, and mammals. Haeckel produced sketches to illustrate these steps. These became influential but he was subsequently forced to admit that he falsified them to bolster the theory.[36]

Furthermore, if the human foetus develops its early life cycle up the ladder of an evolutionary past, it might be assumed that its immediate environment should also reflect this. But the amniotic fluid in the human womb is very different from any possible primitive sea in which life is supposed to have begun. The embryo derives its food from the mother through the umbilical cord and not from this fluid. Nor does the embryo use gills to extract oxygen from the fluid. Its supposed gill slits have been shown to be no more than cervical folds with no perforations.

Also the order in which pre-natal forms appear is sometimes the reverse of that which a theory of vestigial structures would suggest. For instance, the human circulatory system is supposed to have started as a simple duct, part of which developed into a heart. Yet in the embryo the heart develops before the blood vessels. Teeth generally appear in more primitive forms of life than tongues, but in mammals it is the other way round.

In recent years an instrument, called a fetoscope, has been developed which, when inserted into the uterus, permits the observation and photographing of every stage of the human embryo during its development. As a result, it is now known that at every stage the foetal development process is uniquely human.[37]

9.13 PUNCTUATED EQUILIBRIUM vs GRADUALISM

The difficulties inherent in explaining the absence of missing links have prompted a search for explanations.

Three possible theories have been proposed:

1. _Explosive evolution._ It is suggested that a sudden eruption of evolutionary activity occurred early in the history of life, but this then died down and gave way to a steady state.

2. _Saltationism._ This was first advocated by Goldschmidt in 1940.[38] It is based on the idea that new biological types ('hopeful monsters') which are strikingly different from their parents arise by genetic mutation. These types make a first step in the direction of some new adaptation, which is then perfected by further small changes. Brief bursts of gradual, albeit rapid, evolution alternate with long periods of stasis.

3. _Punctuated equilibrium._ This was first proposed by Eldredge and Gould in 1973. Rather than viewing gaps as results of imperfections in the record, they believe they should be regarded as inevitable phenomena of nature. This theory is a form of saltationism which envisages evolution as occurring in small peripherally located populations, which then spread widely and undergo little further change. The prominent evolutionist Richard Dawkins appears to support this view.[39]

None of these theories can provide a mechanism for crossing major biological gaps. No mutation studied by geneticists has revealed any possibility for genetic changes of this magnitude. They are unsatisfactory last-ditch attempts to rescue the uniformitarian theory.

9.14 ADVANTAGES OF THE CREATION THEORY FOR EXPLAINING BIOLOGICAL CHANGE

If all life was due to special creation, one would expect living things to show the following characteristics:
1. To be too intricate and complex to appear by chance.
2. To appear in the record without ancestors.
3. To remain distinct from one another.
4. To resist change into different kinds by modern breeding or genetic experimentation.
5. To show no changes bridging basic taxonomic units such as families and higher categories.
6. To reveal mutations as being often neutral, harmful, or degenerative.
7. To show all basic types of living organisms contained in the fossil record even if some ancient types were extinct.
8. To show relatively cosmopolitan basic kinds in their first appearance in the fossil record.

All these points accord with the facts. They give strong prima facie support for a creationist explanation of biological origins.

9.15 SUMMARY

The micro-evolution of living things is well established, but macro-evolution is not. The indications are dominantly against it. There is negligible chance that life forms can make major advances through mutations, especially in view of the infinity of positive changes which would be required, often simultaneously, to progress from single-celled creatures to mammals. The inadequacy of any mechanism based on mutations is underlined by the total absence of 'missing links'. Some gaps in the fossil record are especially wide, such as fish-amphibia, reptile-mammal, and from earthbound to flying creatures. Even more telling are the much larger number of unbridgeable gaps between relatively similar creatures, such as between ordinary and electric eels and between the presumed stages of horse evolution.

Almost all creatures lack a fossil record suggestive of any different ancestry at all. Elephants, giraffes, whales, and bombardier beetles are obvious examples. Inherited behaviour patterns in some insects ensure not only their own survival, but that of the plants on which they depend. This is inexplicable without the input of prior information into the insect's genetic makeup. Similarly, prior information would be needed to develop complex organic constructions such as spiders' webs, and the human eye and brain.

Offspring cannot inherit characteristics acquired by their parents in the latters' lifetime. The existence of homologous structures does not necessarily argue for common ancestry. Nor do apparently vestigial structures support evolutionary theory.

These are some of the problems that have forced evolutionists to modify the theory. One way has been to substitute the concept of punctuated equilibrium (evolution in jumps) for uniformitarian grandualism (evolution by continuous change). Although this notionally reduces the number of missing links, it cannot explain their total absence.

REFERENCES

[1] 1959. [2] Blackmore and Page 1989, pages 93-95. [3] Bowden 1991, pages 195-211. [4] 1971. [5] 1988. [6] Lammerts 1971. [7] Gish 1975. [8] Riegle 1971, pages 33-48. [9] 1972. [10] Bowden 1991, page 12. [11] Zimmerman 1966, pages 122, 123. [12] 1984, page 219. [13] 1988. [14] Gish 1986, pages 72, 73. [15] Gish 1979, page 85. [16] Keane 1991, page 96. [17] ibid., page 96. [18] Coffin 1969, pages 408, 447; 1983a, pages 242-244, 354, 428. [19] Gish 1985, page 116. [20] Cousins 1973; Denton 1985, page 184. [21] Baker 1976, page 13. [22] Tier 1970; Chadwick 1991. [23] 1952, page 104. [24] Gish undated. [25] Tier 1970. [26] Tier 1970; Clark 1971b. [27] Tier 1970. [28] ibid. [29] 1976, pages 17, 18. [30] Denton 1985, pages 328-330. [31] 1984, page 415. [32] Denton 1985, page 146. [33] ibid., pages 148, 149. [34] ibid., pages 149, 150. [35] ibid., page 151. [36] Assmuth and Hull 1915, pages 14, 15. [37] Gish 1986, page 252. [38] page 390. [39] 1982, page 102.

CHAPTER **10**

THE ORIGIN OF MAN

10.1 PRIMATES

Man is placed within the order primates according to the classification scheme shown in Table 10.1.

TABLE 10.1 **THE PRESUMED ANCESTRY OF MAN**		
ORDER: PRIMATES		
SUBORDER: PROSIMII	SUBORDER: ANTHROPOIDEA	
	Platyrrhines	Catarrhines
Lemurs, Lorises, Tarsiers	New World Monkeys	Old World Monkeys Apes Man

Primates are supposed to have descended from insectivorous ancestors, and catarrhines from prosimians, but transitional forms are unknown between either pair. The fossils described below all fall into the catarrhine group.

10.2 RAMAPITHECUS

Teeth and parts of a jaw found in India in 1932, dated to 14 million yeasr ago, were given the name *Ramapithecus*. It was considered to be intermediate between apes and man mainly because its incisors and canine teeth (front teeth) are relatively small in relation to cheek-teeth, and the curve of its jaw (the dental arcade) is parabolic rather than U-shaped, both characteristics distinguishing human from ape anatomy. Subsequent research has shown that the variation between *Ramapithecus* and the ape *Dryopithecus* is less than within a single population of chimpanzees in Liberia, and that *Ramapithecus* lacks the supposed dental arcade. Even stronger evidence against

Ramapithecus being a hominid (in the line notionally leading to men but still subhuman) is the existence of the baboon *Theropithecus galada* in Ethiopia today. Although this has many of the facial and dental characteristics which have caused *Ramapithecus* to be classed as a hominid, it is clearly only an ape with no genetic relation to man. Without it there is no evidence of any hominid in the gap between the supposed branching point of man and ape and the australopithecines.[1]

Since many evolutionists believe man's ancestors branched off from apes about 30 million years ago, and the next supposed ancestors — the autralopithecines, are dated at one to three million years ago, there remains a gap of more than 25 million years during which hominids were supposedly evolving, yet not a single fossil hominid of that period has been discovered.

10.3 AUSTRALOPITHECUS

The next proposed intermediates were *Australopithecus africanus* (literally 'African southern ape') discovered in South Africa by Dart in 1924,[2] and *Zinjanthropus bosei* discovered by Mary Leakey, wife of Louis Leakey, in Olduvai Gorge, Tanzania in 1959, which has subsequently been classified as a variety of *Australopithecus*.

All the australopithecines possessed small brains, the cranial capacity averaging 500cc or less, which is characteristic of gorillas and about one-third of that for man. They unquestionably had the brains of apes. They also had ape-like skulls and jaws. The argument for their being hominid rests mainly on their dentition. Their similarity to humans resides in the fact that their front teeth, incisors, and canines are relatively small and the curve of the jaw is more paraboloid and less U-shaped than is typical of modern apes. Also, the fragments of the pelvis, limb, and foot bones seem to indicate that they walked habitually upright.

However, a research team under Solly Lord Zuckerman and Charles Oxnard studied all available australopithecine fragments and concluded that they are not related to anything living today, man or ape, but are uniquely different. To the extent that resemblances exist with living forms they tend to be with the orang-utan.[3] The most reasonable conclusion is that australopithecines were neither ancestral to man nor intermediate between man and apes.[4]

10.4 DONALD JOHANSON'S 'LUCY'

Donald Johanson's team in 1973 found a knee joint near Hadar in the Afar Triangle of Ethiopia which he took to be of a bipedal hominid 3 million years old. In the following year they discovered three jaws and about 40% of a fossilized female skeleton, a little over a metre tall and with a brain size of 380–450cc. They called it 'Lucy'. Johanson claimed it to be a bipedal hominid $3\frac{1}{2}$ million years old. In 1975 he found parts of thirteen more individuals. They were given the name *Australopithecus afarensis*.[5]

There are, however, reasons for considering these fossils to be merely apes. A key point is the degree to which they walked upright, that is, their bipedality. Zuckerman and Oxnard had concluded that the australopithecines did not walk erect in a human manner. But they notionally lived only 2 million years ago and so should be $1\frac{1}{2}$ million years more man-like than Lucy. There is no evidence that they are. The proposed bipedality of the knee joints of the first Hadar specimen and of Lucy have been disputed. It may be that *A. afarensis* and other australopithecines were no more adapted to bipedal locomotion than are chimpanzees and gorillas, which do occasionally walk bipedally.[6]

10.5 SKULL 1470

The whole evolutionary scheme for man was thrown into confusion by the discovery by Richard Leakey's team of an apparently human skull, labelled *Skull 1470* near Lake Turkana in Kenya, which he claimed to be nearly three million years old on the evidence of stratigraphy and the potassium-argon analyses of tuffs interlayered in the deposits in which they were found.[7] Skull 1470 lacks the heavy brow ridges of Peking Man, and the wall of the skull is thin as in modern man. The cranial capacity is about 775 cc, much less than modern man's 1,500, but the age and sex of the skull's owner are unknown. Leg bones found in the same strata appeared to indicate bipedality, indicating that if they belonged to the same individual ás the skull, all could be hominid.

Later publications are less positive about its hominid character. Although Leakey had originally called it *Homo* sp. indet.,[8] in 1978 he assigned it to *Homo habilis*, while his co-author Alan Walker believed that it should be classed as *Australopithecus*.[9] The designation *Homo habilis* derived from some fossils found by his father Louis Leakey in Olduvai gorge which he believed to be more advanced than australopithecines. The bipedality of some fossils assigned to this proposed species have, however, been adjudged to be akin to that of apes, and so best designated *Australopithecus*. It thus appears doubtful whether *Homo habilis* walked upright or possessed other characteristics that would warrant placing it in the genus *Homo*. It seems more likely that it was an ape, although it may have differed considerably from the orang-utans, gorillas, or champanzees of today.[10]

10.6 HEIDELBERG MAN

This is a jaw found in 1907 in a sand pit at Mauer, near Heidelberg, Germany. The bank in which it was found contained twenty-four layers, the fossil being in the lowest of them, some 324 metres below the surface. The jaw is very large with a huge ascending ramus and no chin. It is generally dated to the second interglacial period. The remains are so limited that reconstructions are highly speculative. It seems to have been a large ape.

10.7 JAVA MAN

A Dutch physician named Dubois in 1891 found a skull cap along the bank of the Solo River near the village of Trinil, Java. About a year later he found a human femur about 15 metres away and also two molar teeth. In 1898 he discovered a pre-molar tooth which he believed should have been included with his first finds. The collection came to be known as *Pithecanthropus erectus*, or popularly as Java man, and is assigned an age of about half a million years by evolutionists.

Dubois concealed the fact for thirty years that he had also discovered at nearby Wadjak and at approximately the same level two human skulls (known as the Wadjak skulls). Had he revealed this it is most unlikely that his Java Man would have been accepted as a 'missing link'. Before his death he admitted that Java man was nothing more than a large gibbon.[11] Skulls found by von Koenigswald in 1936–39 forty miles from Trinil were labelled *Pithecanthropus II*, but were dominantly ape-like and similar to those of chimpanzees and gibbons.[12] The only justification for assessing *Pithecanthropus* as anything more than an ape was the association of a human femur with the other remains.

10.8 PEKING MAN

Fragments of about thirty skulls, eleven mandibles (lower jaws) and about 147 teeth were found at Choukou-tien about twenty miles from Peking in the 1920s and 1930s. Apart from a few highly fragmentary limb bones nothing else was found. All of this material except for two teeth disappeared in the period 1941–45 and none of it has ever been recovered.

The concept of *Sinanthropus pekinensis* was erected by Dr. Davidson Black, Professor of Anatomy at Union Medical College, Peking, on the basis of one of the molars found in 1927. More fragments were recovered in the next few years from a vast cavern in a limestone cliff with 46 metres of filling whose roof collapsed, burying its fillings. The Sinanthropus remains and the bones of about 100 different animals are found throughout the deposit. All the skulls were damaged and lacked the lower jaw. Their cranial capacity varied from 900 to about 1,200cc, about midway between the values of higher apes and of man.[13]

Boule and Valois[14] described one of the skulls in detail, assigning it to *Pithecanthropus* and stating that it was still very ape-like. The lower jaw is ape-like except for the parabolic dental arcade. Likewise the teeth were mainly, but not entirely, ape-like in character. They concluded that *Sinanthropus* was a large primate more closely allied to man than any other known great ape. They also found that the differences between *Sinanthropus* and *Pithecanthropus* were less than existed within a single species such as Neanderthal man, and for this reason suggested that the two creatures be included within one genus and called respectively *Pithecanthropus erectus* and *Pithecanthropus pekinensis*. Today most evolutionists place *Pithecanthropus* and *Sinanthropus* in a single species: *Homo erectus*.

Davidson Black died in 1934 and was replaced by Franz Weidenreich, who made models of three skulls based on finds made in 1936. They are respectively of a female gorilla, a female *Sinanthropus*, and of a northern Chinese. Since almost all of the original materials are lost, these models remain one of the chief sources of evidence we have today. The suggestion is that *Sinanthropus* forms the bridge between the other two. But the model of *Sinanthropus* is a speculative interpretation only, and although it has been influential, it is hardly admissible as evidence.

There are other problems with the view that *Sinanthropus* can be a missing link. All the bones found are skulls and the obvious conclusion is that they were brought into the cave as spoils or trophies by an unknown hunter. All authorities agree that the *Sinanthropus* individuals must have been killed by hunters. All the skulls have been smashed at the base so that the brains might be extracted and perhaps eaten. The identity of the hunters is unknown, but it seems most likely that they were true men. If this is so, the skulls cannot represent a species which is their ancestor.

Further doubt on the reliability of the Peking finds was cast by a Roman Catholic priest, Revd Patrick O'Connell who was in China during all of the time that the excavations were being carried out. He believed that the disappearance of the *Sinanthropus* remains was by design rather than accident. The Japanese did not interfere with the work at Choukoutien, and Weidenreich and his Chinese palaeontologist colleague Dr. W. C. Pei continued the work until Weidenreich left in 1940. O'Connell believes that Pei may have destroyed the fossils before the Chinese government returned to Peking in order to conceal the fact that the models did not correspond to them.

When we consider the description of the site, doubts are increased. The almost universally accepted version of the Choukoutien setting is that the *Sinanthropus* fossils were found in rubble filling a huge cavern, whose roof had collapsed. The human fossils found at an upper level in the same site supposedly originated from an upper cave. There is, however, little evidence that a cave existed at either level.

O'Connell believes that it was the site of large-scale limestone quarrying and burning in ancient times. This is evidenced by the presence of thousands of both roughly shaped fragments of limestone and of quartz stones, the latter having been brought from a distance (no quartz is found at Choukoutien) and covered with a layer of soot, indicating lime burning. The fossils of ten human individuals of modern type were found at an upper level.

Taking all this evidence together, the most reasonable explanation seems to be that the modern individuals were killed by a landslide caused by the undermining of the limestone cliff during quarrying operations and that this same landslide buried the *Sinanthropus* skulls. O'Connell concludes that the latter were the skulls of either large macaques (large monkeys) or large baboons killed and eaten by workers at the ancient quarry.

A combination of preconceived ideas and a desire for fame seem to have elevated a monkey-like creature to the status of an ape-like man.[15]

10.9 NEBRASKA MAN

In 1922 a tooth was discovered in western Nebraska

which was first thought to combine the characteristics of a chimpanzee, *Pithecanthropus*, and man. It was named *Hesperopithecus* but later study revealed it to be the tooth of an extinct peccary or pig.[16]

10.10 PILTDOWN MAN

In 1912, Arthur Smith Woodward, director of London's Natural History Museum, and Charles Dawson, a medical doctor and amateur palaeontologist, announced the discovery of a mandible and part of a skull in a gravel pit at Piltdown, Sussex. The two were combined and called *Eanthropus dawsoni* 'Dawn Man', known popularly as 'Piltdown Man'.

By 1950 a method had become available for assigning a relative age to fossil bones, based on the amount of fluoride they absorb from the soil. When the Piltdown bones were tested, it was found that the jawbone contained practically no fluoride, and the skull relatively little. This led to them being studied in more detail. It was then found that the bones had been treated with iron salts to make them look old, and scratch marks on the teeth indicated that they had been filed. It revealed that Piltdown Man was an outright hoax. The fact that it had deceived the whole scientific community for almost fifty years is a salutary reminder of the fallibility of even the greatest authorities.

10.11 NEANDERTHAL MAN

Neanderthal Man was first discovered over a century ago in a cave in the Neander Valley near Dusseldorf, Germany. He was first classified as *Homo neanderthalensis* and considered to be a semi-erect subhuman. This misconception seems to have been due to evidence that he was crippled with arthritis and rickets. It is now known that *Homo neanderthalensis* walked upright and was fully human. He has been reclassified as *Homo sapiens*. The conventional estimate is that he lived from about 100,000 to 25,000 years ago.

Other undoubted human remains from Swanscombe,

Kent have been assigned a date of 250,000 years.[17] This estimate, like those of the Peking and Neanderthal remains, is based on the belief that the Pleistocene period had a duration of 2-3 million years. Nothing in the fossils need lead to this conclusion. The fallacies of this chronology are considered elsewhere in this book.

10.12 CROMAGNON MAN

Three skeletons were found at Cromagnon in Dordogne, France, in 1858. They were of an old man, a young man and a young woman. They were tall, with strong muscular development, as proved by their bones, while their skulls were large and well-formed, with a cranial capacity similar to that of modern men. They were associated with some remarkably realistic cave paintings of animals. They are post glacial and unquestionably human.

10.13 THE DIFFERENCES BETWEEN APES AND HUMANS

There are a number of characters possessed by all humans and lacked by all apes:

1. Humans have a spinal column with an S-shaped curve as seen in profile, making for a completely erect posture and bipedal walking. These result from the position of the acetabulum (hip socket) in relation to man's centre of gravity. For an ape to move to a bipedal stance would require a relative movement of the acetabulum. Any intermediate position would be disadvantageous.

There is an evolutionary contention that the human body has inadequacies because the viscera are supported only by a musculature, which is only suitable for an animal going on all fours.[18] The change to bipedality and upright stance, it is claimed, means that the weight is not properly supported so that undue exertion can lead to the tissues giving way, resulting in a hernia. But this suggestion is speculative only and cannot be supported from any study of anatomical detail.

2. Relatively short arms in relation to leg length.

3. A nose with a prominent bridge and elongated tip.

4. Teeth are aligned in a parabolic curve and lack gaps. Apes tend to have their opposite cheek teeth more parallel and there is always a small gap between their upper canine teeth and adjacent incisors and between the lower canines and the adjacent premolars. The canines in apes are more elongated and tusk-like than in man.

5. No thumbs on feet.

6. Humans have a smaller baby:adult weight ratio and are more helpless in relation to adults than are any apes.

7. Red lips formed by extending mucous membrane from inside the mouth.

8. A language fundamentally different from the way animals communicate. All humans have a fully developed language; no animal does.

10. Is a worshipping being.

Brain size is not a good distinguishing criterion because it varies with sex and age. More important is brain surface which cannot easily be interpreted from fossils. For instance, one South American squirrel monkey has a brain twice the relative size of man's in relation to the size of its body.

It is quite consistent both with the fossil record and with these differences to believe that there has always been a clear distinction between apes and humans.

10.14 SUMMARY

Humans are generally believed to be descended from primates via Catarrhines, and to have some Old World monkeys as their closest relatives in the animal kingdom. Supposed human evolution has been traced through numerous fossil finds. Those given earliest positions in the sequence: Ramapithecus, Australopithecus, Heidelberg man, Java man, and Peking man seem to have been apes with some points of similarity to humans. The tooth ascribed to Nebraska man proved to have belonged to an extinct pig and the Piltdown skull was a hoax. Neanderthal men have some ape-like characteristics but are sufficiently within the range of *Homo sapiens* to be classified as true men. Others, including the Swanscombe skull, and Cromagnon men seem most reasonably classified as fully human. There are too many basic differences between the remains of humans and those of even the most similar apes, to sustain the idea of their common ancestry.

REFERENCES

[1] Gish 1986, page 140. [2] quoted by Gish loc. cit., page 144. [3] Zuckerman 1970, page 93; Oxnard 1974, 1975. [4] Gish loc. cit., page 151. [5] Johanson and White 1979, 1980. [6] Gish 1986, page 162. [7] 1973a, Walker and Leakey 1978; Gish 1986, pages 164-166. [8] 1973b. [9] Walker and Leakey 1978; Gish 1986, page 166. [10] Gish 1986, page 168. [11] Gish 1979, pages 123-127. [12] Gish 1986, page 183. [13] Gish 1979, page 92. [14] 1957, pages 133-140. [15] Gish loc. cit., page 199. [16] Gregory 1927. [17] Eckhardt 1972. [18] e.g. Halstead 1984.

CHAPTER 11

EVIDENCES FOR HUMAN ANTIQUITY

11.1 HUMAN REMAINS IN OLDER GEOLOGICAL DEPOSITS

It is common to believe that humans have evolved upwards from primitive beginnings during the Quaternary period and that there has been no world-wide Flood. But there is growing evidence that human remains existed in earlier rock strata and that early man had science and technologies which in some ways matched those of today, and an awareness of origins which accords closely to the biblical account. There was a universal belief that a great Flood destroyed the world, that the pre-Flood world was technically and culturally sophisticated and that some of this sophistication was remembered in the post-Flood world.

A number of records exist which show human traces in geological strata earlier, and in some cases much earlier, than the Pleistocene and Recent geological deposits in which the vast majority of human remains are found. The existence of only one of these would contradict the view that man's origins are only associated with the most recent deposits.

Human bones and teeth have been found in coal. These include a skull in lignite, presumably of Tertiary age first described in 1842 in the collection of the Freiberg Mining Academy in Germany,[1] two molars from Tertiary coal from a mine at Bear Creek, Montana, discovered in 1926,[2] and a child's jawbone in Miocene coal in Tuscany discovered in 1958. Still lower in the geological record, human skeletons were found in Cretaceous rocks near Moab, Utah.[3]

11.2 HUMAN FOOTPRINTS IN OLDER ROCKS

A shod human footprint has been found in Cambrian

rock over some crushed trilobites on which it appears to have trodden. This alone upsets the concept that man did not exist until about 600 million years after these rocks were laid down.[4] Unshod human footprints were found and measured in a crinoidal limestone in Indiana, USA as early as 1822.[5] The geological stratum involved is not named, but crinoids are mainly Palaeozoic, although also found throughout the Mesozoic.

11.3 HUMAN ARTIFACTS IN OLDER ROCKS

Human artifacts have been reported in rocks supposedly older than human life on earth. White[6] has assembled the evidences. Since coal is the sedimentary material most often seen by many people, most examples have been found in it. A lady in Morrisonville, Illinois, found a gold chain still connected to the coal by both ends in 1891.

An iron pot with its impression in coal was found in Oklahoma, an incised steel cube in coal in Austria, and artificially pointed sticks in a lignite in Germany. The Oklahoma and Austrian coals were estimated to be 300 million years old, and the German lignite Tertiary between 2 and 70 million years. Both of these antedate the presumed origin of man on Earth.

Spanish conquistadores found an iron nail 15 centimetres long in a Peruvian mine encrusted with rock. Iron was not known to the Indians at the time, though its antidiluvian use is recorded in Genesis 4:22, which suggests it may have been a pre-Flood remnant. Another nail was found in Cretaceous rock in Britain. These items appear to be genuinely *in situ* and show no sign of having been inserted later into their positions.

Turning to other types of rock, in 1851 workmen discovered a bell-shaped metal pot in solid rock 5 metres below the surface that they were blasting on Meeting House Hill near Dorchester, Massachusetts. It had inlaid floral designs in silver which showed a great deal of artistic ability and metallurgic technology.[7] A baked clay figure measuring about 3.8 centimetres in length was found at a depth of about 90 metres in Pliocene strata at Nampa, Idaho in 1889.[8]

All these finds go to indicate the presence of human remains in rocks far older than current theory allows and indicate a probable human presence on earth as early as the Palaeozoic.

11.4 FLOOD TRADITIONS

The historicity of the Flood is confirmed by six New Testament passages and it is either stated or implied to be supernatural.[9] It is presented as a unique event, never to be repeated.

There is no tradition so widespread among all the peoples of the world. Stickling[10] reported that anthropologists have collected fifty-nine Flood legends from the aborigines of North America, forty-six from Central and South America extending from Alaska to Tierra del Fuego, thirty-one from Europe ranging from Greece to Ireland and Iceland, seventeen from the Middle East, twenty-three from Asia, and thirty-seven from the South Sea Islands, Australia and New Zealand. Such legends are rarer in Africa though can be found from Egypt to Nigeria and from the Congo to the Cape, and Filby records seven.[11] As the tribes migrated further and further from Ararat, the stories become more and more distorted. This substantiates the view that they have a common origin and are not exaggerated tales of local catastrophes.[12]

These Flood legends generally agree on three main features:

1. That water destroyed all the human race and all other living things,

2. That an ark or boat provided a means of escape,

3. That a family was preserved to perpetuate the human race.

Beyond this they tend to differ, some considerably. The tradition in Greenland is of one man being saved, among the Papago Indians of Arizona one man and a dog, in Alaska one man and animals, among the Bataks of

Sumatra two people, among the Incas six people, in Cuba a family, and in Mexico and Hawaii a family and animals. A wide variety of names are given to the man, but Noh in the Sudan, Nu-u in Hawaii, and Nu-Wah in China, are similar to the biblical Noah.

Chinese tradition assigns the Flood to 2,300 BC. The hero escapes with his wife, three sons, and three daughters. The written symbol for 'ship' in the Chinese language is made up of a boat with eight mouths, showing that the first ship carried eight people.[13] The Indian Vedas have two Flood accounts. In the Rig-Veda, Manu (another similar name) builds the ark himself. Most accounts record the use of a boat, but the Algonquins of north-eastern USA believe it was a turtle.[14]

The most detailed records, as might be expected, are from the Middle East and the eastern Mediterranean.

Berossus, a Chaldean priest contemporary with Alexander the Great, reported that the Flood occurred in the reign of the tenth king of Babylon, a recognizable analogy with the Bible record of ten antediluvian patriarchs. The god Chronos warned Xisuthros, king of Babylon, to build a ship to save his family, friends and animals. He specified its size as 5 stadia long by 2 wide (approximately 1,000 × 400 metres). This is far larger than the biblical 300 × 50 × 30 cubits, which is equivalent to 133 × 22 × 13 metres and sounds much more reasonable. When the Deluge was waning, Xisuthros sent out birds. The first two returned but not the third, as in the biblical account.

Xisuthros disembarked with his wife, daughter and pilot, raised an altar, sacrificed to the gods, and then disappeared to heaven with them. The others disembarked from the ark, did not find Xisuthros but heard a voice from heaven enjoining piety and explaining that he, his wife, daughter, and pilot had already received the award of piety and gone to live among the gods.

The voice then told them to return to Babylon, dig up the writings buried at Sippara and make them known among men, telling them that they had landed in Armenia.

They followed these instructions, went to Babylon, dug up the writings, founded numerous temples, and restored Babylon.

The Egyptian tradition was recorded by Manetho about 250BC and included a world-wide catastrophe from which one man named Toth escaped.

The Greeks had a tradition that Zeus destroyed the world by inundation but that a man, Deucalion, was saved. They also had a legend of the island of Atlantis beyond the Pillars of Hercules which in a single day and night of misfortune sank beneath the sea. Plato deals with this tradition in his unfinished dialogue 'Critias', introducing a plan of Zeus' to destroy the world for its wickedness though he never completed the part which would have dealt with the Flood itself.

The Roman Flood tradition is in Ovid's 'Metamorphoses'. Jupiter destroys the human race with a flood because of its wickedness. The rainbow was a messenger of Juno to maintain water in the clouds. All living things were destroyed except for a righteous man, also called by his Greek name Deucalion, and his wife Pyrrha who were saved in a ship. After this the waters abated and they reoccupied the land.

The most remarkable Flood story outside of the Bible is that which forms a part of the Gilgamesh Epic. This is a cuneiform inscription on clay tablets which was found in the ancient library at Nineveh of Assurbanipal, king of Assyria from 668 to 626BC. Austen Henry Layard started in 1845 to dig up this site and sent more than 20,000 clay tablets and fragments to the British Museum. George Smith, a British Orientalist, in 1872 accidentally discovered the Gilgamesh account on a number of them. This caused an immediate sensation.[15]

The importance of this record is its early date and the very close agreement with the Genesis account. Both ascribe the Flood to a divine decision. Both give the dimensions of the ship, although they differ in details.

Gilgamesh gives the floor space as about one 'iku' (3,600 square metres) with a height of 120 cubits (55 metres) in seven decks. It records that the Flood lasted seven days; in the Bible the embarkation alone takes seven days. In both accounts a raven and dove are sent out, though in Gilgamesh the third bird is a swallow and the order is different. Both end with a thank offering which is favourably received by God or the gods respectively. The rainbow of Genesis is represented by the great jewels of Ishtar. The mention of the rainbow in both is remarkable in that it suggests that it must have been a new phenomenon. Finally, in both accounts there is a covenant guaranteeing no repetition of a destructive flood and a blessing on the hero and his wife.

Many scholars explain the coincidence between the Genesis and Gilgamesh accounts by according priority to the latter. Some hold that the story was brought from Mesopotamia by Abraham, some that it was transmitted to the Israelites during the so-called Amarna period in Egypt, and others that it was obtained in Babylon at the time of the Exile. Assurbanipal ruled from 668 to 626 BC and the Gilgamesh tablets must predate this. Although concrete evidence is lacking either way, the Mosaic account has at least as great a claim to be the earlier.

The historicity of the Scriptural account is perhaps supported by a significant coincidence of anniversaries. The Ark came to rest on 17th of Nisan.[16] A millenium later the Israelites kept the first Passover on 14 Nisan, crossing the Red Sea to form a new nation on 17 Nisan. More than a millenium later again, the synoptic gospels place Christ's resurrection on 17 Nisan. The second and third of these events are clearly historical. It is thus reasonable to assume that the first is too. This conclusion is strengthened by the fact that the first and third are theologically linked through baptism.[17] It is unlikely that so important a doctrine would not have been based on true happenings.

11.5 GEOGRAPHICAL NOMENCLATURE

Some place names indicate that the location of the Ark's resting place has been retained in human records.

The Bible states that the Ark landed on the mountains (plural) of Ararat, indicating that the name was used for a district and not for a particular peak. It seems to be identical with the Urartu of ancient inscriptions, a term applied to the land that the Greeks called Armenia and is frequently referred to in Assyrian records.

Some place names in Armenia are clearly connected to the Bible story, though we cannot be sure if they were given immediately after the Flood or centuries later by tradition. Josephus says that the Armenians called the Ark's landing place *Apobaterion* — 'the Place of Descent or Disembarking', and quotes Nicolaus of Damascus as calling the mountain *Baris*,[18] but this name today refers to a town now variously written Izbarta, Sparta or Isparta in western Asia Minor (which seems too far away from the Ararat area to have any connection). Epiphanius locates the landing place among the *Gordyean* hills of Armenia, saying that one peak, higher than the others, had the name *Lubar* which, he says, means 'descending place'. *Gordyean* probably means Kurdistan. The traveller William de Rubruquis about AD 1253 said that in Armenia there was a little town called *Nachuan* near mountains called *Masis* and beyond these yet another place called *Cemainum* which means 'eight', in memory of the eight people saved in the Ark.[19] The Armenian historian, Moses Chorenensis, is quoted as saying that the place was known locally as *Nachidsheuan* — 'the place of descent'. There is still a district and town in Armenia called Nakhichevan, (possibly the same as Nachsivan which means the burial place of Noah) some 130–160 kilometres south-east of Ararat, and a small town called Nahievan some 65 kilometres south-west of the Ararat range. The name *Tabriz*, for the Iranian city nearby, may be a corruption of *Ta Baris* — possibly 'mountain of the ship'. Moses Chorenensis also speaks of a place called *Seron*, 'the place of dispersion' because from there the descendants of Noah began to disperse.[20]

11.6 GENEALOGICAL EVIDENCE FOR MANKIND'S RECENT ORIGINS

Evidences for Creation and the Flood are supported by those derived from genealogy.

Genesis 5 gives a genealogy which extends from Creation until after the Flood; Genesis 10 and 11 bring it down to the time of Abraham. The sequence of Abraham's descendants is given in several places in the Old Testament and is complete to the time of Our Lord. These genealogies are intimately connected to the rest of biblical history and so its historicity is linked to theirs. If they are true, an evolutionary account of human origins cannot be sustained because a. the time required by the genealogies is too short to allow for it, and b. the first humans were mentally and physically at least equal to those of today.

Genealogies also exist for other nations which generally accord with those in Scripture. It is significant that Egyptian, Babylonian, and Celtic records all agree on an original creation, on ten antediluvian patriarchs, on the occurrence of the Flood, and on the approximate time between that event and recorded history. The pagan Irish historians dated every important event from the year of the Creation 'Anno Mundi' — not far removed from Ussher's 4004 BC. Irish Celtic, British Celtic, and Saxon records all contain king lists which purport to go back to the time of the Flood and the scattering of the nations from Babel (see Appendix 1).

11.7 EVIDENCES FROM CHINESE SACRIFICIAL SYSTEM AND SCRIPT

Researches by Ethel Nelson and Richard Broadberry[21] have shown that some aspects of early Chinese civilization retain echoes of man's origins which are remarkably concordant with the early chapters of Genesis.

China had a sacrificial system which began even before

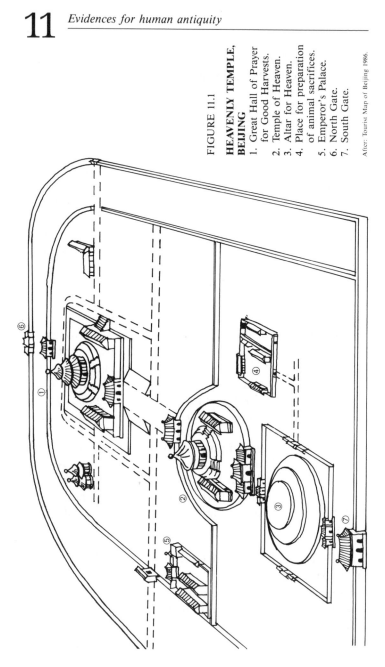

FIGURE 11.1

HEAVENLY TEMPLE, BEIJING

1. Great Hall of Prayer for Good Harvests.
2. Temple of Heaven.
3. Altar for Heaven.
4. Place for preparation of animal sacrifices.
5. Emperor's Palace.
6. North Gate.
7. South Gate.

After: Tourist Map of Beijing 1986.

its dynastic rule in 2205 BC and only ended when the Manchus were deposed in 1911. God was originally viewed as a heavenly emperor and the creator of Heaven, Earth, plants, animals and man. His name was Shang-Ti, notably similar to the Hebrew El Shaddai. Every year the Chinese Emperor conducted, on behalf of the nation, a 'Border Sacrifice', burning a bullock to Shang-Ti on the Altar of Heaven in Peking. Early records speak of this rite having been performed at Mount Tai in Shantung at the eastern border of China. Then there came to be two border sacrifices: to the Earth at the summer solstice on the northern border of the country, to Heaven at the winter solstice on its southern border. Gradually the latter came to be more important.

This sacrifice was clearly important to Confucius (551–479 BC) because he compared a comprehension of the ritual to the efficient ruling of the Chinese Empire. He was a worshipper of Shang-Ti and used his influence to preserve the purity of the worship services to the God of Heaven. He evidently spent much time researching into its true meaning, although without achieving a definite conclusion.

In the fifteenth century AD the service was moved to three edifices in an extensive park in the southern part of Peking. They are in a north-south line. The northernmost is the great Hall of Prayer for Good Harvests, which was completed in AD 1420. In the centre is the smaller Temple of Heaven (Figure 11.1). *This contains no idol*, but a tablet on the north wall inscribed with Chinese characters meaning 'Heavenly Sovereign Shang-Ti'. The southernmost edifice is the Altar of Heaven where the sacrifices were conducted. This is a triple-tiered circular white marble eminence 250 metres in diameter. Each tier is surrounded by balustrades. The uppermost level can be reached by a series of steps on each of four sides. The Border Sacrifice was performed annually throughout the centuries long after its original significance had been forgotten and obscured by

Confucianism, Taoism, and Buddhism. It clearly has close analogies with the sacrificial system of the Old Testament.

The earliest Chinese pictograms indicate that this sacrificial ritual must have been based on an original knowledge of the biblical Creation and Fall. Because pictograms altered substantially over the centuries, it was necessary to refer to their earliest known forms. These appeared on bronzeware ceremonial vessels and oracle bone scripts. Many of the earliest pictograms appeared to be inspired by events in the Garden of Eden in a way that would be hard to explain if humans had no such remembrance. They give a picture of a divinely created man and woman in a garden which had four rivers, contained a forbidden tree, was visited by the Devil, was the scene of human death, and involved the subsequent death of a sheep to secure forgiveness and righteousness.

The word for 'border' has a number of pictograms. All denote the border of this garden, and more specifically the east gate. They show God and a sheep, and one includes a kneeling worshipper. They suggest that the sacrifice outside of Eden's closed east gate, where the cherubim stood,[22] was the original 'border sacrifice' initiated by Shang-Ti himself. The fact that the early imperial sacrifices were in the *east* of China echoes this. All looked forward to the sacrifice of the 'seed of the woman' on behalf of all the descendants of Adam. Finally, the pictogram for 'hiding place', also indicating the 'final safe place for humans', is a combination of those for 'conceal' and 'three mouths' (three persons) — an echo of the Trinity.

The Chinese 'border sacrifice' and some pictograms give some confirmation of the biblical account of origins.

11.8 EVIDENCES OF EARLY ARTISTIC SOPHISTICATION

There is considerable evidence that humans had access to technologies which go far beyond their simple, even primitive, lives before about 2,000 BC. These imply a considerable history of development, and suggest the possibility that the skills may have been in part inherited from still more ancient times, perhaps from memories of an antediluvian world. There are notable examples in art, architecture, and astronomy.

PRIMITIVE ART. European Upper Palaeolithic art first appeared with the advent of the Cromagnon men in the *Aurignacian* period, variously estimated to have begun between about 20,000 and 14,000 BP. It developed in the *Gravettian* period, and fruited in a veritable Renaissance in the *Magdalenian* period which is thought to have ended before 8,000 BC. Frescoes from these periods have been found in caves all the way from the Dordogne to Natal, and especially in France, Spain, and Italy.

Probably the most outstanding example of Aurignacian art is that in the Lascaux caves in south-western France, first discovered in 1940. The walls and ceilings have frescoes of rhinoceroses, bison, deer, oxen, and small horses. Bulls are grouped as they would be in the wild; deer are running. The pictures show quite remarkable vigour of handling, sureness of line, and perfection of form. The artists had skill and sensitivity comparable to the best found today.

The Altamira caves in northern Spain, discovered in 1879, have frescoes showing wolves, bison, reindeer, wild boars, and horses. They are estimated to be of *Magdalenian* age. Their antiquity was doubted when they were first discovered because they are so magnificently observed and drawn. They incorporate the natural vaultings in the walls and roof in the design. The roof paintings must have been done by men by the light of a wick burning in melted animal fat under difficulties at least as severe as those suffered by Michelangelo when he worked on the barrel vaulting of the Sistine Chapel.

The paintings were begun with charcoal or flint-inscribed outlines. The artist added colour with fingers, fur, twigs, or moss, or even blew dry colours through a hollow reed or bone tube, or rubbed on the colours after mixing them with animal fat and rolling them into crayons.

A number of such crayons were found at Altamira. The most commonly used colours were red, yellow, and orange from iron oxides, and brown and black from heated animal fat and charcoal. The sketching and colour application were done in bold, sure strokes, with few apparent mistakes or corrections. The presence of stones bearing corrected sketches indicates the existence of an 'art school' at Limeuil (south-western France).

These paintings show levels of artistic sensitivity and, allowing for the differences in facilities, of technical competence comparable to those of today. They must make us doubt that the human body and mind have experienced any evolutionary change since that time.

PYRAMIDS OF EGYPT. The purpose of the Egyptian pyramids was to protect tombs. This has little justification in modern eyes, especially since it was almost never successful in preventing subsequent robbery. Paradoxically, however, they present a remarkable architectural achievement at a very early date.

The largest pyramid is that of Cheops at Giza. It was built by the fourth-dynasty pharaoh of that name in about 2,600 BC. It is a masterpiece of technical skill and engineering ability, although completed by men working with the simplest implements without draft animals or even the wheel. It contains 2,300,000 limestone blocks each weighing up to 15 tonnes, and fifty-six large granite blocks in critical positions. The latter were cut from the water-worn rocks of the Aswan cataract, some 500 miles upsteam from Giza. They were quarried by cleavage, and then cut out by inserting wedges down lines of holes. The facing was done by hammer-dressing, using rounded masses of quartz hornstone held in the hand without any handle. In order to get a hold for moving the blocks without bruising the edges, projecting lumps or bosses were left, which were subsequently struck off when the block was in place. The blocks were transported from Aswan to Giza by rollers and river transport.

The pyramid was built on absolutely level step-like terraces cut into the irregular sides of a hill. The builders laid out the 5-hectare site so evenly that experts using modern instruments have found that the south-eastern corner of the pyramid stands only 1.2 centimetres higher than the north-western corner. This was apparently achieved by using connected water-filled trenches. The blocks were fitted together with exact precision. The pyramid is aligned to the points of the compass with an accuracy of less than 4 minutes of arc. The length of its four sides are respectively 230.26m (N), 230.45m (S), 230.39m (E), and 230.36m (W). Their maximum difference is therefore only 19cm, or an accuracy better than 1 part in 1,200.

The interior is an architectural marvel. The walls and casing stones show finer joints than any other masonry in Egypt and possibly in the world.[23] The pyramid contains a self-sealing burial chamber with a roof specially designed to bear the vast weight of overlying stone and two narrow shafts to the outside air.

This fourth dynasty was the finest period of Egyptian workmanship in every respect. The accuracy of layout and construction of the Pyramid of Cheops was never again achieved in pyramids, and is evidence of remarkably advanced technology at a very early date.[24]

STONE CIRCLES AND ROWS. Ancient races needed information about the Sun's movements to make accurate calendars and about the Moon's movements to predict eclipses and tides. The latter were especially important for navigation in potentially dangerous areas such as the Scottish coast and islands.

The answer was to build stone rings and rows. Neolithic peoples in the third millenium BC and the Bronze Age Beaker Folk after about 1900 BC constructed them throughout Britain, Ireland and Brittany, with well over a thousand rings in Britain alone. They vary in size from small circles a few metres in diameter to the Avebury ring which is over 300 metres across. They were laid out in accurate geometrical shapes: circular, flattened circular, egg-shaped, and elliptical, as shown on Figure 11.2.[25]

The shapes followed two rules. First, the basic unit of measurement was the megalithic yard (82.97 plus or minus 0.09cm). All linear dimensions had to be multiples of this and the perimeters had to be multiples of the megalithic rod ($2\frac{1}{2}$ megalithic yards). On the smaller scale of stone carvings the builders frequently used a smaller unit, the megalithic inch ($\frac{1}{40}$ of the megalithic yard or 2.07cm). Measurement accuracy approached one part in 1,000. These units were universal throughout Britain, Ireland and Brittany, implying wide intercommunication.[26]

Secondly, all layouts were based on right-angle triangles. Megalithic people had an extensive knowledge of practical geometry and used the 3, 4, 5 triangle extensively. They also knew the 5, 12, 13 right-angle triangle, the 8, 15, 17 and the 12, 35, 37. There is a suspicion that they knew the 9, 40, 41. They had in addition discovered many other triangles that satisfied very closely the Pythagorean relation.[27]

Their most remarkable construction is undoubtedly Stonehenge. Although authorities differ, it appears to have been built in three stages, probably beginning in the third millenium BC and ending by 1550 BC.[28] Although there has been some loss and damage, it remains a veritable cathedral of stones, some up to 50 tonnes in weight. From the centre outwards it consists of an eliptical group of sarsen trilithons (two vertical stones bridged by a horizontal lintel), a circle of Prescelly bluestones, a circle of massive sarsens, and then three circles of holes which may at one time have held posts. The outermost circle of holes includes four stones called Station Stones. The whole is surrounded by a circular bank and ditch, which are the oldest part of the monument.

The sarsens were probably obtained from Marlborough Downs about 30 kilometres to the north. The bluestones came from the Prescelly Mountains in Pembrokeshire,

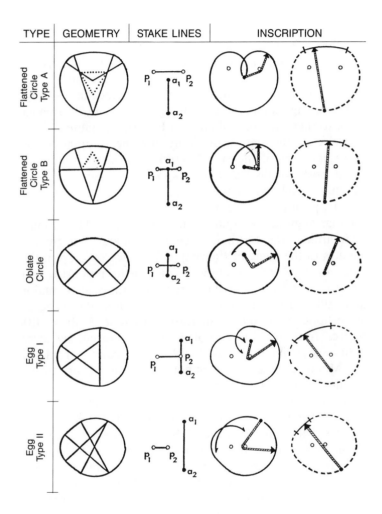

TYPE	GEOMETRY	STAKE LINES	INSCRIPTION

FIGURE 11.2

The geometry, stake lines, and scribing method probably used for laying out the five different designs of megalithic ring.

Source: Cowan 1970, page 322; Copyright 1970 by the AAAS.

whence they must have been transported by sea, land, and river. Hawkins and White[29] estimate that the total building effort must have cost some 1.5 million man days, a vast outlay at a time when England's population was probably less than 300,000. It probably represented at least 1% of the gross national product. The lintels of the trilithons are linked to the uprights by carved mortice and tenon joints.[30] Their construction involved sophisticated locating, lifting, and levelling comparable, although on a much smaller scale, to that used in building the Egyptian pyramids.

Twelve of the significant stone alignments point to extreme positions of the Sun. These include sunrise and sunset at both solstices and were apparently associated with obtaining a reliable annual calendar. Twelve more point to extreme positions of the moon.[31]

Lunar alignments require some explanation. The Moon's orbit around the Earth is inclined by about 5 degrees 8 minutes to the angle of the ecliptic ($23\frac{1}{2}$ degrees). From the point of view of an observer on Earth, moonrise and moonset can vary between extreme positions at a 'major standstill' when it is about $28\frac{1}{2}$ degrees from the plane of the ecliptic to a 'minor standstill' when it is about $18\frac{1}{2}$ degrees from it. One complete cycle of variations takes 18.61 years. Simultaneously with these major variations, the Moon experiences a minor variation of up to $9\frac{1}{2}$ minutes through the effects of gravity.

The Moon's angular deviation from the angle of the ecliptic therefore reaches a maximum of 5 degrees $17\frac{1}{2}$ minutes when the Earth and Sun are aligned with the Moon (in syzygy) and a minimum of 4 degrees 58 minutes when they are at right angles with it (in quadrature). Since eclipses require the linear alignment of Sun, Moon, and Earth, their occurrences coincide with the maximum values of this perturbation and can be predicted from them.

Although few megalithic sites are aligned to every movement of the Sun and Moon, in aggregate they include all solstitial solar alignments and extreme lunar standstill alignments. They usually contain sight lines from stones in the circle to identifiable points on the horizon. The stone lines at Mid Clyth (Caithness) and the stone circle at Temple Wood, (Argyllshire), for instance, are aligned respectively to moonrise and moonset and both include the maximum of the minor variation. The sight lines are accurate to less than one minute of arc (that is, equivalent to 3 centimetres viewed at 100 metres). Thom gives dates for them between about 1830 and 1730 BC.[32]

The Moon's minor variation was unknown to the Greeks. It was first measured by Tycho Brahe (born AD 1546), although its existence had been suspected by the Arab astronomer Aboul-Hassan-Aly-ben-Amajour about AD 918. But it appears that the megalithic builders not only knew of it but were able to determine the exact time at which it was at a maximum over 2,500 years earlier still. This involved brilliant mental capacity. It necessitated working out, from observations made on either side of the maximum, where an observer would have to stand in relation to the standing stones to see the Moon at maximum declination. The achievement is the more amazing because the actual technique is simple, requiring only ropes and measuring rods.[33]

Evidence for early astronomical sophistication can also probably be discerned in the location of Stonehenge at 51 degrees 17 minutes north of the equator. This latitude makes a right angle between the major axis oriented to the extreme solar horizon points and an axis, marked by the 'station stones', aligned to extreme lunar horizon points. If the site was moved south or north by as little as 50 kilometres, to say, Oxford or Bournemouth, the astronomical geometry would be changed. It would only repeat at the same latitude south of the equator, approximately that of the Falkland Islands. The Stonehenge builders had, therefore, placed this geometrically-celestially-elegant pattern at the only latitude in the northern hemisphere which made its unique geometry possible.[34]

That this choice was not accidental seems to be confirmed by the Callanish stone circle on the Isle of Lewis, whose stones also form an astronomical calendar. This lies just 1.3 degrees south of the 'Arctic Circle' of the Moon, the latitude where at its extreme declination the Moon remains hidden just below the southern horizon. At Callanish, the full Moon at midsummer stands about 1 degree above the southern horizon once every 18.61 years. A row of stones points to its rising, transit and setting at this time.

The megalithic builders therefore combined building skills with considerable geometrical and astronomical knowledge. They knew how to keep records of dates and numbers. They understood in some detail the effects of latitude on solar and lunar movements. Their knowledge of the Moon's minor perturbation must be considered the intellectual peak of the early Bronze Age in north-west Europe.[35] It is not too much to infer from this that they may have understood the sphericity and approximate circumference of the Earth over 1,400 years before Eratosthenes' measurements in about 200 BC. Such indications of early intelligence argue against the view that humans were only just emerging from a primitive evolutionary ancestry, and raise the strong possibility that some knowledge was inherited from a remoter, perhaps antedeluvian, past.

11.9 SUMMARY

There are a number of lines of evidence that human life was on the Earth well before the Pliocene period and that it was relatively sophisticated even at the beginning. This supports the biblical idea that man was created perfect and has since declined.

Human bones, teeth, footprints, and artifacts have been reported from rocks earlier than the Pliocene. Flood traditions are widespread in every continent, almost all agreeing that it caused universal destruction and that one family escaped by boat. Place names around Mount Ararat indicate a local belief that it was where a boat landed.

Biblical genealogies begin at Creation and indicate that

the Earth can only be a few thousand years old. Some non-biblical genealogies also support this conclusion. Ancient Chinese religious rituals and forms of writing appear to confirm not only a young Earth but also some details of the Genesis creation story.

Early artifacts indicate a high level of human intelligence. Allowing for the differences in technology, Stone Age paintings reflect artistic skills similar to those of the present day. The Egyptian pyramids and European megalithic observatories testify to high standards of observation, and considerable competence in mathematics and architecture in the third millenium BC. These argue against the view that the human brain has improved by natural selection since those times.

REFERENCES

[1] Whitcomb and Morris 1974, page 176. [2] White 1978, page 108. [3] Gish 1975. [4] Baker 1976, page 9. [5] White 1978, pages 108, 109. [6] ibid., pages 110-112. [7] von Fange 1974. [8] White loc. cit., page 110. [9] Matthew 24:37-42; Luke 17:26, 27; Hebrews 11:7; 1 Peter 3:20, 21; 2 Peter 2:4-5; 3:5-7. [10] 1972. [11] 1970, pages 49-53. [12] Keane 1991, page 58. [13] Noorbergen 1978, page 6. [14] Rehwinkel 1967, page 134. [15] Rehwinkel 1967, pages 153, 154. [16] Genesis 8:4. [17] 1 Peter 3:20. 21. [18] Filby 1970, page 45. [19] ibid., page 44. [20] ibid., page 115. [21] 1986. [22] Genesis 3:24. [23] Encyclopaedia Britannica 1990. [24] Encyclopaedia Britannica 1911. [25] Cowan 1970; Thom 1978, page 18. [26] Thom and Thom 1978, pages 30-44. [27] Thom 1973, page 9. [28] Atkinson 1956, pages 58-94; Heggie 1981, page 146. [29] 1973, pages 73, 74. [30] Thom and Thom 1978, page 141. [31] Hawkins and White 1973, page 107. [32] 1967, pages 97, 156; 1973, pages 112, 113. [33] Thom 1973, page 18. [34] Hawkins and White 1973, pages 189, 190. [35] Wood 1978, page 113.

PART III

THE AUTHORITY OF SCRIPTURE

CHAPTER **12**

SCRIPTURAL AUTHORITY: INTERNAL EVIDENCE

12.1 BIBLICAL AUTHORITY

The Scriptures of the Old and New Testaments claim divine inspiration throughout but contain two distinct types of message. The first type is those messages which claim to be the direct utterances of God. This includes the Decalogue and over 2,000 statements introduced by such phrases as 'the word of the LORD came to . . . ' or 'thus saith the LORD'. The actual words of Christ in the New Testament belong to this category. Although their arrangement in the text may be due to the author, the message is directly from God.

The second type of message consists of narratives, teachings, and poetry composed by the human writers themselves, but which are arrangements of Scripture quotations, historical records, oral accounts, or personal observations. The Pauline epistles and the book of Acts are examples of this method. Rice[1] has defined the first type as 'prophetic' and the second as 'Lucan', choosing these terms because the prophets frequently spoke words given them directly by God, whereas Luke selected and arranged a number of sources.

The Bible authors wrote mainly in Hebrew and Greek although Aramaic is occasionally used.[2] Translations can be valid only to the extent that they reproduce the true sense of the original. As the different writers present a subject under different aspects and relations, there may appear to be discrepancies and contradictions, but reverent study, with clearer insight, shows the underlying harmony.

There are a number of lines of evidence that the Bible is the infallible Word of God.

12.2 TESTIMONY OF THE INTERNAL CLAIM

The internal claim to divine authority is so frequent that to quote all the passages would require a book. It is both directly stated and implicitly assumed in both Old and New Testaments. Direct statements are made by David, Jeremiah, Ezekiel, Luke, and Paul.[3] Peter goes so far as to state that the Scriptures are surer than the evidence of the senses.[4]

Scriptural authority is also assumed in many passages where there is no direct statement. Both Moses and John warn against adding or subtracting from it.[5] David refers to the law as everlasting,[6] and Amos says that God will reveal all His works through His prophets.[7]

The outstanding testimony comes from our Lord. He clearly supports the authority and everlasting nature of every word,[8] refers to Old Testament passages as authoritative both before and after the Resurrection,[9] and equates God with the authorship of the first two chapters of Genesis.[10] He settles a dispute by taking two words from a psalm, calling them the Law and saying that it cannot be broken.[11] He even makes the exact moment of His own death depend upon the fulfilment of one verse,[12] and continues to quote the Scriptures even after the Resurrection.[13]

12.3 TESTIMONY OF ITS UNITY

About forty writers, widely differing in occupation and experience, scattered from Egypt to Babylon, and from Rome to Midian, wrote over a span of 1,500 years. Yet when brought together the writings show one Author and one theme.

12.4 TESTIMONY OF ITS ENDURANCE

The Bible claims that its words will last forever.[14] Despite frequent attempts over 2 millenia to destroy, ban, or restrict its circulation, it remains the world's best seller. Opposition has tended to increase, rather than decrease, its popularity.

12.5 TESTIMONY OF SCIENCE

Although the Bible is not a textbook on science, except the science of salvation, every statement shows a knowledge which can only have come from a deep creative intelligence. Although man's discoveries do not all apparently agree with it, the trend has always been for advancing science to confirm it. This is evidence that the Creator must be its author. It contains statements about the nature of the universe and such details as health laws, unknown when it was written, which were only discovered much later by human science and partly through following its guidance.

The Bible's understanding of cosmology can be seen not only in direct statements about Creation and the Flood but also in many intimations which show that the authors, even if they did not always understand all they wrote, were in fact inspired by a source of knowledge which can only have come from the Creator. A number of examples of this can be quoted.

Hipparchus in the second century BC believed that the number of stars in the sky was less than 3,000, and Ptolemy in the second century AD counted 1,056. However, 400 years earlier Jeremiah had stated that the stars were innumerable.[15] This was repeated by the author of Hebrews in the first century AD,[16] and finally confirmed by modern telescopes.

The Bible states that the Earth is spherical,[17] that it hangs unsupported in space,[18] and that the atmosphere has the character of a tent with wind and water vapour in a circulating cycle.[19] Only since the Renaissance have these facts been appreciated.

The Earth's 'foundations' are said to be 'fastened'.[20] The Hebrew word for foundations literally means 'sockets' and the word for fastened means 'to be sunk'. The Earth's surface crust lies above its mantle from which it is separated by a break known as the 'moho'. The crust consists of two major rock layers — the 'sial' forming the continental masses and the 'sima' on which they stand. The sial is bedded into the sima over a junction resembling 'sockets'.

Biblical health laws reveal a knowledge of the human body which implies the insight of a Creator. This is now being increasingly demonstrated from scientific evidence. The main causes of death in Western countries are atherosclerosis and cancer. They are almost always due to diets high in cholesterol and saturated fats, the former entirely, and the latter partly, from animal products. The Mosaic law forbade the human consumption of animal fat.[21]

Another example is the injunction about infant circumcision. Modern medical science has verified that the greatest risk of haemorrhage from incisions occurs between two and seven days of life. This is because at birth a baby's intestines contain no bacteria and these only proliferate in the 4th to 7th days. These bacteria are needed to form the vitamin K which is important in forming clotting proteins in the liver. After the seventh day, the operation becomes increasingly traumatic as the child's consciousness of pain increases. It can only be because of prior knowledge of the human body that Scripture enjoins circumcision on the eighth day.[22]

12.6 TESTIMONY OF THE JEWS: Acts 7:36; Jeremiah 31:36, 37; Leviticus 26:32, 33; Numbers 23:9

The existence of the Jewish people is a standing testimony to the historicity of the Scriptures. Their observance of the Passover and the Mosaic law are perpetual reminders of their Egyptian bondage and of the Exodus. The Jewish diaspora among the nations is a reminder of Old Testament prophecies that they would be thus scattered.[23] Their unchanging attachment to Jerusalem continually recalls the central place of its temple in worship. The Arch of Titus in Rome is a standing witness to the fall of Jerusalem in AD 70. Its representation of the vessels of the Tabernacle links Gentile history incontestably to the religion given by God on Mount Sinai more than 3,000 years ago.

12.7 TESTIMONY OF FULFILLED PROPHECY RELATING TO FOREIGN NATIONS

The antiquity and prophetic character of the Old Testament writings has always been accepted by the Jews. In recent years this has been strongly confirmed by the discovery of the Dead Sea Scrolls. These were leather scrolls wrapped in linen cloth and placed in jars in numerous caves in the marly cliffs at Qumran, a mile or so west of the north-western corner of the Dead Sea. They date from the first century BC to the first century AD, thus antedating by centuries previously known texts, which they closely confirm.

The caves contained fragments of every Old Testament book except Esther. No fewer than twelve manuscripts of Isaiah and ten of the Psalms were found in a single cave. A significant find with bearings on the date and authorship of the book of Daniel was that fragments show the change from Hebrew to Aramaic in 2:4 and from Aramaic to Hebrew in 7:28-8:1, exactly as in our modern texts of Daniel.

a. BABYLON. Isaiah 13:19-22.

Isaiah prophesied between about 745 and 686 BC. There is no manuscript or traditional evidence that his book is not a unity or that his book was written later than this time. Babylon rose to its zenith under Nebuchadnezzar between 606 and 561 BC. Isaiah predicts that it would be destroyed, left desolate and uninhabited and that no Arab would pitch his tent or shepherd leave his sheep there.

The site of Babylon is still a desolation. The ground is infertile through impregnation with salt. The area is inhabited by wild creatures and is avoided by Arabs after dark for fear of evil spirits. This future was almost inconceivable when Isaiah wrote. The city fell in 536 BC to Cyrus, king of Persia, after which it declined to obscurity.

b. NINEVEH. Zephaniah 2:13-15; Jonah 3:3.

Zephaniah probably wrote during the reign of Josiah (640–609 BC). His allusions to Judah's low state of morality seem reasonably to place his book before the great reformation in 621 BC. He prophesied that Nineveh, called by Jonah a century earlier 'an exceedingly great city', would become desolate, parched, and inhabited by flocks and wild animals. It was completely destroyed by Babylon in about 607 BC and the site was only with difficulty discovered in the nineteenth century. Thus the prophecy was exactly fulfilled although it would have appeared very unlikely when given.

c. EGYPT. Ezekiel 29:14, 15; 30:13-15.

Ezekiel wrote between 592 and 570 BC around the time of the fall of Jerusalem to the Babylonians under Nebuchadnezzar in 586 BC. He was living in exile in Babylon over 1,000 kilometres from Egypt, which he had probably never seen. He states that four things will happen: the idols of Memphis will be destroyed, Thebes will be destroyed and fired, the multitude of Thebes will be cut off, and there will no longer be a native prince from Egypt.

Both Memphis and Thebes were then important cities. Herodotus tells us that Cambyses destroyed idols when he conquered Egypt in about 525 BC. This destruction probably included Memphis because it was the Egyptian capital. Memphis ultimately was surpassed by nearby Cairo, so that by the beginning of the twentieth century AD the ruins of the city, including the great temple of Ptah and the dwelling of Apis, were traceable only by a few stones among the palm trees, fields and heaps of rubbish.[24] Thebes was finally destroyed by Cornelius Gallus during the reign of Augustus and became a collection of villages, which it remained until modern times.

At the time the prophecy was written, Egypt was a world power ruled by the 26th dynasty, the last native Egyptian. After this, the country lost international influence and then for 2,000 years lacked a native ruling dynasty, and has never had a ruler who possessed the power of former kings.

d. TYRE. Ezekiel 26:3-14.

These verses were written before Ezekiel heard of the fall

of Jerusalem, probably in early 585 BC (Ezekiel 33:21). They contain six prophecies:

1. Nebuchadnezzar will destroy the mainland city of Tyre (26:8).
2. Many nations will oppose Tyre (26:3).
3. She will be made a flat bare rock (26:4).
4. Her debris will be thrown into the water (26:12).
5. Fishermen will spread nets over the site (26:5).
6. She will never be rebuilt (26:14).

The fulfilment:

1. Nebuchadnezzar started a siege of Tyre in 585 BC and finally destroyed the mainland city in 573 BC. When he broke the gates down he found the city almost empty. The majority of the people had moved by ship to an island about half a mile off the coast and fortified a city there.

2. Alexander the Great sacked Tyre in 332 BC. During the wars of his successors it was captured from Antigonus by Ptolemy I, the ally of Seleucus in 312 BC. It passed into the dominion of Seleucus in 287, and was again captured by Ptolemy II Philadelphus in 275. It was often contested during the Crusades and was in the hands of Europeans until AD 1291, when it was finally yielded to the Muslims.

3, 4. When Alexander attacked Tyre, the people retreated from the mainland site to the fortified offshore island. He scraped the old site clean, throwing the debris into the sea to make a causeway to the island, leaving it bare rock.

5. The old (deserted) site has long been used by fishermen to spread their nets.

6. That site has never been rebuilt to this day.

12.8 TESTIMONY OF FULFILLED MESSIANIC PROPHECY

Much the greatest amount of fulfilled prophecy relates to the Messiah. There are two main reasons why this is especially strong evidence for Scriptural authority. First, the prophecies are both numerous and highly detailed, extending to some of the minutiae of Jesus' life on Earth. Secondly, the prophecies are incontestably earlier than their fulfilments. Even before the discovery of the Dead Sea Scrolls, it was universally accepted that the Old Testament books in which they occur were in existence before our Lord's first coming.

		PROPHECY	FULFILMENT
A	**Prophecies concerning Jesus' birth**		
1	Born of the seed of woman	Gen. 3:15	Gal. 4:4
2	Born of a virgin	Isa. 7:14	Matt. 1:18, 24, 25
3	Son of God	Ps. 2:7	Matt. 3:17
4	Seed of Abraham	Gen. 22:18	Gal. 3:16
5	Son of Isaac	Gen. 21:12	Luke 3:34
6	Son of Jacob	Num. 24:17	Luke 3:34
7	Tribe of Judah	Gen. 49:10	Luke 3:23, 33
8	Family line of Jesse	Isa. 11:1	Luke 3:23, 32
9	House of David	Jer. 23:5	Luke 2:4
10	Born at Bethlehem	Mic. 5:2	Matt. 2:1
11	Presented with gifts	Ps. 72:10	Matt. 2:1, 11
12	Herod kills children	Jer. 31:15	Matt. 2:16
B	**Prophecies concerning Jesus' ministry**		
1	Preceded by a messenger	Isa. 40:3	Matt. 3:1, 2
2	Year Christ begins ministry	Dan. 9:25	Matt. 4:16-20
		Isa. 61:1, 2	
3	Ministry to begin in Galilee	Isa. 9:1	Matt. 4:12-17
4	Will perform miracles	Isa. 35:5, 6	Matt. 9:35
5	Teaching in parables	Ps. 78:2	Matt. 13:34
6	Enters Jerusalem on a donkey	Zech. 9:9	Matt. 21:7-10
C	**Prophecies of Jesus' last days**		
1	Betrayed by a friend	Ps. 41:9	Matt. 10:4
2	Sold for 30 pieces of silver, which was thrown down in God's house and used to buy a potter's field	Zech. 11:12, 13	Matt. 27:3-7
3	Forsaken by disciples	Zech. 13:7	Mark 14:50
4	Accused by false witnesses	Ps. 35:11	Matt. 26:59, 60
5	Dumb before accusers	Isa. 53:7	Matt. 27:12
6	Wounded and bruised	Isa. 53:5	Matt. 27:26
7	Smitten and spat upon	Isa. 50:6	Matt. 26:67
8	Mocked	Ps. 22:7, 8	Matt. 27:31
9	Hands and feet pierced	Ps. 22:16	John 20:25-27
10	Crucified with thieves	Isa. 53:12	Matt. 27:38
11	Made intercession for persecutors	Isa. 53:12	Luke 23:34
12	Rejected by His own people	Isa. 53:3	John 7:5, 48

		PROPHECY	FULFILMENT
13	Friends stood afar off	Ps. 38:11	Luke 23:49
14	People shook their heads	Ps. 109:25	Matt. 27:39
15	Stared upon	Ps. 22:17	Luke 23:35
16	Garments parted and lots cast	Ps. 22:18	John 19:23, 24
17	Suffered thirst	Ps. 69:21	John 19:28
18	Gall and vinegar offered Him	Ps. 69:21	Matt. 27:34
19	Made forsaken cry	Ps. 22:1	Matt. 27:46
20	Committed Himself to God	Ps. 31:5	Luke 23:46
21	Bones not broken	Ps. 34:20	John 19:33
22	Heart broken	Ps. 22:14	John 19:34
23	His side pierced	Zech. 12:10	John 19:34
24	Darkness over the land	Amos 8:9	Matt. 27:45
25	Buried in rich man's tomb	Isa. 53:9	Matt. 27:57-60

D Prophecies after Jesus' death

| 1 | Resurrection | Ps. 16:10 | Acts 2:31 |
| 2 | Ascension | Ps. 68:18 | Acts 1:9 |

Such a wealth of detailed foresight is virtually inconceivable unless inspired by an Author who knew the future.

12.9 TESTIMONY OF BIBLE'S POWER TO TRANSFORM CHARACTER: 1 Peter 1:23; Hebrews 4:12; Psalm 119:11

The Scriptures claim an ability to transform character, and by common consent this is true. It has inspired most of the world's material and moral improvements and has enobled individuals and societies which have followed it.

12.10 SUMMARY

There are many lines of evidence not only for the authority, but also for the infallibility, of the Scriptures. They make these claims for themselves in both Old and New Testaments, sometimes by statement, but more often by assumption. They have a remarkable unity, despite the variety of authors and the 1,500 years they span. They have endured despite continuous opposition. They show inerrant scientific insights, although written at a time when modern science was unknown. The existence of the Jewish people is a continuing testimony to the accuracy of their history as given in the Old Testament.

The capacity of the Scriptures to foretell the future has often been verified, notably about the fate of nations, and above all, about the Messiah. Finally, the Bible has demonstrated a unique ability to transform character and lives.

REFERENCES

[1] 1983, page 16. [2] e.g. in Daniel 2:4-7:28. [3] 2 Samuel 23:1, 2; Jeremiah 1:4-9; Ezekiel 2:7; Luke 1:70; 2 Timothy 3:16. [4] 2 Peter 1:20, 21. [5] Deuteronomy 4:2; Revelation 22:18, 19. [6] Psalm 119:152. [7] Amos 3:7. [8] Matthew 5:18. [9] e.g. Matthew 24:15; Luke 16:31; 24:27. [10] Matthew 19:4, 5. [11] John 10:34, 35. [12] Psalm 69:21. [13] Luke 24:25-27. [14] Psalm 12:7; Isaiah 40:8; Matthew 24:35; 1 Peter 1:23-25. [15] Jeremiah 33:22. [16] Hebrews 11:12. [17] Isaiah 40:22. [18] Job 26:7. [19] Isaiah 40:22, Ecclesiastes 1:6, 7. [20] Job 38:6. [21] Leviticus 3:17. [22] Genesis 17:12; McMillen 1970, pages 91, 92. [23] Leviticus 26:33; Psalm 44:11; Jeremiah 31:10; Ezekiel 12:15. [24] *Encyclopaedia Britannica*, 1911, article on Egypt.

CHAPTER 13

THE CASE FOR BIBLICAL LITERALISM

13.1 IS GENESIS 1-11 LITERAL?

The first eleven chapters of Genesis record Creation, the Fall, the Flood, and the early history of man until the call of Abraham.

They read factually, going straight into a description of the real world. There is no suggestion that they are recounting events belonging to another world or level of reality. They contain sixty-four geographical terms, eighty-eight personal names, forty-eight generic names, and at least twenty-one identifiable cultural items (such as gold, bdellium, onyx, brass, iron, gopher wood, bitumen, mortar, brick, stone, harp, pipe, cities, towers). Every one of these items presents us with the possibility of establishing the reliability of the account. The list contrasts, for example, with the paucity of such references in the Koran. The tenth chapter alone has five times more geographical data of importance than the whole of that book.

The account is in narrative prose, frequently using the Hebrew 'waw' consecutive with the verb, the direct object sign, and the relative pronoun. It stresses definitions, and spreads events in sequential order.

The phrase 'these are the generations of' implies straightforward history. It is used not only of Aaron and Moses,[1] Terah,[2] Jacob,[3] Noah,[4] but also for the heaven and the Earth.[5]

All the New Testament books refer to these eleven chapters, and each chapter is specifically referred to. Jesus referred to each of the first seven chapters.

13.2 IS THE SIX-DAY CREATION HISTORICAL?

The first two chapters of Genesis describe the original six-day creation.

The days fall into two cycles of three, followed by a Sabbath, as shown on Table 13.1.

TABLE 13.1	**The Creation Week**
THE FIRST CYCLE	THE SECOND CYCLE
Day 1: Earth and light	Day 4: Sun, moon, and stars
Day 2: Sea and air	Day 5: Sea and air creatures
Day 3: Land vegetation	Day 6: Creatures of the earth
(including terrestrial waters)	(including the horse, the
	serpent and man). Garden of
	Eden including Euphrates
Day 7: Climax and end, Sabbath rest	

The account reads as straightforward history and is treated as fact throughout Scripture.

There are a number of reasons which demand that it be factual. Other Scriptures depend its historicity for validating their message. Psalm 104 uses it to demonstrate God's creative power and majesty. Our Lord answers a question about divorce by citing God as its author.[6] Peter and James both refer to it as factual.[7] Paul, in Romans 5, rests his entire argument on Adam being a literal person. Only if one man is the source of universal sin can one man be the source of universal salvation.[8] He also cites the story of Adam and Eve as the basis for instruction on behaviour in churches.[9] Sequences of events clearly inspired by Genesis 1 occur in a prophetic context in Revelation 8 and 9 and in an apocalytic context in Revelation 16. Since the last two are factual rather than figurative, they carry the implication that the first must also be (see Appendix 2).

The apparent conflict between the creation story and the findings of evolutionary science has led to attempted harmonizations. Five main theories have been proposed: the Gap Theory, the Age-Day Theory, the Pictorial-Day Theory, the Literary Theory, and Theistic Evolution.

13.3 THE GAP THEORY

The Gap Theory has also been called the Restitution Theory and the Ruin-Reconstruction Theory.

It states that the Earth originally created in Genesis 1:1 was populated with plants, animals, and pre-Adamic men, but because of the fall of Lucifer (that is, Satan) it was destroyed by God in a universal cataclysmic flood. It was simultaneously plunged into darkness and thus *became* 'without form and void'.[10] This first destruction is thought to account for the vast geological ages including the fossils. The Earth's present landscape is seen as a relic of this pre-Adamic destruction. The six literal days of Genesis 1:3-31 are therefore a re-creation to provide a home for man.

The theory justifies this view by reading the first three verses of Genesis in such a way that a. *reshith* (literally 'beginning' or 'first' used as a noun) here means 'When God began to . . .' rather than 'In the beginning', implying that there could have been an earlier creation, b. *bara* (literally 'create') here means that God 'made' the heavens and the Earth out of pre-existing matter rather than 'creating' it *ex nihilo*, and c. *hayeth* (literally either 'was' or 'became') here means that the Earth 'became' rather than 'was' without form and void. The effect of these variant translations would clearly be to favour the idea of a pre-Adamic creation.

But can the Hebrew words bear this interpretation? The answer is almost certainly no.

Reshith is always used as a noun and never translated 'began' in the Old Testament, and so there is no support for this reading. *Bara*, the word used here, is the usual word for 'create' and is never used for 'make'. *Asah* is the usual word for 'make' but can sometimes be used for create. *Bara* and *asah* can sometimes be used synonymously as in Genesis 1:26 and 27 where both are used of the creation of man. But there is no justification for translating *bara* as 'made' in the first three verses, particularly when New Testament references such as Hebrews 11:3 support the idea of creation *ex nihilo*. Regarding *hayeth*, Hebrews makes no distinction between 'became' and 'was' and so there might be a case for translating it 'became' in verse 2. However the word is almost invariably translated simply as 'was', and so the preponderance of evidence is against this translation.

There are also a number of obvious practical objections to this theory:

1. Adam was given dominion over all living creatures.[11] If the Gap Theory is correct, there were many creatures who lived before his time over which he would never have ruled.

2. If carnivorous creatures were living and dying not only before Adam but even before the fall of Lucifer, death cannot have been due to his fall. Yet Scripture ascribes the Earth's 'groaning and travailing in pain' to this cause.[12]

3. The use of the term 'very good' to describe the created Earth in Genesis 1:31 seems unreasonable if it had already once been the domain of Satan and the graveyard of millions of creatures.

4. If all original plants and animals were destroyed they would probably have no genetic relationship to existing types. Most living things in the world today, however, are clearly descended from those found in the fossil record. If pre-Adamic men existed, there can have been no provision for their spiritual needs. Such a possibility is irreconcilable with the rest of Scripture.

5. If the geological record is explainable by a pre-Adamic flood, it leaves nothing for explanation by Noah's Flood. Geology reveals no chaotic period between human times and the preceding Tertiary age.

6. Finally, it seems incredible that the majesty and sublime simplicity of the Creation account which forms the basis of so much else in Scripture, can merely relate to a secondary event, while the earlier and more important origins receive only a passing reference.

13.4 THE AGE-DAY THEORY

This is also called the 'Divine-Day Theory' or 'Concordism'.

It affirms that the days of Genesis are to be interpreted metaphorically as long periods of time. It is based on the idea that the word *yom* can mean other things than a literal twenty-four-hour day. For instance, *yom* means 'daylight' in Genesis 1:5, 'daylight' in contrast to 'night' in verse 14, and 'the entire period of creation' in 2:4. The expression 'evening and morning' is considered to be figurative, either referring to consecutive periods of rest and creation or to a 'cosmic' day of great length. The statement in 2 Peter 3:8 that 'one day is with the Lord as a thousand years, and a thousand years as one day' is seen as supporting this figurative interpretation.

The advantage claimed for this theory is that it allows time for a uniformitarian explanation of the geological column by means of a series of long stages. But this view cannot bear detailed examination, for the following reasons:

1. *Yom* almost invariably refers to literal days when used with an ordinal such as 'first', 'second', etc. It is usually quite clear from the context when it is being used figuratively. The straightforward narrative style of the creation story argues that it is not.

2. The reference to 'evenings' and 'mornings' of each day indicates that they were literal twenty-four-hour days.

3. The Sabbath commandment contains a direct statement that it commemorates a six-day creation. Since the Sabbath is itself a literal day, this only makes sense if the preceding six days were also literal. The tables of stone on which the commandment was written are central to Old Testament worship and unique in being written by the finger of God Himself. Any figurative interpretation of the creation story thus brings into question the whole basis of Old Testament religion. The ten-commandment law is also basic to the New Testament and continues in the post-millenial Earth.[13] John sees the heavenly counterpart of the ark of the covenant, which by assumption included the ten-commandment law.[14] Thus the religion of both Old and New Testaments, including their eschatology, is inseparably linked to a six-day creation.

4. The Age-Day Theory cannot explain the conventional

scientific view of evolution. If each day represents an aeon, how could the vegetation survive through the long third day until the sun appeared? Even this would not be enough. In order to pollinate, it would have to survive through the whole fourth day into the fifth before insects were available. This would be impossible. Also, the order of Genesis 1 does not accord with the fossil record. The palaeontological sequence is approximately: bottom dwelling sea mollusks — fish — vegetation — reptiles — birds — mammals. In Genesis the highest forms of vegetation precede the lowliest sea creatures, and the most complex bird precedes the lowliest reptile.

This theory is thus at variance with both the Genesis account and evolution.

13.5 THE PICTORIAL-DAY THEORY

This is also known as 'Moderate Concordism'. It follows the Gap Theory in believing in a prior creation as described in Genesis 1:1, but adheres to literal days by teaching that the process was *revealed* to Adam in this time. It is based on the claim that the Hebrew words *bara* (create) and *asah* (make or do) which are used throughout Genesis 1 can have the sense of 'reveal'.

Similar objections, however, apply.

1. *Bara* is nowhere used in the Old Testament for 'show' ('shew'), 'reveal', 'disclose', or 'unveil'. *Asah* is translated 'make' or 'do' over 1,800 times, and 'show' forty-three times. In forty of these it is used in the abstract sense of showing mercy, kindness, goodness, love, terror, might, or salvation. The other three instances where it means 'show' are Numbers 14:11, Judges 6:17, and Psalm 88:10. Its objects are here respectively 'signs', 'sign', and 'wonders'. In each case the reference is to miracles performed at the time of observation, not to past events subsequently revealed to an observer.

2. The theory does not give due weight to the assumption throughout Scripture that the events of the first week are straight historical narrative. It makes a sublime state-

ment of the creation into a device for explaining something completely different.

3. The wording of the Sabbath commandment is also stongly indicative. The word 'asah' is used three times in Exodus 20:9-11:

'Six days shalt thou labour, and *do* (*asah*) all thy work: but the seventh day is the sabbath of the Lord Thy God: in it thou shalt not *do* (*asah*) any work, thou, nor thy son, nor thy daughter, thy manservant, nor thy maidservant, nor thy cattle, nor thy stranger that is within thy gates: for in six days the Lord *made* (*asah*) heaven and earth, the sea, and all that in them is, and rested the seventh day: . . . .'

Although in these verses the English word 'do' appears twice and 'make' once, all are translations of *asah*. If the word for human labour does not have the sense of 'revealing', that for God's labour in the same passage cannot.

13.6 THE LITERARY THEORY

This is the theory that the best way to understand the six-day creation story is as a 'tract for the times' designed by a Hebrew author to counter the paganism and idolatry that surrounded his people at the time of the Exodus and settlement of Canaan. It was to underline the warning of Deuteronomy 4:19:

'And lest thou lift up thine eyes unto heaven, and when thou seest the sun, and the moon, and the stars, even all the host of heaven, shouldest be driven to worship them, and serve them, which the Lord thy God hath divided unto all the nations under the whole heaven.'

This tract, it is claimed, was aimed to answer four questions:

1. Was there one God or many gods? The creation account deals especially with the prevalent problem of ancient heliolatry. It teaches monotheism by relegating the heavenly bodies to the fourth day of creation, and substituting the phrases 'greater light' and 'lesser light' for the more connotative Hebrew words *shamash* (sun) and *qamar* (moon). This emphasizes that they were only

created objects in order to support the warning against worshipping them.[15]

2. What is the nature of man? The creation account emphasizes that every man and woman is made in God's image and has the potential for direct relations with Him. It counters the prevalent pagan view than man was a mere plaything of the gods.

3. Is the universe rational? The creation account teaches that God is a God of order, not of chaos. It does this in part by the frequent use of numbers with great significance to ancient man: 3, 7 and 10. For example, the creation was in two cycles of three days ending with a seventh. The statements 'it was good' and 'it was so' each occur seven times. 'God said', 'to make', and 'after their kind' each occur ten times.

4. Who is God? The creation account emphasizes the absolute sovereignty of the one true God, while at the same time indicating His plurality.[16] This was intended to counter surrounding paganism which had a multiplicity of gods often in conflict with each other.

The literary theory stops here. The purpose of the chapter does not go beyond these objectives. It is only a well-designed tract, not history.

While the points above are incontestable, they cannot be the whole story. The chapter must also be historical. A clear reason for this is its inseparable associations with central biblical doctrines: the Sabbath and marriage. The Sabbath involves the six-day creation in the Decalogue. Marriage is inseparable from the whole New Testament message. The intertwined relations of husband and wife, Christ and the church, bridegroom and bride are strongly dependent on the Genesis account of Creation. The relation between Adam and Eve is quoted in the New Testament as a model of theological truths, especially concerning the Trinity and the Church.[17] This model would lose its central meaning if the Creation story was not factual.

13.7 THEISTIC EVOLUTION

Theistic Evolution is perhaps the most widespread of all views on evolution today. It accepts the spiritual message of the Bible but believes that the early chapters should not be taken literally but interpreted in the light of their overall function. It contends that God controlled the Earth's origins through an evolutionary process. It believes that the Bible speaks of the origin of the universe and its make-up, not to present a scientific treatise but in order to state the correct relationships of man with God and with the universe. It employs the terms of the cosmology in use at the time of the writers to explain that God created the world not as the seat of the gods, as was taught by other cosmogonies and cosmologies, but for the service of man and the glory of God. It does not deal in detail with the origin and make-up of the universe because its aim is not to teach how the heavens were made but how one goes to heaven. It therefore views the Bible and science as different but complementary sources of knowledge.

Therefore, theistic evolution has the advantage of denying neither science nor the Bible. It accords with the assumption, originating with Thomas Aquinas, that natural science and theology can be separated and their mutual interdependence disregarded in arriving at truth. Its popularity today is less due to its intrinsic merit than to the wide publicity it has enjoyed. It tacitly underlies most standard scientific texts and popular presentations of scientific facts.

But it cannot be sustained. It shelves the central debate between Genesis and science by implicitly subjecting the former to the judgement of the latter. The Creation and Flood stories are so interwoven with the whole of the rest of Scripture that they cannot be dissociated from it. Its truth stands or falls by theirs. The Bible differs irreconcilably not with science, but with current scientific views of the origins and age of the Earth, life, and humanity. Until these questions are resolved, there can be no agreement between the two sources of knowledge.

13.8 CREATIVE EVOLUTION

Creative Evolution, also called the 'Life-Force', was conceived to fill the ethical vacuum left by the theory's removal of a purposeful and creative force in the universe. It is not so much a theory to harmonize evolution with the Scriptures as a dynamic mechanism to explain its upward progress. The originator was Henri Bergson, a French philosopher, who taught that a creative urge or 'elan vital', rather than natural selection, was at the heart of evolution. His vision was poetical rather than philosophical, working by analogy and suggestion rather than by rigorous argument. He had a great influence on biology and psychology, and on such writers as Ralph Waldo Emerson, Samuel Butler, George Bernard Shaw, and Marcel Proust.

A similar view was advocated by the French cleric and scientist Pierre Teilhard de Chardin. He attempted to combine evolution and the Catholic faith. Like Aquinas, he started from the belief that humans, by their reason and apart from Scripture, may rightly view the world in which they live but that they need revelation for faith and religion. He taught that human life was impelled by the Life Force towards greater complexity and greater consciousness. He called this the 'Law of Complexity Consciousness', now sometimes referred to as 'Teilhard's law'. It goes something like this. Human consciousness of matter has evolved in parallel with its advancing complexity. The Earth is mantled by a number of 'spheres': the barysphere (molten interior), the lithosphere (hard crust), the hydrosphere (water in sea and air), and the atmosphere. The biosphere (zone of living creatures) has evolved from these. The final layer, called the 'noosphere', or 'mind layer' represents the next stage of evolution, the arrival of thinking humanity. This transforms the Earth's previous state. In the future, Christ's intervention will raise consciousness, gathering and transforming everything until an 'Omega point' when God will be all in all. This is the final synthesis of evolution and Christian faith.[18]

But this fails to solve the fundamental question: if the Life Force has a mind, then it is really a god; if not, it cannot have purpose. Creative Evolution is really a form of pantheism which sees the Life Force as a part of the nature which it activates. It conflicts with biblical teaching in rejecting the historicity of Genesis, failing adequately to distinguish the Creator from his creation, and ignoring specific biblical teachings on judgement and eschatology.

13.9 SUMMARY

When the Scriptures use figurative language, as in describing visions, dreams, and parables, it is made clear they are doing so. They do not speak of either the Creation or the Flood in this way, but treat them as quite historical.

The lack of agreement between these accounts and the apparent findings of science has led to a number of attempts at harmonization. These have been made by Christians who respect the Bible but who also to some extent support current evolutionary theory. They seek to interpret the Scriptures in the light of its teachings. They vary, however, in the degree of historicity which they accord to the Genesis account of origins.

The Gap Theory and the Age-Day Theory accept the six-day creation as literal but attempt to interpret the wording in a way which would allow room for an evolutionary explanation. The Pictorial-Day Theory and the Literary Theory see the account as essentially poetic and figurative, but to contain historical truths which they seek to elaborate in harmony with evolution. Theistic Evolution and Creative Evolution regard the account as purely figurative and make little attempt to harmonize it with evolution. Although they hold Christian beliefs, they seek to portray evolution as the key to understanding God's working in nature and history.

None of these theories can satisfactorily bridge the gap. All accord ultimate priority to evolutionary theory. This forces them to depart from the literal and obvious meanings of some Hebrew words and to neglect Scriptures related to them.

REFERENCES

[1] Numbers 3:1. [2] Genesis 11:27. [3] Genesis 37:2. [4] Genesis 6:9. [5] Genesis 2:4; Young 1977. [6] Matthew 19:4, 5. [7] 2 Peter 3:5; James 3:9. [8] Romans 5:12-19. [9] 1 Timothy 2:13, 14. [10] Genesis 1:2. [11] Genesis 1:26. [12] Romans 8:22. [13] Isaiah 66:23. [14] Revelation 11:19. [15] Deuteronomy 4:19. [16] Genesis 1:26. [17] Ephesians 5:22, 23; 1 Corinthians 11:7-12. [18] Teilhard de Chardin 1959, pages 257-299; Brown 1969, pages 240-242.

PART IV

A CREATIONIST MODEL

CHAPTER 14

THE PRE-FLOOD EARTH

14.1 CREATION WEEK

The Genesis record of origins can perhaps be harmonized with scientific findings along the lines of the following brief provisional outline:

On Day 1 the Earth was created from nothing as a formless mass covered by water. Then non-solar light was created and time separated into night and day. The primitive materials were moulded into physical and chemical forms suitable for habitation and use by man and other forms of life. Archeozoic rocks originated on this day.

On Day 2 the atmosphere was formed from the materials of Day 1, air being separated from water. There must have been much warm water vapour possibly due to a different land and sea distribution and a non-solar source of heat and light. Water was divided into two portions: atmospheric and oceanic.[1] This second day is the only one which does not have the statement 'God saw that it was good', presumably because nothing new had been created; there had only been a rearrangement.

Day 3 saw the emergence of land from sea and the creation of vegetation with soil and an appearance of age. It must also have ensured the availability of terrestrial waters. These activities would have been accompanied by the formation of the Proterozoic rocks which always rest on Archeozoic. (The subsequent Cambrian and later rocks, due to the Flood, locally rest directly on the Proterozoic over an unconformity). This left the Earth in its primitive state ready for animal and human occupation.

Day 4 brought the Sun, Moon, and stars which started plant photosynthesis and root growth. This must have included the provision that light from distant stars was already visible on Earth.

Days 5 and 6 saw the creation of the animal kingdom and humans.

14.2 THE PRE-FLOOD PHYSICAL WORLD

The physical world before the Flood was pronounced by God to be 'good'. It had mountains,[2] rivers,[3] and seas,[4] and so must have experienced geological processes somewhat like those of today. It appears likely that there was only one large proto-continent. We presume that the land lacked the barren wastes, bleak and sterile hills, bitter cold and searing heat of the post-Flood Earth. There were probably no polar ice caps. The movement of continental 'plates' and all post-Proterozoic geological deposition cannot have begun before the Flood.

The fossil record shows that the antediluvian flora and fauna differed from today's a. in being more widely distributed over the Earth's surface, b. in having a greater number of genera and species, and c. in being better grown specimens. They indicate a mild climate at all latitudes. There must have been zonal differences but not the present extremes. We know this because many fossil creatures were cold blooded and could not have lived under cold conditions. Also, there is no geological system which does not contain coral limestone or some other evidence of warm conditions. Many of these 'warmer' rocks extend far into high latitudes. Carboniferous limestone and coal are the nearest known rocks to the North Pole. They outcrop all around the polar basin, and from the dip of the beds, must underlie the pole itself.

The atmosphere must have been substantially different from that of today. The waters 'above the firmament' were placed there by divine fiat, not by the hydrological cycle of the present day. Such a vast expanse of water vapour would necessarily have had a profound effect on terrestrial climates and therefore on geological activity. It seems to have maintained a warm atmosphere and provided moisture for plants without obscuring the Sun, Moon, or stars. There was no rain but a mist watered the ground.[5] The first appearance of a rainbow after the Flood indicates that cloud and rain must have started at this time.

Patten[6] suggests that the Earth's atmosphere had three to five times as much H_2O as today's, concentrated in the lower troposphere with a humid blanket 1,000-1,500 metres thick and ranging from 1,500 to 3,000 metres above sea level. The richness of the plant life and the vast amount of carbonate rocks and of coal and oil pools subsequently deposited suggests that the antediluvian atmosphere must have contained six to eight times as much carbon dioxide as today (now about 0.35%). This would probably have helped atmospheric moisture to maintain a greenhouse effect and relatively high temperatures. This effect was probably also sustained by a relatively high level of carbon dioxide in the atmosphere at that time. It has been estimated, for instance, that halving the CO_2 in the atmosphere would lower the Earth's temperature by 3.8 degrees Celsius.[7]

It seems likely that there was a thicker ozone canopy. Ozone is produced by the action of ultraviolet rays on ordinary oxygen atoms, and decomposed by chemical reaction with oxides of nitrogen, and of recent years, with fluoro-chlorocarbons. It is distributed throughout the atmosphere, but mainly between 10 and 50 km in altitude. Maximum concentrations are at about 48 km in equatorial, and about 35 km in polar, latitudes.[8] The ozone canopy serves as a shield, protecting the troposphere and the Earth's surface from most of the ultraviolet radiation coming from the Sun.

The pre-Flood ozone canopy probably contrasted with that of today in being a. considerably thicker and more concentrated in the upper atmosphere due to reduced mixing, and b. slightly higher in elevation due to greater barometric pressure. Therefore the atmosphere would have retained almost all the long-wave solar radiation received by the Earth. Temperatures would have been warm from pole to pole, daily ranges probably being only 1.1-2.2 degrees Celsius.[9]

14.3 THE ORIGIN OF SPECIES

The Bible is definite that the main 'kinds' of life were all created separately. There must have been many of these. As we have seen, each 'kind' could embrace a wide variety of forms, approximating to those within a single gene pool.

14.4 THE ORIGIN OF HUMANS

Humans were an independent creation, undescended from any other.

Genesis 2:7 says:

'And the Lord God formed man of the dust of the ground, and breathed into his nostrils the breath of life; and man became a living soul.'

It is sometimes contended that 'dust of the ground' is the Bible's way of referring to evolutionary descent. One reason this cannot be so is that in the next chapter the same phrase is used of man's fate: 'for dust thou art, and unto dust shalt thou return'.[10] It must bear the same meaning in both places.

Adam was given the power of speech initially to enable him to talk to God. He first used it to name all the creatures. Language appears to have been universally comprehensible until the confusion of tongues at the Tower of Babel.

Death did not have a naturalistic origin but was a result of sin. Adam was warned that eating of the tree of knowledge of good and evil would bring death, and Paul states that the one was the cause of the other.[11]

Humans were created to be vegetarian. Their prescribed diet was grains, fruits, nuts, and legumes.[12] Meat eating was only allowed after the Flood but with a restriction on the consumption of blood,[13] and fat.[14] That the human body is better adapted to this than to a flesh diet is another indication for an original fiat creation. Animals were also created vegetarian.[15] Since the fossils of carnivores appear almost throughout the geological strata, some of the animals must have become flesh eaters after the Fall but before the Flood.

The origin of clothing is also significant. Adam and Eve, because of new-found guilt, hid their nakedness by sewing fig leaves together and making themselves aprons.[16] The record, however, goes on to say that God later covered them with skins,[17] a foreshadowing of later teaching about covering evil by blood sacrifice. The purpose was moral rather than practical, differentiating the biblical from any secular explanation of the origin of dress.

14.5 THE PRE-FLOOD PATRIARCHS

Genesis 5 records the line of ten patriarchs from Adam to Noah. This list received support from the list of ten antediluvian kings, written in 2170 BC, on the *Weld Prism* which was discovered in 1922 at Larsa, a few miles north of Ur. It has further external confirmation from Berossus' statement that the Flood came in the reign of the tenth king of Babylon.[18] The ages for these patriarchs given in the King James Version and subsequent English translations of the Bible are shown on Table 14.1:

NAME	AGE AT BIRTH OF FIRST SON	AGE AT DEATH
1 Adam	130	930
2 Seth	105	912
3 Enos	90	905
4 Cainan	70	910
5 Mahalel	65	895
6 Jared	162	962
7 Enoch	65	365 (did not die)
8 Methuselah	187	969
9 Lamech	182	777
10 Noah	500	950 (Flood occurred when he was 600)

TABLE 14.1 **The Patriachial List in Genesis 5**

There is no way of determining the actual dates unless these lists are complete and end at a known reference point from which backward calculations can be made. The problem is that the lists are not complete and there is no such reference point. Upwards of 200 authors have attempted calculations, which give dates for the Creation varying from 3,483 to 6,984 years before the Christian era. The most widely known is Ussher's date of 4,004 BC.[19]

Although Table 14.1 gives 1,656 years as the interval between the Creation and the Flood, there are reasons for questioning this figure. These are considered in chapter 15.

The pre-Flood population of the world is of course unknown, but even 1,656 years would be more than adequate for vast numbers. We have seen rapid rises of population in the past century but they could have been much larger then. People had greater vitality and were longer lived. Add to this the favourable climatic conditions, the fact that food supplies were more plentiful and accessible to all, that a world of virgin soil and unlimited riches beckoned man to take possession, and one has the best possible conditions for rapid population growth. It was clearly also possible for these numbers to have penetrated to the far corners of the Earth.

14.6 EARLY CIVILIZATION

There is biblical evidence for pre-Flood civilization. Adam practised agriculture and managed animals. Cain built a city[20] which demands a level of competence far above savagery. Early men also had tents, owned cattle, played harp and organ, and worked brass and iron.[21] This picture contrasts strongly with the ideas of primitive early human life which one would derive from evolutionary theory. The Genesis record tells of a time of human abundance and prosperity in near-ideal natural conditions. Moral decay brought materialism, promiscuity, and violence to such a point that God destroyed the world by a Flood. This model is clearly irreconcilable with one which sees human development as an upward evolutionary process.

14.7 SUMMARY

A Scriptural model of Earth history must progress from Creation to the pre-Flood situation. The Earth at that time seems to have resembled that of today except in having a more equable climate and in being more productive and less degraded. There was a wide variety of plants and animals even at high latitudes. The human population must have been much smaller.

There were ten antediluvian patriarchs, beginning with Adam and ending with Noah. A straightforward calculation of the patriarchal genealogy gives 1,656 years as the duration between Creation and the Flood, but there is no way of being certain of this figure and it is probably an understatement. There was a moral decline apparently associated with the abundance and prosperity the Earth then offered. This brought the divine judgement of the Flood.

REFERENCES
[1] Genesis 1:20. [2] Genesis 7:20. [3] Genesis 2:10. [4] Genesis 1:10. [5] Genesis 2:5, 6. [6] 1970. [7] Whitcomb and Morris 1974, pages 253, 254. [8] Strahler 1969, pages 119, 120. [9] Patten, loc. cit. [10] Genesis 3:9. [11] Romans 5:12. [12] Genesis 1:29. [13] Genesis 9:3-5. [14] Leviticus 3:17. [15] Genesis 1:30. [16] Genesis 3:7. [17] Genesis 3:21. [18] Rehwinkel 1967, page 142. [19] Green 1894. [20] Genesis 4:17. [21] Genesis 4:17, 20-22.

CHAPTER 15

THE FLOOD

15.1 THE DATE OF THE FLOOD

Archbishop Ussher's date for the Flood is 2348 BC. The call of Abraham is now generally assigned to about 1920 BC, about 400 years later. But there are a number of reasons for thinking that this gap may be too short and that the Flood must have been somewhat earlier.

First, the patriarchal chronology in Genesis 11 does not give absolute dates and leaves a gap. Verses 12 and 13 in this chapter exclude Cainan from the list given in Luke 3:36. One omission suggests there could be others. His inclusion would extend the time.

Secondly, Ussher's calculations were based on the assumption that when Genesis says so-and-so 'begat' so-and-so, it means a direct father-son relationship. But 'begat' is the KJV translation of the Hebrew *yalad* and the Greek *gennao*, which can refer to an ancestral relationship. 'A was 100 years old when he begat B' can mean 'A was 100 years old when he had the son who became the ancestor of B.' Hebrews 7:9, 10 tells us that 'Levi . . . paid tithes in Abraham. For he was yet in the loins of his father, when Melchisedec met him'. This seems to say that Abraham was Levi's actual father, but he was in fact his great grandfather, so two whole generations are missed. In Matthew 1:8 we read that Joram begat Uzziah, but three generations are omitted.[1] In 1 Chronicles 26:24 we are told that 'Shebuel the son of Gershom, the son of Moses, was ruler over the treasures' in the days of David. This skips 400 years between Gershom and Shebuel. Finally, Exodus 6:20 tells us that Amram and Jochebed were the actual parents of Aaron and Moses, but according to Numbers 3:17-19, 27, 28 the family of the Amramites numbered 8,600 in Moses' day. Only two explanations are possible: either Amram and Jochebed, although called parents, were ancestors of Aaron and Moses and separated from them by 300 years, or else Amram was not a son but a descendant of Gershom. In either case more generations intervened and hence more time elapsed than a strict father-son sequence would allow. Furthermore, a strict equation of 'begat' with a father-son relationship would make all post-diluvian patriarchs, including Noah, contemporaries of Abraham. This does not accord with Joshua's statement that his fathers 'dwelt of old time beyond the River'.[2] Thus the time covered by the genealogies may be considerably longer than a simple reading would suggest.

Thirdly, the genealogies in Genesis 5 and 11 are symmetrical in form, each having ten patriarchs with the tenth having three sons. Matthew 1 is likewise symmetrical with three groups of fourteen patriarchs. This symmetry was apparently more important to the authors than chronological exactness.

The cumulative effect of these considerations is to allow for some 'stretching' of the time between the Flood and Abraham. But this stretching cannot be very great. It is probably hundreds or at most a very few thousands of years. More would not accord with other indications in Scripture. Not all the post-diluvial patriarchs can have their times extended at all. The judgement of Babel occurred in the days of Peleg when the human race was apparently geographically confined and linguistically uniform. This argues that it was less than, say, a few hundred years after the Flood. This eliminates half of the post-diluvian patriarchs before time stretching can begin. Since Terah was the actual father of Abraham, we are left with only three names — Reu, Serug, and Nahor between them and the Tower of Babel. It seems unreasonable to ascribe to them and any unnamed generations surrounding them a period longer than hundreds of years.

There is no evidence for questioning the pre-Flood chronology, but the above arguments against an assumption that the post-diluvian genealogies are complete may also apply to the antediluvian period. The time from

Creation to the Flood may have been substantially longer than the calculated 1,656 years.

Some evidence that the tilt of the Earth's axis may have changed,[3] would, if verified, support a Flood date in the third millenium BC (see Appendix 3).

15.2 THE SIZE OF THE FLOOD

There are two main views about the size of the Flood: either it was a vast cataclysm accounting for most of the geological series from Cambrian to Pliocene, or else it was a limited inundation in Pleistocene or Recent time which did not leave important traces. Variants of the latter view are that it was a local inundation in Mesopotamia,[4] a rise in sea level between the Upper Palaeolithic and Mesolithic civilizations,[5] and or the high sea level at the commencement of the Ice-Age known as the 'Calabrian Transgression' in Europe.

The Scriptural record argues strongly for the first alternative, that the Flood was an immense global cataclysm. No limited flood could satisfy its cosmic impact. Every high hill was submerged to a depth of 15 cubits. All living things on dry land were destroyed.[6] The heavens as well as the Earth were changed.[7] The ark was big even by modern standards,[8] and much larger than would have been required for a local inundation in Mesopotamia. In both the Genesis and Babylonian accounts it went north. A local flood in Mesopotamia would have driven it south.

The Flood was a global catastrophe which had a global cause and therefore produced worldwide geological effects. It was clearly the greatest natural convulsion since Creation. It all but obliterated every living thing. If the Bible is historical, the Flood must have been the most significant natural event of all time. It must have a prominent place in any system of geological explanation.

15.3 THE DURATION OF THE FLOOD

Scripture states that the Flood lasted 371 days, or a little over a year. This is in keeping with its universality and cannot be reconciled with a Local-Flood theory. The sequence of events is summarized on Table 15.1.

TABLE 15.1 **Chronology of the Flood**[9]	
References are from Genesis; numbers refer to days. It is assumed that a month was of 30 days.	
Rain falling, deeps ejecting (7:12)	40
Rain stopped, deeps closed, but waters still covering (7:24) giving a total of 150 days for 'prevailing'	110
Decreasing from 17th day of 7th month to 1st day of tenth month (8:5)	74
Time before Noah sent out raven (8:6-7)	40
Time before Noah sent out dove for first time (8:8)	7
Time before Noah sent out dove second time (8:10)	7
Time before sending out dove for third time (8:12)	7
Remaining time until 1st day of first month of 601st year (7:11; 8:13)	29
Time from removal of ark's covering to end of the experience (8:14)	57
TOTAL	371

The first 40 days saw an opening storm. During the next 110 the water stayed at approximately maximum depth. At the end of this it was shallow enough for the ark to rest. The waters then receded for 74 days with mountains becoming increasingly visible. The last 147 days saw the exposure of increasing land while the waters finally receded.

This scenario suggests an outline model for the Flood of four phases: a beginning storm, a period of standing water, a period of decreasing water with uplands only visible, and a final retreat with more land exposed. Winds and other atmospheric forces could have strongly affected the land in both of the last two periods.

The following outline, based on this, is tentative in the extreme and subject to revision in the light of increasing knowledge.

15.4 THE BEGINNING STORM

The Flood began with heavy rain and the upwelling of water and probably magma from the ocean floors, causing powerful tsunamis (waves generated by submarine earthquakes and volcanoes). These are the most destructive waves of all and have been known to attain speeds of over 640 kilometres an hour and reach heights of over 40 metres. They cause extensive coastal damage and loss of life. They must have assisted the rain in eroding the land and removing sediments to lower ground and into the sea.

Ocean waves then invaded the land. These can likewise be immensely destructive. They have been recorded as moving masses weighing many tonnes. At Cherbourg, France, for instance, storm waves hurled 3.5-tonne stones over the breakwater and moved 65-tonne concrete blocks 20 metres. In 1872 at Wick, Scotland, a concrete block and the breakwater to which it was attached with a combined weight of 1,350 tonnes, were shifted by waves, and their 2,600-tonne replacement suffered the same fate a few years later.[10] Air compressed in joints and cracks acts as if a wedge was suddenly driven in to the rock. Recession of the water is accompanied by an explosive expansion of air. This driving of water into cracks not only exerts great mechanical stress but in soluble rocks may greatly accelerate solution.[11]

River floods on land have caused similar damage. Some have moved individual boulders of upwards of 350 tonnes in currents turbid with particles several centimetres in diameter, and excavated canyons 20 metres deep in a single storm.[12] The Bible Flood must have been many times more powerful because it lasted much longer.

Genesis says that the 'fountains of the great deep were broken up, and the windows of heaven were opened. And the rain was on the earth forty days and forty nights'.[13] It lasted 40 days.[14] After 150 days 'the fountains of the deep and the windows of heaven were stopped',[15] and the waters then decreased continuously. Thus the breaking up of the fountains of the deep lasted 150 days. The best interpretation of the apparent discrepancy over the duration of the rainfall seems to be that the rain from the waters above the firmament[16] caused a rise for 40 days after which they maintained a constant depth for a further 110 days. The Koran makes the interesting statement that the Flood came by opening 'the gates of heaven with pouring water and caused the Earth to gush forth springs'.[17] It is likely that water from the Earth's crust was hot. The forces generating the Flood were therefore clearly many times greater than the most extreme conditions of our own age.

The pre-Flood landscape must have had substantial hills and valleys. Psalm 104:6-9, apparently referring to Creation, implies that the mountains were relatively easily submerged, and so may have been lower than those of today. Pangaea was probably composed of 'Basement Complex' rocks from the Archaeozoic and Proterozoic geological systems which form the foundation of present continents. They include some metamorphosed sediments but these at most contain only minute and simple fossils.

As the Flood progressed, the creatures of the deep sea bottom, notably trilobites, brachiopods, mollusks, graptolites, and corals would have been overwhelmed, churned, and buried by the inorganic materials dislodged from the bed. The resulting deposits appear to represent the deposition of the first three systems called Lower Palaeozoic: the Cambrian, Ordovician, and Silurian, giving vast thicknesses of marine sediments of all sorts. They include some volcanic materials, in the British Isles especially in the Ordovician.

15.5 THE PERIOD OF STANDING WATER

The early Palaeozoic deposits were then upheaved in the phase known as the Caledonian orogeny (mountain-making) and became the source of the material for the next massive erosional stage. This laid down the Upper Palaeozoic systems: Devonian and Carboniferous rocks. It could be called the 'period of standing water' because of the large proportion of relatively still water deposits it contains, especially shales and limestones.

The characteristic Devonian fossils are fish, crustaceans, and mollusks. The fish are often found in masses with very little disturbance as though buried very rapidly in one event, possibly associated with a sudden rise in water temperature. That such fossils do not represent an evolutionary development is underlined by the fact that some 'less advanced' fossils appear above 'more advanced' ones in the stratigraphic succession.[18]

Carboniferous strata are mainly sandstones, limestones, and coal measures, derived from the land and deposited in inshore waters. The limestones are often associated with chalk and corals. All are built of sea creatures and therefore indicate abundant soluble calcium bicarbonate in the water. Coal measures represent the first occurrence of large masses of vegetation in the geological record, and indicate abundant atmospheric carbon dioxide. They may have been transported in the form of great rafts which were deposited and buried in relatively quiescent waters. Their formation into coal was apparently due to heat and pressure in the relative absence of oxygen.

Carboniferous rocks contain the fossils of the first land animals. They do not appear before this presumably because the sea beds were the first areas affected by the breaking up of the deeps, and hydrodynamic selectivity kept creatures of the same size and specific gravity approximately together. The settling velocity of particles in water increases as their size and sphericity increases and as water density decreases. Organisms in the lowest strata tend to be spheroidal and, because composed of calcium carbonate, quite dense. The first ostrachoderms (armoured fish), which are lighter, are in the Ordovician. Above this the order is as might be expected: creatures showing increasing mobility, decreasing density, and higher elevation of habitat as one ascends the geological column.

The third great orogeny, generally referred to in Europe as Hercynian and in Britain as Armorican, followed the Carboniferous. It folded and uplifted the earlier deposits, exposing them to a further cycle of erosion and deposition. The resulting sediments begin with the Permian strata. These are conventionally associated with a major glaciation because of their resemblance to tillites and the presence of striations but, as discussed in chapter 6, these are as likely to be submarine slump deposits. Some sandy deposits, hitherto considered to be wind-laid are more likely to have been laid down in shallow water.[19]

Upwelling of lavas from the Earth's crust beginning in this period also appears to have initiated the breakup of Pangaea. Its northern part became Laurasia, its southern part, Gondwanaland. Laurasia then split into North American and Eurasian parts, and Gondwanaland into South America, Africa, India, Australia, and Antarctica. These separations must have enlarged rapidly during the Flood to form the present ocean basins. They have extended ever since at a slower rate.

15.6 THE VIOLENT WINDSTORM

The Mesozoic period follows the Permian and is divided into the Triassic, Jurassic, and Cretaceous systems. Because of the abundance of reptile fossils in the last two, they are sometimes referred to collectively as the 'Age of Reptiles'. The Flood seems to have been receding, some rocks being marine and some subaerial.

The Triassic rocks reflect a time of geological quiescence but of intense atmospheric activity. The strata are marine in southern Europe but in northern Europe they are considered to have been laid down in an area of inland drainage. Some of the sandstones are thought to have been deposited as dunes under desert conditions, and then buried under pebbly and ultimately clayey materials from surrounding uplands. Others were apparently laid down on shallow submarine shelves by agitated sea water.[20] This is why the period might be called 'The Great Windstorm'.

Higher Triassic strata extending across wide stretches of northern Europe contain deposits of rock salt and gypsum, in Britain locally up to 400 metres thick. They are thought to be due to high evaporation from large temporary lakes. It is often considered difficult to compress thick evaporite deposits into a short span of time, but it is not necessary to assume that they were formed in environments like those of the present world. They may have been transported from some previous location where they existed since Creation. Alternatively, they may have been formed by intense application of heat for evaporation of large quantities of water in a short time rather than by solar heating acting over a long time. Evaporite layers have been ascribed to evaporation from lagoons. However, none deriving from this cause are known from rocks before the Miocene and many later evaporites are too thick to be explainable in this way. They may have been due to unusual conditions of vaporization and separation of precipitates during the volcanic uphevals accompanying the Deluge. Some salt accumulations, such as salt domes, are definitely tectonic.[21]

Jurassic and Cretaceous rocks contain vast thicknesses of limestone. Although their index fossils are mainly marine, they contain many reptiles and some mammals. These are high in the sequence probably because of their greater mobility. This would have enabled them to escape temporarily to higher ground as the waters rose, only occasional individuals being swept away and entombed in earlier sediments. Even if they were overwhelmed, they would simply have been drowned and then carried about on or near the surface until finally decomposed by the elements. Occasionally groups might have been buried together if suddenly overwhelmed in a cave or on a hilltop.

The Mesozoic strata conclude with another episode of mountain building, known as the Alpine, followed by a final, mainly marine, depositional stage — the Cenozoic. This itself included further uplifts and volcanic activity with lava flows in areas such as Arabia, the American desert, and the Giant's Causeway in Northern Ireland.

15.7 THE PERIOD OF RECEDING WATER

Cenozoic strata are subdivided into the Tertiary and Quaternary. The former includes the Eocene, Oligocene, Miocene and Pliocene, the latter the Pleistocene and Recent. The Eocene deposits are often fossiliferous limestones similar to those of the preceding Mesozoic period but Oligocene and later deposits tend to be shales and fine textured sediments indicative of slack-water deposition, according with the final stages of a Flood recession. They are not separated by strong stratigraphic breaks but are distinguished from each other on the percentages of their fossils which occur as living forms today. All could have been contemporary. Any species could be ancestral to or descended from any similar form. Zones in the strata are therefore not necessarily due to evolution but to hydrodynamic sorting and the capacity of the creature to escape from the Flood waters. Mammals were better at escaping, especially the bigger ones.

The Flood ended with a drying of the earth and the deposition of the Pliocene strata. The retreating waters must have caused intense erosion. Psalm 104:7 says they 'fled' and 'hasted away'. The retreat was accompanied by the strong atmospheric cooling which introduced the Ice-Age.

15.8 SUMMARY

Although there is room for doubt in interpreting some Hebrew words, Scripture appears to place the Flood in the third millenium BC. It was a worldwide cataclysm rather than a local inundation on the Middle East.

It seems to fall into four periods: a beginning storm for 40 days, a phase of standing water for 110 days, and a violent windstorm followed by receding water which together lasted 221 days. The transitions between phases could approximately accord with major tectonic upheavals. Conditions throughout differed widely from anything seen since. The beginning storm was immensely destructive and involved the deposition of vast thicknesses of sediments fossilizing mainly the bottom-dwelling marine creatures. This is presumed to represent the early Palaeozoic strata. The period of standing water saw the sudden destruction and entombment of fish and masses of probably rafted vegetation. This accords to the late Palaeozoic period. The third period notionally covers Mesozoic rocks. It witnessed the wind deposition of sandstones, a chemically accelerated precipitation of evaporites and a massive destruction of reptile populations. The final period of receding water is thought to coincide with the deposition of Tertiary rocks. These are largely products of slack-water deposition and contain almost all the mammal fossils. The final retreat of the water caused intense surface erosion and alluvial deposition.

REFERENCES

[1] 2 Chronicles 21-26. [2] Joshua 24:2. [3] Setterfield 1987, pages vi-x; Bowden 1983. [4] Woolley 1952, pages 22, 23. [5] Filby 1970, page 137. [6] Genesis 7:19-23. [7] 2 Peter 3:3-7. [8] Genesis 6:15. [9] Abbreviated from Whitcomb and Morris 1974, page 3. [10] Bascomb 1959. [11] Thornbury 1954, pages 432, 433. [12] Whitcomb and Morris 1974, page 260. [13] Genesis 7:11, 12. [14] Genesis 7:4, 17. [15] Genesis 8:2. [16] Genesis 1:7. [17] Sura 54:12. [18] Wells and Kirkaldy 1966, page 199. [19] Brand 1976, pages 4-7. [20] Brand 1976, pages 4-7. [21] Whitcomb and Morris 1974, pages 412-417.

CHAPTER 16

THE ICE-AGE

16.1 THE POST-FLOOD EARTH

In spite of the magnitude of the effects of the Flood, the newly emerged Earth had some similarity to the antediluvian one. This is indicated by the fact that rivers named Tigris and Euphrates existed both before and after, and the availability of 'pitch' for the ark, suggests an environment similar to today's Mesopotamia. (This has no necessary implication of fossil organic origin since the Hebrew word for 'pitch' in Genesis 6:14 is 'kopher' which means a covering material.)

The post-Flood Earth would, however, have differed from today's in two important respects:

a. the oceans would have been much warmer and therefore ice-free.

b. the land would have been colder. There are two reasons for this. First, volcanic dust and aerosols were blocking the sun's radiation from reaching the Earth. Measurements of Greenland ice cores have shown that over the past 1,400 years high levels of volcanic activity can be correlated with low temperatures in the northern hemisphere. For example, lower atmospheric temperatures coincided with a high content of volcanic dust between 1880 and 1915.

Secondly, the 'greenhouse effect' would have been less, due to the lower atmospheric carbon dioxide after the beginning of the Ice-Age. This would have resulted from a fairly rapid fall at the end of the Flood. The amount of CO_2 in both atmosphere and ocean was probably relatively high during the Flood as a result of the abundant antediluvian biosphere. The post-Flood vegetation would rapidly reduce this since it would absorb much and would initially have had few decaying residues to recycle CO_2

back into the atmosphere. It would also be progressively absorbed into the oceans as they cooled, since its solubility increases as water temperature drops. The process would have been accelerated by the proliferation of phytoplankton and zooplankton feeding on the abundant nutrients in the sea after the Flood. These would fix CO_2 in their structures, further reducing it in both ocean and atmosphere.

The lower postdiluvian CO_2 has been confirmed by a study of air bubbles trapped in the deeper ice of the Greenland and Antarctic ice sheets (Sundquist 1987). Scientists claim it was then about 200ppm (parts per million), which compares with a pre-industrial value of about 275ppm and a current value of 350ppm.[1]

16.2 THE ADVANCE OF THE ICE

The first recognition of the importance of glaciation in forming the landscapes of northern Europe and North America was by Louis Agassiz in 1840, but it was some time before the idea gained general acceptance. It is now recognized that there were a number of glacial advances interrupted by retreats. In Europe, Penck and Brueckner[2] suggested four advances: Guenz, Mindel, Riss, and Wurm, based on correlating river terraces in the Alps with terminal moraines (distal accumulations of ice-dumped material). Four advances are likewise recognized in central North America: Nebraskan, Kansan, Illinoian, and Wisconsin. Only the last has deposits with a strong topographic expression: moraines, drumlins (small hills shaped like half-pears with the wide end facing the direction of ice movement), eskers (sinuous ridges), and striations on underlying rocks. The earlier ones are all till plains (more or less level plains composed of glacial sediments). The sequence of four major advances is not found everywhere. Where it is, each has been subdivided into several advances and retreats known respectively as stadials and interstadials.

Since most information exists about the northern hemisphere, the rest of this chapter will deal only with the glaciations there, although analogous conditions occurred in the southern hemisphere. Oard[3] has developed a Creationist model for the Ice-Age and the following discussion is based on his work.

After the Flood, the strong contrast between the warm oceans and the cold land would have raised atmospheric instability. This would have increased winds and rainfall/snowfall especially at the margins of the continents. A veritable 'snow blitz' could thus occur. Once the ice cover had developed, it would make the lands even colder and accelerate the process of glaciation.

A high rate of volcanic activity would probably have continued at least until the glacial maximum. Oceans would remain warm, and ice sheets would build up on land. The oceans would cool only slowly because, in the absence of ice, they would absorb more solar heat in summer. Winters would be warmer than today's because of the legacy of the warm flood water and the absence of polar ice caps. Any tendency for the ocean's surface layer to freeze would be inhibited by mixing with deeper layers. On the other hand, summers would be cooler than at present because the warm oceans would generate more cloud and rain over the land.

Heavy precipitation would occur equatorward of the ice sheets, making for a relatively lush vegetation in high latitudes. The warmer winters and cooler summers would explain the disharmonious associations of, for instance, cold-loving animals such as reindeer, musk oxen, and woolly mammoths with hippopotami.

Ice would increase and reach a maximum thickness towards its margins where precipitation was highest. Till would also reach a maximum in these areas. In North America it varies in thickness from about 10 metres in New Hampshire to about 52 metres in Iowa. The time to glacial maximum would depend on how long conditions favoured an increase in ice volume. Although volcanic eruptions would have decreased, the land would be kept cold by the higher cloudiness, the highly reflective character of the wide snow cover, and the low atmospheric carbon dioxide.

Measurements of the depth attained by the ice are based on analogies with Greenland and the Antarctic, the height of nunataks (ice-sculpted hillocks whose summits stood above the level of the moving ice), evidences from coastal terraces, and calculations based on the measured isostasy of glaciated areas. They give a figure of about 800 metres. The total amount of moisture available over the land areas between 40 degrees and 60 degrees north can be calculated to have given an annual increment of precipitation of 1.4 metres, more than three times the present average. This would give the 800 metre depth of ice in about 500 years.

The maximum ice and hence the steepest ice slopes would be near to the margin of the ice sheets, because the track of depressions would bring the maximum snowfall to these areas. This greater marginal thickness makes it easier to explain why these areas would be especially subject to periodic surges and retreats. Glacial flow depends on the thickness of the ice and the slope over which it moves. It can materially increase and even become a surge when there is a layer of water at the base. Volcanic dust and other impurities in the ice can give a more rapid rate of internal deformation. Rapid surges of ice could engulf plants and some animals and duplicate the probable effects of slow glacial advances. They would also produce multiple till deposits, superposed simultaneously in layers.[4] Water-laid sediments separating till layers can often be explained not as multiple successions, but as due to the former presence of glacial melt streams coupled with shifting ice divides and changing ice flow directions.

The spread of polar ice at the glacial maximum would have 'compressed' the climatic belts towards the equator. This would have brought rainfall now characteristic of the Westerlies zone of northern Europe and North America into what are now the semi-arid and arid areas lying equatorward of them. The increased rainfall in these areas could help account for the extensive fossil river systems to be seen in them.

16.3 THE RETREAT OF THE ICE

The critical factor determining when the ice would reach its maximum extent would be ocean temperature. This would steadily fall. It would initiate a decline in the ice sheets when it fell below about 10 degrees Centigrade. Assuming it was 30 degrees C at the end of the Flood, the cooling by 20 degrees C to this threshold value, when applied to the present oceanic volume of c1.3 $\times$ 10^9 km3, represents a heat loss of 2.6 $\times$ 10^{25} calories. Likely rates of radiation loss to space and atmospheric heat transport from low to high latitudes, would give 500 years as the probable time required for this. This accords with the calculations based on probable rainfall and maximum ice depth and therefore represents the time from the end of the Flood to the glacial maximum.[5]

Once the sea temperature fell below 10 degrees Centigrade, oceanic evaporation would be reduced, fewer clouds would form at high latitudes, precipitation would decrease, and more solar radiation would penetrate to the surface of the ice sheets. The ice would begin to retreat. This would lead to what one might describe as a 'big chill'. When the sea temperature approached the 4 degree Centigrade average of today, ice would begin to form in it near to the poles, accelerating the cooling. The atmosphere would become drier and colder than today as long as the ice sheets remained. This would accentuate the contrast with the tropics, raising the air pressure in polar regions, driving the Jet Stream further south, and generating high winds around the southern margins of the ice sheets. The fossil dune and loess tracts now found in these areas would form at this time.

Once the oceans had cooled, deglaciation would be relatively rapid. The big chill would produce much colder temperatures in winter, but summers would be warmer than during the build up of the ice sheets, although cooler than today. Winter snowfall would be light, so that most of the summer sunshine and heat, then increased by clearer skies and less aerosols, would be available to melt the ice sheets. Oard[6] estimates, from the best assumptions possible about the albedo of the ice surface and the probable cloudiness, that the average melting rate in Michigan towards the southern edge of the ice sheet would be at the rate of 10.4 metres per year, a deglaciation in 50–87 years. The interior of the ice area would melt in about 200 years, so that the whole Ice-Age would have occupied only about 700 years.

This relatively rapid melting would have generated a large volume of terrestrial water, perhaps ten to twenty times as much as would occur in a similar time period today. The resulting downcutting of valleys must have been very violent. It explains the extensive fossil valley systems with their flights of erosional terraces found near to glacial margins in many parts of the world. These terraces are conventionally ascribed to long interglacial periods, but have been locally observed to form very quickly. They may be due to episodic changes in channel geometry and sediment load rather than to long-term climatic change.[7]

River discharge generally increases with the wave length of meanders. Their large size in old periglacial rivers shows that they must have carried much more water than today, in some areas more than sixty times as much. This accords with the idea of a rapidly retreating ice sheet.

Another fact supporting the relatively rapid sequence of events described above is the massive extinction of megafauna that occurred in immediate post-glacial times. These large animals thrived during the Ice-Age because the climate was wetter and the winters milder than today. This gave adequate food. As the ice sheets melted, the colder and drier winters would have stressed the largest animals most. Some were destroyed by man, some buried by floods. The vast numbers of mammoth remains in northern Europe, especially Russia, testify to a sudden cataclysmic freeze at this time. This could have been associated with a rapid freezing of meltwater floating on top of the salt water of the Arctic Ocean, and derived from Asian mountains across the low ground of northern Siberia. The mechanism, however, which preserved so many mammoth skeletons, some with the flesh still on them and some even containing undigested food in their stomachs, is still unknown.

The arguments for a single, rather than multiple Ice-Ages, are substantial. First, the drastic climatic changes which would be required in high latitudes to generate the amount of ice involved bespeak a unique event which would be unlikely to recur several times in the same way. Secondly, much of the evidence is from layers of non-glacial materials and palaeosols (buried soils) between glacial deposits. Non-glacial layers occur more rarely and are of more restricted extent than would be expected from long interglacial periods. Also, they can often be explained by some local depositional factor.

Palaeosols are mainly confined to unglaciated areas. Most humid-region soils have four horizons: A — the organic surface layer, B — the zone of concentration of chemicals and clay washed down from the surface, C — the transitional zone of weathered materials above bedrock, and D — unweathered bedrock. Since the A horizon is often eroded away or destroyed by oxidation and the C horizon does not differ much from bedrock, most palaeosols have to be interpreted from the presence of B horizons. This is seldom irrefutable. Other processes can develop them, such as the upward translocation of material from the water table or the accumulation of fine material over impermeable sediments. Only very rarely is a sequence of tills found with palaeosols between them, and these often only take the form of a weathered or chemically altered zone on the surface of glacial detritus in one limited locality.

16.4 THE END OF THE ICE-AGE

The Ice-Age concluded with a general warming. Post-

Flood human settlement in tropical and subtropical latitudes would have been little affected by the ice, but the subtropics would have experienced increased rainfall because of the equatorward migration of the Westerlies climatic belt in front of the ice. This would have made areas such as the Fertile Crescent better watered than now.

The climatic belts would have migrated polewards as the ice retreated. This would have been followed by a migration of human settlements into middle latitudes. Since then, despite minor fluctuations, the Earth has had the climate and patterns of settlement we know today.

16.5 ICE-AGE CHRONOLOGY: ORBITAL PERTURBATIONS

Glacial geologists believe that the Ice-Age started about two million years ago and ended about 10,000 years ago, and that stadial maxima occurred about once every 100,000 years. There is no agreement concerning their exact number, but the usual estimate is about twenty.

This long time scale is based mainly on several lines of evidence which appear to reinforce each other: the Milankovitch planetary hypothesis, oxygen isotope ratios, radiometric dating, and current sedimentation rates. This time scale cannot, however, be harmonized with the few thousand years of the Bible account.

The Milankovitch hypothesis is based on a correlation of three perturbations of the Earth's movements around the sun: the eccentricity of the orbit, the precession of the equinoxes, and the obliquity of the ecliptic. When the current rates of change of these three perturbations are combined and extrapolated back into the past, they give temperature minima for high latitudes which are thought to correlate with glacial maxima.

These perturbations cannot, however, account for the large changes in temperature and rainfall that would be needed to initiate an ice-age of the magnitude which occurred. It would have required much more cooling and snowfall than would result from the small changes in summer sunshine at high latitude that the theory allows. Even doubling the present snowfall would not be enough. The annual temperature change would have to have been quite large, that is, 12 degrees Celsius cooler summers than today's. Calculations of the perturbations at today's rates does not explain the relatively sudden once-for-all onset of the Ice-age.

16.6 ICE-AGE CHRONOLOGY: OXYGEN ISOTOPE RATIOS

The ocean bed is covered with ooze which is continuously fed by a 'rain' of fine particles. The rate is assumed to have remained relatively unchanged throughout geological time. The shells of micro-organism populations, each with a known range of tolerated living temperatures, are distributed throughout this ooze and can be brought up in the cores. Data for oxygen isotope ratios is derived from this.

There are two main isotopes of oxygen: ^{16}O and ^{18}O. The heavier ^{18}O is slightly less volatile than ^{16}O. It is therefore believed that during glacial periods it constituted a slightly higher proportion of oceanic waters. Variations of the $^{16}O/^{18}O$ ratio are found in the micro-organisms in chronological layers in the ooze. Cores from these layers are measured to determine this ratio as a key to ocean temperatures. These temperatures are then correlated with the advances and retreats of glaciations on land. The conclusions from this method are believed to corroborate the Milankovitch chronology.

The method, however, has a number of difficulties that bring its conclusions into serious question.

1. It supposedly shows that ice-ages repeat about every 100,000 years. This matches only the eccentricity variations in the Earth's orbit, which is by far the smallest of the three perturbations, changing the solar radiation on Earth by at most 0.17%. This is insufficient to generate an ice-age.

2. The oxygen isotope method assumes that sea temper-

atures have been relatively homogeneous in the oceans at any one time. But they can vary widely, up to 10 degrees Celsius at mid and high latitudes, with depths tending to be cooler than the near-surface waters. This can upset conclusions based on the assumed local uniformity of ocean temperatures.

3. Planktonic animals can change depth at times, so that they may have lived in temperatures different from those on the ocean floor.[1]

4. The ocean floor may not have been undisturbed. There can also have been erosion, mixing of materials by bottom-feeding worms, dissolution of deposited calcium carbonate, or a combination of these. The dissolution of calcium carbonate can change the oxygen isotope ratios by dissolving the shells that are isotopically lighter.

16.7 ICE-AGE CHRONOLOGY: LAND SURFACE INDICATIONS

The most recent ice advance is thought to have peaked at around 18,000 years ago and ended about 8,000 years ago. The last date is derived from radiometric and fossil-dating methods. But a number of considerations argue that these dates are too long. Many Ice-Age deposits look fresh and uneroded. Glacial striations are exposed on rocks that have been little weathered since they were made. Drumlins and eskers often retain near perfect form. Cirque lakes have only small notches in their outer rims. The age of Niagara Falls, which were initiated by the final retreat of the ice, can be assessed from the time required for their erosional retreat from a known original position. This cannot be more than 3,000-4,000 years.[2]

16.8 SUMMARY

The end of the Flood must have left the Earth much changed from what it had been before. The atmosphere had lost its vapour canopy, causing the land to be colder at high latitudes. The Flood had left the seas much warmer. This temperature contrast must have caused atmospheric instability which would have led to much higher rainfall and snowfall around their interface. Large ice sheets would have formed on land.

Summers would have been relatively cool because of the higher cloudiness and the volcanic dust and aerosols left behind by the Flood events. Winters would have been milder because of the warmer oceans and the absence of polar ice caps.

The seas would have gradually cooled and the land warmed as the summer skies cleared. The glacial maximum would have been reached when the cooling seas failed to generate enough snowfall to balance an increasing summer melting of the ice sheets.

The build-up of the ice could have taken of the order of 500 years and the retreat of the order of 200, giving an Ice-Age total of about 700 years. Reasons are given for defending this brief chronology against the Milankovitch hypothesis, the apparent evidence from ocean-bed cores, and the view that some layers between sequential glacial deposits indicate long time lapses.

The loci of glacial retreat would be associated with high winds forming loess deposits and dunes, and with strong meltwater flows eroding valley systems. A sudden sharp onset of winter cold in flood conditions at this time could explain the wholesale destruction of large mammals in northern Eurasia.

REFERENCES
[1] Oard 1990, page 43. [2] 1909 Tafel 1 endpaper. [3] 1990. [4] Flint 1971, page 159. [5] Oard, loc. cit., page 209. [6] Oard, page 222. [7] Schumm 1977, pages 210-221. [8] Berger and Gardner 1975. [9] Oard, loc. cit., pages 169-171.

CHAPTER 17

CONCLUSIONS

17.1 THE CASE FOR CREATIONISM

Although creationist and evolutionist models of our natural world do not differ over observed facts, there is a wide difference between their interpretations.

The evolutionary view today is of a universe originating in something like the Big Bang and developing myriads of astral fragments from one of which our solar system derived. The Earth developed from this beginning as a formless mass about 4.5 billion years ago. Life arose on it spontaneously and from primitive beginnings evolved into its present form over a period of something like $3\frac{1}{2}$ billion years.

The creationist view runs counter to this. It teaches a six-day creation with a different order of events. The atmosphere, oceans, and vegetation preceded the Sun, Moon, and stars. All types of plants and animals were separately created, and except for variations within individual gene pools, have not evolved. Although sharing many characteristics with animals, humans also differ from them too profoundly for common ancestry to be credible. The time scale for the Earth's existence is only a few thousand years. This not only accords with divine revelation, but has scientific support.

The history of Western thought shows how a rift developed between science and ethics and how the resulting loss of a unitary world view led to a neglect of the ethical component of scientific enquiry. This neglect undermined any resistance to the rapid acceptance of the theory of evolution, which now permeates not only science but many aspects of thought and behaviour. It has also diminished interest in Bible study.

Science points at least as strongly to creationism as to evolution. The law of entropy argues against the possibility of upward progress by evolutionary means. It is becoming clear that the Big Bang, although it may provide a framework for explaining some observed phenomena, is inadequate to explain the origin of the universe. The possibility that the speed of light has decreased tends to support the idea of a young Earth and a non-expanding universe.

There are many facts which cannot be explained by current theories of the origin of the solar system. These include the differences in chemical composition between the Sun and planets, the distance from the Sun to the outermost planets, and the reverse spin on two of the planets and eleven moons.

In geology, the marine origin of all early strata suggest a flood. The gaps between apparently conformable strata, claimed to represent millions of years, are based entirely on the view that the fossils evolved and do not accord with local stratigraphic evidence. Where apparent glacial or wind deposits occur in marine strata, they have sometimes been proved also to be marine. Although almost no fossils at all occur in Precambrian rocks, examples of all today's phyla except vertebrates appear suddenly and without antecedents in the Cambrian. This cannot be explained in evolutionary terms. A convincing case can be made for the view that the geological strata from Cambrian to Pliocene are due to a single catastrophic flood. This is supported by their dominantly marine provenance, and also by the relatively low salt content of the oceans and the youth of their floors.

Many questions surround radiometric dating, a major line of evidence cited in favour of an old Earth. The amount of helium in the Earth's crust is too little to accord with its presumed long-term radioactivity. Daughter as well as parent isotopes of a radioactive element may have been present at the starting date. Decomposition rates may have varied and neutron flux occurred. Pleochroic haloes argue for an instantaneous creation of some Precambrian rocks and a rapid deposition of subsequent sedimentary strata.

17

The Pleistocene and Recent geological periods are generally thought to have included several ice ages covering about two million years, but this chronology is based on questionable evidence. The main scientific clock — radiocarbon dating — is unreliable beyond about 5,000 years. Time calculations in terms of backward extrapolation of the Earth's present perturbations provides an inadequate explanation of the dramatic nature of the changes that initiated the Ice-Age. These changes can be better understood in terms of the aftermath of an immensely destructive flood whose retreat left warm oceans and a drastically changed atmosphere. The Ice-Age could have occurred within hundreds rather than thousands of years.

In biology it is not possible to establish the idea of the spontaneous generation of life. External information is needed for this and for any further evolution of cells. The argument for progress through natural selection of favourable mutations is at variance with the fact that almost all are harmful. Thus the chances of a favourable mutation becoming dominant by natural selection over a long period are negligible. Missing links are totally absent from the fossil record. Organisms cannot inherit acquired characteristics, so there is no mechanism through which physical changes not in an original gene pool can be propagated. The fossil evidence points to creationism.

17.2 POSSIBLE SCIENTIFIC ADVANCES USING THE CREATIONIST MODEL

The effectiveness of Darwin's *Origin* was in part due to the number of meticulously-researched case studies it contains. It effectively established micro-evolution but not macro-evolution. Only by following this same method further can the scientific truth or error of the latter theory be effectively tested.

It is important to keep reviewing the relation between the Scriptures and science. There are a number of ways in which this could be approached. They could include:

1. Studying the Bible's exact wording about nature and mankind's part in it.

2. Continuing the search for a world-view which incorporates both Scriptural authority and systematic observation of nature. The general principle has been outlined by Odajnyk:[1]

' . . . because every theory depends on an understanding of what man is, what society is, what should be the relation between them, and what the reason and purpose of each of these is, no theory can claim infallibility unless it is able to provide answers to these fundamental questions of existence.'

3. Seeking testable creationist or evolutionist positions critical to the debate. For instance,

a. IN GEOLOGY:

i. Some sediments called glacial and wind-borne have been subsequently shown to be of marine formation. This supports the flood explanation. Others remain to be tested.

ii. Some continuous rock surfaces are part-buried, part-exhumed. It can be useful to test the amount of destruction of the surface of the exhumed part against the assumed date of exhumation. The length of time required for this destruction will give conclusions relevant to the creation/evolution debate.

iii. The Bible account of the Flood suggests that the water may have been hot. The possibility that this could be partly the cause of some 'fossil graveyards' could be explored.

iv. Turbidites can be deposited very rapidly. The mechanisms of deposition need to be explored.

b. IN METEOROLOGY. The history of atmospheric carbon-14 needs to be investigated. It relates closely to past changes in the Earth's magnetic field and atmospheric changes at the time of the Flood.

c. IN BIOLOGY:

i. Present creation and evolution of life in the form of models, make a prediction based on each model, and then test the predictions against scientific evidence. Fossils are the key, specifically the presence or absence of missing links.

ii. Symbiosis is far more common than parasitism in nature. It would be useful to place more emphasis on finding harmonies and less on conflicts.

iii. Waste in nature may be due to design. Trees produce a great excess of seeds, frogs of spawn. What would be the consequences of the absence of such excesses?

d. IN PHYSICS:

i. Much chronology currently depends on radiometric dating. Its assumptions need to be re-examined, for instance, with investigations relating to the origins of pleochroic haloes.

ii. Further investigation is needed into possible past changes in the speed of light and of the angle of the Earth's axis in relation to the plane of the ecliptic.

e. IN HISTORY:

i. Flood legends require further investigation together with records relating to it from Anatolia and neighbouring areas. Rehwinkel[2] has given a comprehensive review of these.

ii. There is now much evidence from archaeology bearing on human origins. It is important to relate these to the Bible account.

f. IN THEOLOGY:

There are many undiscovered truths in the Scriptures. Evolution has undermined belief in their infallibility. A revived acceptance of this belief can redirect research into understanding their application to our times.

17.3 FURTHER IMPLICATIONS

Is human history explained by random processes and a slow upward climb or is it a sin-caused decline from an original perfection? The first view would sanctify the competitive qualities making for individual survival; the second, obedience and self-sacrifice. The debate between creationism and evolutionism thus remains a vital concern not only theoretically but for daily life. Our concept of human origins affects the whole way we relate to the cosmos. It governs our thoughts about the future.

The Bible assumes creationism throughout, but teaches it mainly in the early chapters of Genesis. The Adam and Eve story sets the framework for its human implications. Adam's relationship with his Creator, by identifying divine authority and law, gives a framework for all aspects of life. The story centres on moral responsibility. In elevating conscience above material interest, it provides the basic rationale for free social, economic, and political institutions. Adam's responsibility for the natural world provides a model for the environmental challenges of today.

The scientific debate about evolution is marginal to a greater one: about our understanding of the supernatural. This is because our view of origins profoundly affects our understanding of who God is and how He deals with the world. It determines our view of His nature. The principle of atonement is first introduced outside the Garden of Eden. It provides inspiration and moral guidance for human conduct. Through this it influences our approach to science, the arts, education, and theology. Adam's relationship with his family is a guide to all religious and social relations. His relationship with Eve derives lustre and meaning from the fact that it reflects the relationship between God and the Church, and because it even echoes that within the Trinity. The evolution theory, by denying the historicity of Genesis, is absolutely destructive of these insights.

The importance of these questions demands the attention of us all. They govern our vision of the world, and beyond this, of our ultimate destiny. Central is our view of the Scriptures, and the way science relates to them.

There are two alternatives. On the one hand we can see the world as having no meaning and human life as having evolved from primitive beginnings through upward struggle with a view of the future which at best provides some material and cultural advancement for the race, at worst to destruction, but in either case to oblivion for the individual. On the other hand all can be seen as part of a divine plan.

It is vital to consider these things because our life, both here and in the hereafter, can depend on our answer.

17.4 SUMMARY

The case for creationism derives its origin from Scripture, but is also the most reasonable scientific explanation of the world. The success of the theory of evolution has been partly because it arose in circumstances which approved an intellectual separation of science from ethics. This permitted ideas to be accepted in the one which could not accord with the other. A consideration of astronomical, geological, and biological evidences shows that even from a secular scientific standpoint the evolutionary view is unsatisfactory. On the other hand, the case for the authority of Scripture is overwhelming and attempts to harmonize its view of origins with current evolutionary theory are impossible. It is feasible to outline a provisional model which accounts for Earth's history mainly in terms of a universal Flood followed by a relatively short Ice-Age.

REFERENCES

[1] 1965, page 172. [2] 1967, pages 127-164.

APPENDICES

APPENDIX 1. GENEALOGICAL EVIDENCE FROM EUROPE SUPPORTING A YOUNG EARTH

British history is generally considered to begin with the Roman invasion in 55 BC, but early chronicles exist which purport to extend the lists of kings back to the Flood. The earliest period is covered in the works of the ninth-century monk Nennius and the records that he gathered in his *Historia Britonum.*[1] These include a Table of European Nations showing their common descent from Noah through Japheth. Geoffrey of Monmouth in his work *Historia Regum Britanniae* ('History of the Kings of Britain'), written about AD 1138–39, extends this list. He begins with the supposed settlement of Brutus, the grandson of Aeneas, in Britain about the twelfth century BC and goes on to the death of King Cadwallader in AD 689.[2]

Although Geoffrey's history is generally regarded as fictitious, there is archaeological evidence apparently supporting some of it. In the fourth chapter of Book 5 of his *History*, Geoffrey relates that London was occupied by Roman troops who were in their turn besieged by the British king Asclepiodotus. The king offered to preserve their lives if they surrendered. The Venedoti, however, a British warrior tribe, showed no mercy and beheaded the Romans *en masse* at the site of a stream which the Britons called Nantgallum — the modern Walbrook. When the bed of this stream was excavated in the 1860s a large number of human skulls was found which appeared to be the remnants of a great pile. This seems to confirm Geoffrey's account.[3]

All seven separate nations of the Saxon Heptarchy trace the lineages of their various kings back to the same ancestors who themselves claimed to be descended from Noah through Japheth's line. It is unlikely that such agreement is due to accident or collusion because, for instance, Kent and Northumbria were separated by hundreds of miles and their people spoke different dialects and seldom wandered beyond their own borders. King lists are unlikely to be fabrications since any tampering with tribal memories would have been rapidly detected and would have been regarded as a serious offence.[4] Although these accounts must be taken with much caution, they seem to project a view of human origins that does not disagree with the biblical record. It is not unreasonable to suppose that they have a basis in fact.

REFERENCES
[1] Giles undated. [2] Geoffrey of Monmouth 1975; Cooper 1991. [3] Cooper 1991. [4] ibid.

APPENDIX 2. ANALOGIES BETWEEN THE CREATION STORY IN GENESIS AND PROPHECIES IN REVELATION

The Creation story provides the framework for the closely analogous seven-stage sequence of events used for prophetic purposes in the seven trumpets of Revelation 8:7-9:19, and for final judgement in the seven last plagues of Revelation 16. This can be seen by comparing Table N1 with the analysis of Genesis 1 on Table 13.1.

TABLE N1. **Trumpets and bowls in Revelation 8–9 and 16 in relation to the creation story.**

	TRUMPETS	BOWLS
1	Earth (8:7 etc.)	Earth (16:2)
2	Sea (8:8)	Sea (16:3)
3	Rivers, fountains (8:10)	Rivers, fountains (16:4)
4	Sun, moon, stars (8:12)	Sun (16:8)
5	Abyss, king Abaddon, darkness (9:11) (The Jew often equated the sea and the abyss.)	Throne of Beast, darkness (16:10).
6	River Euphrates (9:14)	River Euphrates (16:12) (This river originally flowed by the Garden of Eden.)
7	Voices, thunders etc., (9:15, 19)	Voices, thunders etc. (16:17, 18)

The passages in Genesis and Revelation are parallel. Genesis 1 describes the Creation, Revelation 8 and 9 a series of historical events and Revelation 16 the coming judgement. The final voices and thunders contrast with the post-Creation Sabbath calm. The end of the Bible story thus balances the beginning. Such symmetrical arrangement within the Bible argues that both are connected by a single mind. Since the historical and final events purport to be descriptions of real happenings, it would be illogical to believe that Genesis 1 does not.

APPENDIX 3. EVIDENCE FOR POSSIBLE CHANGES IN THE EARTH'S TILT IN THE THIRD MILLENNIUM BC

Evidence has recently emerged which, if verified, could support a Flood date in the third millennium BC. This relates to possible changes in the inclination of the Earth's axis.

Barry Setterfield, known for his examination of the decrease in the speed of light, has also reviewed the researches of the late G. F. Dodwell, a prominent Australian astronomer.[1]

The inclination of the Earth's axis is known as the obliquity of the ecliptic. The current value is 23 degrees 27 minutes but, according to the formula calculated by the American astronomer Simon Newcomb, it varies over a period of about 40,000 years between extreme values of 22 degrees and 24 degrees 45 minutes.

Dodwell became interested in the changes in this value and collected a total of sixty-six records of the sun's movements covering over 4,000 years from Egypt, China, Rome and elsewhere in Europe. These measurements were made with gnomons, which are vertical sticks on a plane tangential to the Earth's surface. If the angles cast by the gnomon's shadow at midday on the longest and shortest days of the year are measured, then the latitude of the observer is equal to the angle between the post and a line which bisects the two recorded shadow lines (Figure N1).

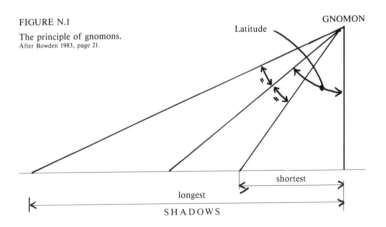

FIGURE N.1

The principle of gnomons.
After Bowden 1983, page 21.

Dodwell discovered that these records did not agree with the variations in tilt which would be expected from the Newcomb formula. In fact they deviated increasingly from the path it would predict, following a log sine curve which ended in a very rapid rise towards a larger angle of ecliptic in about 2345 BC. One explanation of this is that something happened drastically to disturb the Earth's equilibrium at that time.

An unexpectedly rapid fall in the angle of the ecliptic may help explain some phenomena which have hitherto been puzzling. Some Egyptian temples are said to have been aligned towards sunrise or sunset at the summer solstice. The temple of Amen-Ra at Karnak, for instance, is about $\frac{1}{2}$ a kilometre long down the aisle along which the sun shone only one day in the year. Over the years as the sun failed to reach the axis of the temple, it is said that the doors had to be moved further south, while today the sun does not enter the depths of the temple at all. Newcomb's formula gives a maximum tilt of 24 degrees 45 minutes, yet the original alignment of the temple is for a tilt of 25 degrees 12 minutes, an angle which the sun should theoretically never reach. It is perhaps also significant that the original alignment of Stonehenge was slightly to the north of that which later aligned its altar and heel stones towards sunrise at the summer solstice.

A change of this sort in the angle of the ecliptic would, if verified, imply the presence of a strong external force and would have significant climatic effects. It is possible that some such phenomenon may be associated with the Flood.

REFERENCE
[1] Setterfield 1987; Bowden 1983.

FURTHER READING

There is a large and growing literature on all aspects of the creation-evolution debate, and it is hard to select from it. The following list is mainly of books which together would give a general overview of the subject.

There are many works on the inspiration of the Scriptures. A useful bibliography of them is given in Ferguson, Wright, and Packer's *New Dictionary of Theology*, page 631.

A general creationist text for college and school use is Morris's *Scientific Creationism* (1974).

Philosophical and historical questions about the origin and consequences of Darwinism are covered by Clark (1972), Bowden (1982 and 1991), and Chittick (1984).

The astronomical arguments for creationism are given by White (1978), flood geology by Whitcomb and Morris (1974, and later editions), the Ice-Age by Oard (1990), biology by Wilder-Smith (1974) and Denton (1985), and fossil evolution by Gish (1986). The definitive critique on radiometric dating is by Slusher (1973).

Flood traditions are described by Rehwinkel (1951) and Filby (1970), and the story of the Chinese memories of ancient biblical history by Nelson and Broadberry (1986).

Books by evolutionists seeking to meet creationist arguments include those by Kitcher (1982) and the collections of essays edited by Montagu (1984) and Ruse (1982, 1988). Burke (1985) records a debate between Christians who take different sides of the question.

The leading journals for creationist research are the *Creation Research Society Quarterly* published at Michigan State University, and *Origins* published by the Geoscience Research Institute of Loma Linda University, California. A useful numbered series of *Symposia on Creation* is published by Baker Book House, Grand Rapids, Michigan. In Britain, the journal *Origins* is published by the Biblical Creation Society, PO Box 22, Rugby, Warwickshire CV22 7SY, and the journal *Creation* and pamphlets by the Creation Science Movement of 50 Brecon Avenue, Portsmouth, PO6 2AW.

GLOSSARY

Definitions of words as used in this book. Sources include Challinor (1967), Parker (1980), and Whittow (1984).

ACETABULUM: hip socket.

ALPHA PARTICLES: atoms of helium charged positively which are thrown off at high velocity by radioactive elements.

ALPINE: the orogeny that culminated in the Miocene period forming the Alpine system of mountain ranges.

AMINO ACID: a class of organic acids containing the amino group NH_2.

AMNIOTIC FLUID: fluid surrounding a mammal foetus before birth.

AMOEBA-MAN THEORY: the theory that man has evolved by a continuous series of steps from an original ancestor resembling an amoeba.

ANAEROBIC PHOTOSYNTHESIS: the synthesis of living tissue by organisms which draw their oxygen from chemical compounds rather than from the atmosphere.

ANHYDROUS: the state of matter in the absence of water.

ARMORICAN: the phase of mountain building in Western Europe at the end of the Palaeozoic.

ARTHROPOD: a member of the large and diverse phylum of invertebrates including insects, scorpions, spiders, crayfish, crabs, centipedes, millipedes, and the extinct trilobites.

AZIMUTHAL: of or pertaining to the horizontal angle of a bearing clockwise from north.

BACKSIGHT: the point of observation nearest the observer along a surveyed line of sight.

BARYSPHERE: Teilhard de Chardin's term for the molten interior of the Earth.

BASEMENT COMPLEX: a complex basement of rocks, usually consisting of Precambrian rocks.

BEDROCK: the solid rock underlying any loose superficial material.

BETA PARTICLES: electrons thrown off at very great velocity from the nuclei of radioactive substances.

BICUSPIDS: any of eight adult teeth with two-pointed crowns.

BIG BANG THEORY: the theory of cosmology holding that

the hypothesized expansion of the universe began with a gigantic explosion.

BIOSPHERE: the zone on the Earth's surface inhabited by living creatures.

BIVALVE: any mollusk having a shell of two parts or valves, hinged together, as a mussel, clam, etc.

BLACK HOLE: a hypothetical object in space, supposed to be an invisible collapsed star so condensed that neither light nor matter can escape its gravitational field.

BLASTODORM: a layer of cells on the inside of an animal embryo (the blastula) surrounding its cavity (the blastocoel).

BLUESTONES: spotted dolerite stones of a blue colour flecked with white, originating from the Prescelly Mountains, Pembrokeshire, and used for the inner circle and inner horseshoe of Stonehenge.

BO STAR: young star, thought to have been formed only a few million years ago.

BRECCIA: rock consisting of sharp-cornered bits cemented together by sand clay or lime.

BRECCIATION: the process by which breccia is formed.

BROWN DWARF: one of a group of stars that never attain internal temperatures high enough that nuclear burning can supply their entire radiated luminosity. They contract to the point where the electrons become highly degenerate, and reach a limiting radius that depends on the mass and composition.

BRYOZOAN: colony-forming polyp-animals, marine or fresh water. The colony may consist of horny frond-like growth (sea-mats) or beautiful calcareous masses (lace-corals).

C: the speed of light, approximately 299,793 km/sec.

CANINE: a sharp-pointed tooth on either side of the upper and lower jaws, between the incisors and the bicuspids.

CATALYTIC: adjective describing something which speeds up the rate of a chemical reaction by the addition of some substance which itself undergoes no permanent chemical change thereby.

CATARRHINE: having a slender nose with the nostrils placed close together.

CHERT: a hard very fine-grained siliceous rock, black or dull in colour, which splinters easily and fractures along flat planes in contrast to the conchoidal (shell-shaped) fracture of flint. It occurs especially in limestone deposits.

CHITIN: a tough, horny substance forming the outer covering of insects, crustaceans, etc.

CHLOROPLAST: an oval, chlorophyll-bearing body found in cells of green plants.

CIRQUE: a steep hollow depression on a mountainside made by glacial erosion.

COAL MEASURES: coal beds or strata.

COCCOLITH: a minute round or oval discoid plate which once built up the calcareous sheath of a unicellular planktonic alga, found in deep sea dredging and also fossilized in chalk.

CONFORMABLE (STRATA): the unbroken relationship between rock strata which lie one above another in parallel sequence.

CONGLOMERATE: a sedimentary rock consisting of rounded or sub-rounded fragments, usually water-worn pebbles, cemented together by a matrix of calcium carbonate, silica, etc.

CONTINENTAL DRIFT: a concept suggesting that continents can move around the Earth's surface because of the weakness of the suboceanic crust.

CRINOID: a class of marine animals that are flower-like and anchored by a stalk or are free-swimming.

CROSSOPTERYGIAN: fringe-finned fish typically with a blunt head, small rhomboidal scales, and having the vertical column continued into the upper lobe of the tail which is typically longer than the lower one.

CYTOPLASM: all the protoplasm of a cell outside, and surrounding, the nucleus. The cytoplasm is not just a simple, slightly viscous fluid; in it are situated various structures, called organelles, each concerned with different functions of the cell.

DIAGENETIC: adjective describing post-depositional compaction and cementation of near-surface sediments at relatively low temperatures and pressures.

DIPOLE: any system having two equal but opposite electrical charges or magnetic poles separated by a small distance.

DNA: deoxyribonucleic acid.

DOLOMITE: a common rock-forming mineral of calcium-magnesium carbonate.

DOPPLER SHIFT: the apparent change in frequency of sound or light waves caused by relative motion between the source of radiation and the observer.

DREIKANTER: a pebble that has been faceted by sand-blasting.

DRUMLIN: a streamlined elongated hummock or 'whale-back' hillock of glacial drift, generally of till.

ECCENTRICITY OF THE ORBIT: the amount by which the position of the sun differs from the exact centre of the Earth's orbit.

ECHINOID: sea urchin; a class of the Echinodermata with a globular, heart-shaped or discoidal test and a star-shaped pattern of spines.

ECLIPTIC: 1. the apparent annual path of the sun on the celestial sphere; 2. a great circle on the celestial sphere formed by the intersection of the plane through the Earth's orbit with the celestial sphere.

ELECTRINO: an uncharged subatomic particle which has zero or negligible mass and an extremely low probability of interaction with matter.

ELECTRON: the negatively charged particle that forms a part of all atoms.

ENDOSPERM: the nutritive tissue, also called albumen, within the seed of a flowering plant that surrounds and nourishes the developing embryo.

ENTROPY: a measure of the amount of energy unavailable for work in a thermodynamic system. Entropy keeps increasing and available energy decreasing in a closed system.

ERRATIC: a large rock fragment that has been transported by moving ice away from its place of origin and deposited in an area of dissimilar rock types.

ESKER: a narrow sinuous ridge of partly stratified coarse sand and gravel of glaciofluvial origin.

EUCARYOTIC CELLS: complex cells of higher plants and animals.

EXISTENTIALISM: a philosophical and literary movement which holds that humans are totally free and responsible for their acts, and this responsibility causes man's dread and anguish.

FATTY ACIDS: 1. any of a series of organic acids having the general formula $CnH_2n+1COOH$, 2. any of a number of saturated or unsaturated organic acids.

FELDSPAR: a member of the most important group of rock-forming minerals, comprising silicates of aluminium linked together with those of calcium, potassium, or sodium.

FERROMAGNESIAN MINERALS: minerals rich in iron and magnesium, usually dark in colour.

FLAGELLUM (plur. flagella): a whip-like part serving as an organ of locomotion in certain cells, bacteria, protozoans, etc.

FLINT: a very fine-grained black or dark grey variety of chert. It splinters easily giving conchoidal fracture planes. It mainly originates from nodules along the bedding planes of chalk.

FORAMINIFERA: one-celled sea animals with calcareous shells full of tiny holes through which slender filaments project.

FORESIGHT: the point of observation furthest from the observer along a surveyed line of sight.

GALAXY: a vast grouping of star systems held together usually in a circular or elliptical shape.

GAMMA RADIATION: electromagnetic radiation emitted by the nucleus of a radioactive substance, similar to X-rays but shorter in wave length.

GESTALT SWITCH or SHIFT: a change in view of a whole situation, not just its components.

GLACIATION: exposure to or change by glacial action.

GLACIAL ACTION: action of ice or glaciers.

GLACIOFLUVIAL: adjective describing the processes and landforms related to the action of glacial meltwater.

GNOMON: a column or pin on a sundial that indicates the time of day.

GONDWANALAND: the name given by geologists to the super-continent thought to have existed in the southern hemisphere over 200 million years ago and formerly part of the even larger Precambrian continent of Pangaea.

HERCYNIAN: the mountain-building episode of Carboniferous/Permian times.

HETEROCYCLE: a cyclic molecular arrangement of atoms of carbon and other elements.

HOMINID: any form of man, extinct or living.

HOMOLOGY: a biological term for the quality of corresponding in structure. This has led to the view that such correspondence between different creatures derives from a common ancestry.

HYDRODYNAMIC: adjective describing the motion and action of water and other liquids.

HYDROSPHERE: the zone on the Earth's surface which includes the water in sea and air.

HYRAX: any of the several small mammals which superficially resemble guinea pigs, but possess small hoofs.

ICE CAP: a mass of glacial ice that spreads outwards from a centre.

ICE SHEET: a thick layer of ice covering an extensive area.

ICHTHYOLITE: a fossil fish, or fragment of a fish.

ICHTHYOSTEGID: a Devonian amphibian with numerous characteristics of fish, such as bony head, vertebrae and tail, but with amphibian limbs and capability for living in air.

IGNEOUS ROCK: rock formed by volcanic action or intense heat.

IKU: ancient Babylonian areal measure equal to about 3,600 square metres.

ILMENITE: a black opaque mineral, oxide of iron and titanium, $FeO.TiO_2$.

IMBRICATED: overlapping evenly, as tiles or fish scales.

INCISOR: any of the front cutting teeth between the canines of either jaw.

INTERCALATION: an insertion.

INTERGLACIAL: between glacial periods.

INTERSTADIAL: between stages, usually of glaciations.

ISOSTASY: approximate equilibrium in large equal areas of the Earth's crust, preserved by the gravity of the different substances in the crust in proportion to their densities.

ISOTOPE: any of two or more forms of an element having

identical or very similar chemical properties and the same atomic numbers but different atomic weights.

ISOTROPY: having physical properties that are the same regardless of the direction of measurement.

JET STREAM: a narrow band of high altitude westerly winds in the troposphere.

KERATIN: a tough, fibrous, insoluble protein, the principal matter of hair, nails, horn, etc.

KIND: a natural group or division, used in the KJV Bible to define the main subdivisions of living things.

LAURASIA: the northern sector of the hypothetical super-continent thought to have existed after the breakup of Pangaea by continental drift.

LAW OF COMPLEXITY CONSCIOUSNESS: see Teilhard's Law.

LEACHING: the process by which water, in percolating downwards through a soil, removes humus, chemicals and clay, depositing them lower down.

LIFE FORCE: a notional vital force which causes upward evolutionary progress.

LIGNITE: a soft, brownish-black coal in which the texture of the original wood can still be seen.

LINE OF DESPAIR: Francis Schaeffer's term for the psychological threshold below which humanity falls when materialistic philosophy destroys old moral absolutes.

LITHOSPHERE: the crustal component of the Earth in contrast to the atmosphere and hydrosphere.

LOESS: an unstratified, homogeneous, fine-grained, yellowish brickearth considered to be wind-deposited.

LOG SINE CURVE: the wave-shaped graph which results when the size of angles is plotted against the logarithm of their sines.

MACRO-EVOLUTION: the concept that evolution can explain the origin of all living things from the simplest origins.

MAGMA: molten rock.

MAGNETOSTRICTION: the process by which some materials can become magnetized by physical stress.

MANTLE: the layer of the Earth between the crust and the core.

MATRIX: the fine grained material of a rock in which the coarser components are embedded.

MEANDER: a sinuosity or loop-like bend in a river.

MEGAFAUNA: large animals.

MESON: an unstable particle between the electron and the proton in mass, first observed in cosmic rays.

METAMORPHIC ROCKS: rocks which have been altered from their original state by processes such as mountain building and the intrusion and extrusion of magma.

MICRO-EVOLUTION: the concept that evolution has only occurred within the limits of the main subdivisions of the animal and vegetable kingdoms, and not between them.

MICROSPHERE: very small sea creature of spherical shape.

MILANKOVITCH HYPOTHESIS: the hypothesis, due to M. Milankovitch, that solar radiation received at different latitudes over a period of time will give cyclic changes in the Earth's temperature, related to three variables in the Earth/sun geometrical relationship. These are: 1. the eccentricity of the Earth's orbit, with a periodicity of 91,800 years, 2. the obliquity of the Earth's axis to the plane of the ecliptic, which varies between 21 degrees 58 minutes and 24 degrees 36 minutes, with a periodicity of 40,400 years, and 3. the precession of the equinoxes, that is, whether the equinox occurs when the Earth is nearest or furthest from the sun, with a periodicity of about 21,000 years.

MITOCHONDRION (plur. mitochondria): a specialized structure present in all cells with a true nucleus, which primarily functions to store and release energy.

MOHO: abbreviation for Mohorovicic Discontinuity, a seismic discontinuity occurring between the crust of the Earth and the underlying mantle. It occurs at an average of about 35km below the continents and 10km below the oceans.

MOLAR: a tooth adapted for grinding.

MOLLUSK: a member of the large phylum of invertebrate creatures, including oysters, cuttlefish, octopi, mussels, slugs, and snails.

MORAINE: rock material carried, or having been carried, by

a glacier; a terminal moraine is one which marks the limits of its advance.

MUON: a positively or negatively charged subatomic particle with a mass 207 times that of an electron.

MYLONITE: a metamorphic rock produced by grinding and rolling out.

NEUTRINO: a neutral particle having a mass approaching zero.

NEUTRON: a fundamental particle in the nucleus of an atom, which is uncharged and has about the same mass as a proton.

NEUTRON FLUX: the movement of neutrons between different atoms.

NEUTRON STAR: a heavenly object thought to be a collapsed star consisting of many densely packed neutrons.

NOOSPHERE: term originated by Teilhard de Chardin to describe the final 'mind layer' on the Earth's surface when thinking humanity is added to the preceding layers: hydrosphere, biosphere, etc.

NUCLEOTIDE: one of four types of small organic molecules found in a cell. It consists of a nitrogenous base, a pentose sugar, and a phosphate group.

NUNATAK: an isolated rocky peak which protrudes, or at one time protruded, above an ice sheet. Its summit may never have been glaciated.

OLIVINE: a rock-forming silicate mineral which is usually dark green, exhibits no cleavage, and is a member of a continuous series ranging from silicate of magnesium (Mg_2SiO_4) to silicate of iron (Fe_2SiO_4).

OMEGA POINT: the final stage of Teilhard de Chardin's evolutionary sequence when God will be all in all.

OOZE: the fine-textured sediment formed in ocean basins at depths greater than 2,000 metres.

OROGENY: a major period of fold mountain formation.

OSTRACHODERM: any of an extinct group of small fish-like Palaeozoic vertebrates with bony armour. They are allied to hagfishes and lampreys.

OVULE: a small body in seed-bearing plants that contains the egg cell and develops into the seed after fertilization.

OXIDATION: to unite with oxygen as in burning or rusting.

PALAEOSOL: a buried ancient soil.

PARACONFORMITY: a geological unconformity where there is apparently a continuous sequence of strata, but in fact a major time gap between two adjacent beds.

PARADIGM: a model, generally in the sense of a set of interlocking ideas.

PARASITISM: the property of some plants and animals whereby they live on or within others from which they derive sustenance.

PEPTIDE: any of a group of compounds formed from two or more amino acids by the linkage of amino groups in some of the acids, or by hydrolysis of proteins.

PHOTOIC ZONE (or photic zone): the shallow surface layer of the ocean, lying above a level of 60m depth, in which light can easily penetrate and make photosynthesis possible.

PHOTON: a quantum of electromagnetic energy, as of light, X-rays, etc., having both particle and wave behaviour.

PLAGIOCLASE: a common rock-forming mineral consisting of a series of aluminosilicates of sodium and calcium.

PLANKTONIC CELL: the cell of microscopic animal and plant life floating in bodies of water, used as food by fish.

PLATYRRHINE: a monkey belonging to the infraorder Platyrrhini of the Order Primates, distinguished by a flattened nose with widely separated nostrils facing outwards, and including most of the New World monkeys.

PLEIOTROPY: the production by a single gene of two or more apparently unrelated phenotypic effects.

PLEOCHROIC HALOES: very small sunburst-shaped discolorations in rock or wood caused by the decomposition of radioactive materials.

PLUTONIC ROCK: igneous rock of deep-seated origin.

POLYMER: a naturally occurring or synthetic substance made up of giant molecules formed by polymerization.

POLYMERIZATION: the process of joining two or more like molecules to form a more complex molecule whose molecular weight is a multiple of the original and whose physical properties are different.

POLYNUCLEOTIDE: a chain of nucleotides.

POLYPEPTIDE: a substance containing two or more amino acids in the molecule joined by peptide linkages.

PRECAMBRIAN: all geological time before the Cambrian.

PRECESSION OF THE EQUINOXES: the slow change of the relative positions of the Earth's equator and the ecliptic in which the celestial north pole appears to describe a complete circle every 21,000 years.

PROCARYOTES: small simple cells, including bacteria.

PROSIMIAN: any primate within the suborder Prosimia, which includes lemurs, lorises and tarsiers.

PREMOLAR: any bicuspid tooth in front of the molars.

PROTON: a fundamental particle in the nucleus of all atoms, carrying a unit positive charge of electricity, and with a mass approximately 1,836 times that of an electron.

PROTOZOA: any of a large group of mostly microscopic one-celled animals living chiefly in water but sometimes parasitic.

PULSAR: any of several small heavenly objects in the Milky Way that emit radio pulses at regular intervals.

QUASAR: any of a number of extremely distant star-like objects that emit powerful radio waves.

RAMUS: a projecting branch.

RED GIANT: a star with a large extended envelope and a compact hydrogen, carbon, or oxygen core. The size is 10-100 solar diameters and the mean density 0.001-0.000001 grams per cubic centimetre.

RED SHIFT: 1. displacement of spectral lines towards the red end of the spectrum; 2. increase in the wave length of electromagnetic radiation.

RELICT: remaining.

RIBONUCLEIC ACID (RNA): a complex compound of high molecular weight found in both the nuclei and the surrounding protoplasm of living cells. It functions in cellular protein synthesis and replaces deoxyribonucleic acid (DNA) as a carrier of genetic codes in some viruses. It consists of ribose nucleotides in strands of varying length.

RIBOSE: a sugar derived from ribonucleic acids.

SALT DOME: a mass of salt which is injected into overlying sedimentary rocks, thereby piercing and deforming them.

SARGASSUM WEED: a large floating seaweed of the genus so called, found in masses in warm and temperate seas.

SCHISTOSITY: the property of metamorphosed rocks whereby the minerals are segregated into thin layers, platy minerals are reoriented, all traces of former bedding are destroyed, and cleavage is along the new planes.

SEDIMENTARY ROCK: rock formed by the accumulation of material derived from pre-existing rocks or from organic sources. It is deposited in layered sequence and may be consolidated.

SEISMIC SURVEY: the scientific investigation of subterranean rock structures by generating surface pulses and recording them as they return.

SIAL: that part of the Earth's crust which is composed of granitic material rich in silica and alumina. It forms the continental land masses where it overlies the sima.

SIMA: that part of the Earth's crust which is composed of materials rich in silica and magnesium. It underlies both the sial and ocean floors.

SITUATION ETHICS: ethics derived from the guidance of circumstance and not determined from established codes.

SLICKENSIDE: a polished and scratched planar surface in rock or soil.

SOIL HORIZON: a layer more or less parallel to the ground surface whose character is determined by biological, chemical, and mineralogical differences caused by water movements and organic processes. It does not include layers caused by geological deposition.

SPECIFIC GRAVITY: the ratio between the weight of a given volume of a material and the weight of an equal volume of water, expressed in grams per cubic centimetre.

SPECTROSCOPE: an optical instrument for breaking up

light from any source into a spectrum so that it can be studied.

SPECTRUM (plur. spectra): the series of coloured bands into which white light is broken up by passing through a prism.

SPHERICITY: the property of being spherical.

SPHEROIDAL: adjective describing a body that is not quite a sphere.

STADIAL: adjective of stage.

STALACTITE: a tapering pendant of concretionary material descending from a cave ceiling, created by the reprecipitation of carbonates.

STALAGMITE: a columnar concretion ascending from the floor of a cave, formed by the reprecipitation of carbonates.

STAPES: a small stirrup-shaped bone, the innermost of the three bones of the middle ear.

STRATIGRAPHER: worker in stratigraphy.

STRATIGRAPHIC: adjective of stratigraphy.

STRATIGRAPHY: the branch of geology which deals with the composition, sequence, spatial distribution, classification, and correlation of the stratified rocks.

STRATUM (plur. strata): a sedimentary bed, regardless of thickness, consisting of a number of layers.

STRIATION: a tiny groove or scratch on the surface of rock considered to be due to abrasion by rocks frozen into the base of a glacier.

SUPERLUMINAL: speed greater than that of light.

SUPERNOVA: an extremely bright star that suddenly increases 10 million to 100 million times in brightness.

SYMBIOSIS: the living together of two kinds of organisms, especially where such association is of mutual advantage.

TAIL FLUKE: tail lobe of fish or whale.

TALUS: scree.

TEILHARD'S LAW: the law, advocated by Teilhard de Chardin, that humanity is heading towards greater complexity and greater consciousness. He called it the 'Law of Complexity Consciousness'.

TERRACE: a flat or gently inclined land surface bounded by a steeper ascending slope on its inner margin and a steeper descending slope on its outer margin. It usually approximately parallels a river or sea coast.

THEORY OF EVOLUTION: the theory that all present living things are descended by natural processes from very simple forms, the exact origin of which is unknown.

THEORY OF RELATIVITY: the fact, principle, or theory of the relative rather than the absolute character of motion. It includes the statements that the velocity of light is constant, that the mass of a body in motion varies with its velocity, that matter and energy are interconvertible, and that space and time are interdependent and form a four-dimensional continuum.

THERMOCLINE: an intermediate layer of water in an ocean or deep lake, lying between the disturbed upper layer and the relatively stagnant lower layer.

THERMODYNAMICS, first law of: although energy can be converted from one form to another, the total amount remains unchanged.

THERMODYNAMICS, second law of: although the total amount of energy in a closed system remains unchanged, there is always a tendency for it to become less available for future work.

TILL: a type of sediment in which the components have been brought into contact by the direct agency of glacier ice.

TILL PLAIN: a wide area of low relief created by a sheet of till which masks all irregularities in the bedrock relief.

TILLITE: a former till that has become compacted and changed to form a tough sedimentary rock.

TRANSLOCATION: the migration of material in solution or suspension from one soil horizon to another.

TROCHOPHORE (= trochosphere): small translucent, free-swimming larva characteristic of marine annelids (segmented worms) and most groups of mollusks. Trochophores are spherical or pear-shaped and are girdled by a ring of cilia (minute hair-like structures that enable them to swim).

TROPOSPHERE: the lowest of the concentric layers of the Earth's atmosphere in which the bulk of weather is generated.

TSUNAMI: a large sea wave generated by an earthquake or volcanic activity.

TURBIDITE: a sediment deposited in water by a submarine

current. The size of included particles decreases upwards to create a type of graded bedding.

ULTRABASIC: consisting primarily of ferromagnesian minerals and having a low percentage of silica and feldspar.

UNCONFORMITY: a hiatus or break in a sequence of rock strata, marked by a major break in sedimentation or by a structural planar surface separating younger rocks above from older rocks below.

UNIFORMITARIANISM: the belief that the Earth's present surface has received its form mainly as a result of the same type and speed of processes which operate today.

VARVE: a thin laminar bed of sediment divided into a thicker, lower, lighter coloured band of sand grading upwards in to a thinner upper band of silt.

VOLCANIC ROCKS: rocks formed by the solidification of magma on the Earth's surface.

WHITE DWARF: a whitish star of high surface temperature and very low intrinsic brightness usually with a mass about comparable with that of the sun but of such small dimensions that its average density is enormous.

WORLD-VIEW: the whole view of the world, including the reason for its existence and the explanation of its characteristics, held by a person or group.

ZIRCON: a crystalline silicate of zirconium.

ZOOPLANKTON: plankton consisting of animals, as protozoans.

REFERENCES

Aardsma, G. E. (1988). Has the speed of light decayed recently? *Creation Research Society Quarterly*, 18, 39-41.

Acrey, D. O. (1971). Problems in absolute age determination, In Lammerts, W. E. (ed.) *Scientific Studies in Special Creation*, Presbyterian and Reformed Publishing Co., USA, chapter 7, 72-78.

Alberts, B., Bray, D., Lewis, J., Raff, M., and Roberts, K., and Watson, J. D. (1983). *Molecular Biology of the Cell*, Garland Publishing House Inc., New York.

Anderson, J. L. (1971). Abstract of Papers, 161st National Meeting, American Chemical Society, Los Angeles. Deals with the variations in the decay rate of 14C.

Andrews, E. H. (1982). *God, Science, and Evolution*, Evangelical Press, Welwyn.

Appleton, J. (1975). *The Experience of Landscape*, John Wiley and Sons, London.

Assmuth, J. and Hull, E. R. (1915). *Haeckel's Frauds and Forgeries*, published by Joseph Ignatius Fonseca at the Examiner Press, Bombay. Refers to Haeckel's admission that he falsified human embryo sketches.

Atkinson, R. J. C. (1956). *Stonehenge*, Hamish Hamilton, London.

Austin, S. A. (1992). Excessively old ages for Grand Canyon lava flows, *Impact*, Article No. 224, Institute for Creation Research, El Cajon, California.

Axford, W. I. (1968). The polar wind and the terrestrial helium budget, *Journal of Geophysical Research, Space Physics*. 73 (21) 6855-6859.

Baker, S. (1976). *Bone of Contention: Is Evolution True?* Evangelical Press, Welwyn, England.

Barlow, N. (ed.) (1958). *The Autobiography of Charles Darwin*, Collins, London.

Barnes, T. G. (1981). Satellite observations confirm the decline of the Earth's magnetic field, *Creation Research Society Quarterly*, 18, 39-41.

Barnes, T. G. (1983). *Origin and Destiny of the Earth's Magnetic Field*, Institute of Creation Research, El Cajon, California.

Barzun, J. (1958). *Darwin, Marx, Wagner: Critique of a Heritage*, Doubleday Anchor Books, Garden City, New York.

Bascom, W. (1959). Ocean waves, *Scientific American*, 201 (August), 74-84.

Benton, M. J. (1990). *Vertebrate Palaeontology*, Chapman and Hall, London.

Berger, W. H. and Gardner, J. V. (1975). On the determination of Pleistocene temperatures from planktonic foraminifera, *Journal of Foraminiferal Research*, 5, 102-113.

Blackmore, V. and Page, A. (1989). *Evolution: the Great Debate*, Lion Books, Oxford.

Boule, M. and Valois, H. M. (1957). *Fossil Men*, Dreyden Press, New York. Translation of the 1952 edition of *Les Hommes Fossiles*.

Bowden, M. (1982). *The Rise of the Evolution Fraud*, Sovereign Publications, Bromley, Kent.

Bowden, M. (1983). *The Recent Change in the Tilt of the Earth's Axis*, Creation Science Movement Pamphlet No. 236, 50 Brecon Avenue, Portsmouth, PO6 2AW.

Bowden, M. (1988). *Decrease in the Speed of Light*, Pamphlet 262, Creation Science Movement, Portsmouth, PO6 2AW.

Bowden, M. (1991). *Science Vs Evolution*, Sovereign Publications, PO Box 88, Bromley, Kent.

Brand, L. R. (1976). Field and laboratory studies on the Coconino sandstone (Permian) fossil footprints and their paleoecological implications, *Earth, Life, and Time Symposium*, volume 2, 1-28, Andrews University, Michigan.

Brinton, C. C. (1941). *Nietzsche*, Cambridge, Massachusetts.

Brooks, J., James, D. E. and Hart, S. R. (1976) Ancient lithosphere: its role in young continental vulcanism, *Science*, 193 (4258) 1086-1094.

Brown, C. (1969). *Philosophy and the Christian Faith*, Tyndale Press, London.

Brown, R. H. (1979). The interpretation of C-14 dates, *Origins*, Loma Linda, California, 6, 30-44.

Brown, R. H. (1988a). Implications of C-14 age vs depth profile characteristics, *Origins*, Loma Linda, California, 15, 19-29.

Brown, R. H. (1988b). Statistical analysis of the atomic constants, light and time, *Creation Research Society Quarterly*, 25, 91-95.

Burdick, C. L. (1974). *Canyon of Canyons*, Bible-Science Association, Caldwell, Idaho.

Burke, D. C. (1985). *Creation and Evolution: When Christians Disagree*, Inter Varsity Press, London.

Chadwick, D. H. (1991). Out of time, out of space: elephants, *National Geographic Magazine*, 179 (5) 2-38.

Chadwick, O. (1975). *The Secularization of the European Mind in the Nineteenth Century*, Cambridge University Press, Cambridge.

Challinor, J. (1967). *A Dictionary of Geology*, University of Wales Press, Cardiff.

Chambers, R. (1844). *Vestiges of the Natural History of Creation*, (published anonymously, and republished with introduction by Gavin de Beer, Humanities Press, New York, 1969).

Chittick, D. E. (1984). *The Controversy: Roots of the Creation/ Evolution Conflict*, A Critical Concern Book, Multnomah Press, Portland, Oregon.

Clark, H. W. (1971a). The mystery of the red beds. In Lammerts, W. E. (ed.) *Scientific Studies in Special Creation*, Presbyterian and Reformed Publishing Company, USA, chapter 13, 154-164.

Clark, H. W. (1971b). The plants will teach you, In Lammerts, W. E. (ed.) *Scientific Studies on Creation*, Presbyterian and Reformed Publishing Company, USA, chapter 26, 303-307.

Clark, R. E. D. (1972a). *Science and Christianity: A Partnership*, Pacific Press, Mountain View, California.

Clark, R. E. D. (1972b). *Darwin: Before and After, The History of Evolutionary Theory*, Paternoster Press, Exeter.

Clementson, S. P. (1970). A critical examination of radioactive dating of rocks, *Creation Research Society Quarterly*, 7, 137-141.

Coffin, H. G. (1969). *Creation: Accident or Design?* Review and Herald Publishing Association, Washington DC.

Coffin, H. G. (1971). A paleoecological misinterpretation. In Lammerts, W. E. (ed.) *Scientific Studies in Special Creation*, Presbyterian and Reformed Publishing Company, USA, chapter 14, 165-168.

Coffin, H. G. (1983a). *Origin by Design*, Review and Herald Publishing Association, Washington DC.

Coffin, H. G. (1983b). Mount St. Helens and Spirit Lake, *Origins*, Loma Linda, California, 10, 9-17.

Conrad, J. (1917). Heart of Darkness, in *Youth: a Narrative and Two Other Stories*, J. M. Dent and Sons, Limited, London.

Cook, M. A. (1957). Where is the Earth's radiogenic helium? *Nature*, 179, 213-215.

Cook, M. A. (1966). *Prehistory and Earth Models*, Max Parrish, London.

Cook, M. A. (1971). Radiological dating and some pertinent applications of historical interest. Do radiological clocks need repair? In Lammerts, W. E. (ed.) *Scientific Studies in Special Creation*, Presbyterian and Reformed Publishing Co., USA, chapter VIII, 79-97.

Cooper, W. (1991). *After the Flood: the Witness of Early European History*, Pamphlet 274, Creation Science Movement, 50 Brecon Avenue, Cosham, Portsmouth, PO6 2AW.

Cousins, F. W. (1973). The alleged evolution of the horse. In Patten, W. D. (ed.) *Symposium of Creation III*, Baker Book House, Grand Rapids, Michigan, 68-85.

Cowan, T. M. (1970). Megalithic rings: their design construction, *Science*, 168, no. 3929, 321-325.

Cuffey, R. J. (1972). Paleontological evidence and organic evolution, *Journal of the American Scientific Affiliation*, (*Science*), 24, 161, 167-174.

Darwin, C. (1859, 1867, 1875, 1898, etc.). *The Origin of Species*, John Murray, London; (1928) Everymans Edition, with introduction by W. R. Thompson, J. M. Dent and Sons Ltd., London; (1952) Encyclopaedia Britannica Edition ed. by W. Benton, Chicago; (1984) Reprint of first edition, Penguin Books, Harmondsworth.

Davidheiser, B. (1969). *Evolution and Christian Faith*, Presbyterian and Reformed Publishing Company, Philadelphia.

Dawkins, R. (1982). *The Extended Phenotype*, Oxford University Press, Oxford.

Dawkins, R. (1988). Universal Darwinism. In Ruse, M. (ed.) *But Is It Science?* Prometheus Books, Buffalo, NY, chapter 14, 202-221.

Denton, M. (1985). *Evolution: a Theory in Crisis*, Burnett Books, London.

Eckhardt, R. B. (1972). Which of the fossil apes of the past 25 million years was man's ancestor? *Scientific American* 226 (1) 94-103.

Eicher, D. (1968). *Geologic Time*, Prentice Hall, Englewood Cliffs, New Jersey.

Eldredge, N. and Gould, S. J. (1973) Punctuated equilibria: an alternative to phyletic gradualism. In Schopf, T. J. M. *Models in Palaeobiology*, Freeman, Cooper, and Co., San Francisco, 82-115.

Elliott-Binns, L. E. (1956). *English Thought 1860-1900: The Theological Aspect*, Seabury Press, Greenwich, Connecticut.

Encyclopaedia Britannica (1911). 11th edition, Encyclopaedia Britannica Company, New York. Articles on Egypt, Memphis, Philo, Pyramids, Thebes; (1990) 19th edition, University of Chicago Press, Chicago. Article on Egyptian Art and Antiquities.

Evernden, J. F., Savage, D. E., Curtis, G. H., and James, G. T. (1964). Potassium-argon dates and the Cenozoic mammalian chronology of North America, *American Journal of Science*, 262, 145-198.

Ferguson, S. B., Wright, D. F., and Packer, J. I. (1988). *New Dictionary of Theology*, Inter-Varsity Press, Leicester.

Filby, F. A. (1970). *The Flood Reconsidered*, Pickering and Inglis, London.

Fleming, J. (1826). The geological deluge, as interpreted by Baron Cuvier and Professor Buckland, inconsistent with the testimony of Moses and the phenomena of nature, *Edinburgh Philosophical Journal*, XIV, 205-239.

Flint, R. F. (1971). *Glacial and Quaternary Geology*, John Wiley and Sons, New York.

Fosdick, H. E. (1926). *The Modern Use of the Bible*, Student Christian Movement, London.

Fothergill, A. (1989). *Heart of Darkness*, Open Guides to Literature, Open University Press, Milton Keynes, 81-83.

Fowler, W. A. (1956). The origin of the elements, *Scientific American*, 195 (September), 82-91.

Fox, C. S. (1952). *Water: A Study of Its Properties, Its Constitution, Its Circulation on the Earth, and Its Utilization by Man*, The Technical Press, Kingston Hill, Surrey.

Fox, S. W. (1984). Creationism and evolutionary biogenesis. In Montagu, A. *Science and Creationism*, Oxford University Press, 194-239.

Froom, L. E. (1946-48). *The Prophetic Faith of Our Fathers*, 4 volumes, Review and Herald Publishing Company, Washington D.C.

Garton, N. (1991). Private communication.

Geikie, A. (1885). *Textbook of Geology*, 2nd edition, Macmillan, London.

Geisler, N. L. and Anderson, J. K. (1987). *Origin Science: A Proposal for the Creation-Evolution Controversy*, Baker Book House, Grand Rapids, Michigan.

Gentry, R. V. (1971). Radiohaloes: some unique Pb isotope ratios and unknown alpha radioactivity, *Science*, 173, 727-731.

Gentry, R. V. (1986). *Creation's Tiny Mystery*, Earth Science Associates, Knoxville, Tennessee.

Geoffrey of Monmouth (1975). *History of the Kings of Britain*, translated by Evans, S., revised by Dunn, C. W. Everyman's Library, Dent, London.

Geoscience Research Institute (1990). 'Evidences: the Record of the Flood', Videotape, Loma Linda University, California.

Gilbert, A. D. (1980). *The Making of Post-Christian Britain: A History of the Secularization of Modern Society*, Longman, London.

Giles, J. A. (ed.) (undated). *Six Old English Chronicles*, including Nennius and Geoffrey of Monmouth, Bell and Daldy, York Street, Covent Garden, London.

Gish, D. (1975). A decade of creationist research, *Creation Research Society Quarterly*, 12 (1) 34-46.

Gish, D. (1979). *Evolution: the Fossils Say No!* Creation-Life Publishers, San Diego, California.

Gish, D. (1986). *Evolution: the Challenge of the Fossil Record*, Creation-Life Publishers, El Cajon, California.

Gish, D. (1988). Creation, evolution, and the historical evidence. In Ruse, M. (ed.) *But Is It Science?* Prometheus Books, Buffalo, NY, chapter 17, 266-282.

Gish, D. (1992). Bombardier beetle, *God's Wonderful World*, Autumn House, Grantham, Lincolnshire.

Golding, W. G. (1965). *Lord of the Flies*, Faber and Faber, London.

Goldschmidt, R. (1940). *The Material Basis of Evolution*, Yale University Press, New Haven.

Gould, S. J. (1975). Catastrophes and steady state Earth, *Natural History*, LXXX (2).

Gould, S. J. (1988). Is a new and general theory of evolution emerging? In Ruse, M. (ed.) *But Is It Science?* Prometheus Books, Buffalo, NY, chapter 12, 177-194.

Grand Canyon Natural History Association (1976). 'Geological Map of the Grand Canyon National Park, Arizona', Scale 1:62,250. Williams and Heintz Map Corporation, Washington DC.

Green, S. G. (1894). Basis of Scripture chronology, in The Holy Bible, The E and S Teachers' Edition, Eyre and Spottiswoode, London, Aids to Bible Students, 109-111.

Gregory, W. K. (1927). Two views of the origin of man, *Science*, 65 (1695), 601-605.

Gregory, W. K. and Raven, H. C. (1941). Studies of the origin and early evolution of paired fins and limbs. *Annals of the New York Academy of Sciences*, Volume XLII, Article 3, 273-360.

Halstead, B. (1984). Evolution, the fossils say yes. In Montagu, A. *Science and Creationism*, Oxford University Press, 240-254.

Harland, B. (1964). Evidence of late Precambrian glaciation and its significance, in Nairn, A. E. M. (ed.) *Problems in Paleoclimatology*, Interscience Publishers, London.

Hawkins, G. S. and White, J. B. (1973). *Stonehenge Decoded*, Book Club Associates, Souvenir Press, London.

Hayes, C. J. H. (1941). *A Generation of Materialism*, Harper Torch Books, New York.

Heggie, D. C. (1981). *Megalithic Science: Ancient Astronomy and Mathematics in North-West Europe*, Thames and Hudson, London.

Hensley, W. K., Bassett, W. A., and Huizenga, J. R. (1973). Pressure dependence of the radioactive decay constant of beryllium-7, *Science*, 181 No. 4104, 1164-1165.

Hitching, F. (1982). *The Neck of the Giraffe, or Where Darwin Went Wrong*, Pan Books, London.

Holmes, A. (1936). A record of new analyses of Tertiary igneous rocks (Antrim and Staffa). *Proceedings of the Royal Irish Academy*, Dublin 43B, 89-94.

Holt, R. D. (1988). The speed of light and pulsars, *Creation Research Society Quarterly*, 25, 84-87.

Howell, W. (1967). *Mankind in the Making*, Doubleday and Co., Garden City, New York.

Howorth, H. H. (1887). *The Mammoth and the Flood: An Attempt to Confront the Theory of Uniformity with the Facts of Recent Geology*, Sampson, Low, Marston, Searle, and Rivington, London.

Humphreys, D. R. (1988). Has the speed of light decayed recently? *Creation Research Society Quarterly*, 25, 40-45.

Humphreys, D. R. (1990). New evidence for rapid reversals in the Earth's magnetic field, *Creation Research Society Quarterly*, 26, 132, 133.

Hutchinson, G. E. (1957). Future of marine paleoecology, in *Treatise on Marine Ecology and Paleoecology*, Volume II, Geological Society of America Memoir 67.

Johanson, D. C. and White, T. D. (1979). A systematic assessment of early African hominids, *Science*, 203, 321-330.

Johanson, D. C. and White, T. D. (1980). Answer to a report by R. E. F. Leakey and A. Walker: On the status of Australopithecus afarensis (pages 1102, 1103), *Science*, 207, 1104, 1105.

Johnson, H. (1973). *The International Book of Trees*, Mitchell Beazley Ltd., London.

Johnson, M. R. (1988). *Genesis, Geology and Catastrophism*, Paternoster Press, Exeter.

Judge, J. (1969). Retracing John Wesley Powell's historic voyage down the Grand Canyon, *National Geographic Magazine*, (May), 668-713.

Kafka, F. (1955). *The Trial*, Penguin Books, Harmondsworth, Middlesex.

Kafka, F. (1986). *The Castle*, translated from the German by W. and E. Muir, Penguin Books, Harmondsworth, Middlesex.

Keane, G. J. (1991). *Creation Rediscovered*, Credis Pty Limited, PO Box 451, Doncaster, Australia.

Kettlewell, H. B. D. (1959). Darwin's missing evidence, *Scientific American*, 200:3, 48.

King-Hele, D. (1977). *Doctor of Revolution*, Faber and Faber,

London. This describes Erasmus Darwin's *Zoonomia; or The Laws of Organic Life*, published by J. Johnson, London, in 1794.

Kitcher, P. (1982). *Abusing Science: the Case Against Creationism*, MIT Press, Cambridge, Mass.

Kofahl, R. E. and Segraves, K. L. (1975). *The Creation Explanation*, Harold Shaw, Wheaton, Illinois.

Koran, The (1954). *The Meaning of the Glorious Koran*, an explanatory translation by Mohammed Marmaduke Pickthall, A Mentor Book, The New American Library, New York.

Kuhn, T. S. (1962). *The Structure of Scientific Revolutions*, University of Chicago Press, Chicago.

Ladd, H. S. (1957). Paleoecological evidence, chapter 2 in *Treatise on Marine Ecology and Paleoecology*, Geological Society of America Memoir 67, Volume 2.

Lammerts, W. E. (1971). Planned induction of commercially desirable variation of roses by neutron radiation. In Lammerts, W. E. (ed.) *Scientific Studies in Special Creation*, Presbyterian and Reformed Publishing Company, Philipsburg, Pennsylvania, XXIII, 269-284.

Lammerts, W. E. (1983). Are the bristlecone pines really so old? *Creation Research Society Quarterly*, 20, 108-115.

Lammerts, W. E. (1984-87). Recorded instances of wrong-order formation or presumed overthrusts (mainly in the United States): a bibliography, *Creation Research Society Quarterly*, Part I: 21, 88; Part II: 21, 150; Part III: 21, 200; Part IV: 22, 127; Part V: 22, 188; Part VI: 23, 38; Part VII: 23, 133; Part VIII: 24, 46.

Laudan, L. (1988). Science at the bar — causes for concern, In Ruse, M. (ed.) *But Is It Science?* Prometheus Books, Buffalo, NY, chapter 22, 351-355.

Lawson, A. D. (1927). Folded mountains and isostasy, Bulletin of the Geological Society of America, 38, 253-273. Deals with the impossibility of very wide large overthrusts.

Leakey, R. E. F. (1973a). Skull 1470: New Clue to Earliest Man? *National Geographic Magazine*, 143 (6), 818-829.

Leakey, R. E. F. (1973b). Evidence for an advanced Plio-Pleistocene hominid from East Rudolf, Kenya, *Nature*, 242, 447-450.

Libby, W. F. (1963). Accuracy of radiocarbon dates, *Science*, 140, 278-280. Admission of its weaknesses by the originator.

Lyell, C. (1892). *Principles of Geology*, 11th edition, 4 volumes, D. Appleton and Co., New York.

McKee, E. D., Crosby, E. J. and Berryhill, H. L. (1967). Flood deposits, Bijou Creek, Colorado, June 1965, *Journal of Sedimentary Petrology*, 37 (3), 829-851.

McMillen, S. I. (1970). *None of These Diseases*, Power Books, Fleming H. Revell Company, Old Tappan, New Jersey.

Malthus, R. (1798, 1803). *An Essay on the Principles of Population as it Affects the Future Improvement of Society*, J. Johnson, London. Reissued with a foreword by A. Robinson by Macmillan, London, 1966.

Miller, H. (1870). *The Old Red Sandstone*, 7th edition, William P. Nimmo, Edinburgh.

Miller, K. R. (1984). Scientific creation versus evolution: the mislabelled debate. In Montagu, A. *Science and Creationism*, Oxford University Press, 18-63.

Montagu, A. (1984). *Science and Creationism*, Oxford Unversity Press.

Morris, H. M (1974). *Scientific Creationism*, Creation-Life Publishers, San Diego. Kitcher says this is the best contemporary presentation.

Morris, H. M. (1983). *Science, Scripture, and the Young Earth*, Institute for Creation Research, El Cajon, California.

Nelson, E. and Broadberry, R. E. (1986). *Mysteries Confucius Couldn't Solve*, Read Books, South Lancaster, Massachusetts.

Nevins, S. E. (1973). Stratigraphic evidence for the Flood. in Patten, D. W. (ed.) *Symposium on Creation III*, Baker Book House, Grand Rapids, Michigan, 33-65.

Nevins, S. E. (1975). *Evolution, the Oceans Say No*, Symposium on Creation V, Baker, Grand Rapids, Michigan.

Nevins, S. E. (1990). *The Ocean says No! to Evolution*, Creation Science Movement Pamphlet 221, 50 Brecon Avenue, Cosham, Portsmouth PO6 2AW.

Newell, N. D. (1957). Supposed Permian tillites in northern Mexico are submarine slide deposits, *Bulletin of the Geological Society of America*, 68, 1569-1575.

Noorbergen, R. (1978). *Secrets of the Lost Races*, New English Library, Times-Mirror, London.

Norman, T. and Setterfield, B. (1987). *The Atomic Constants, Light and Time*, Invited Research Report, prepared for Lambert T. Dolphin, Senior Research Physicist, Geoscience and Engineering Center, Stanford Research Institute International, 333 Ravenswood Avenue, Menlo Park, California.

Oard, M. J. (1990). *An Ice Age Caused by the Genesis Flood*, Institute for Creation Research, San Diego, California.

O'Connell, P. (1969). *Science of Today and the Problems of Genesis*, Book I. Christian Book Club of America, Hawthorne, California.

Odajnik, W. (1965). *Marxism and Existentialism*, Doubleday, Garden City, New York.

Orwell, G. (1980). *Nineteen Eighty-four*, Penguin Books, Harmondsworth, Middlesex.

Orwell, G. (1951). *Animal Farm*, Penguin (and many later printings), Harmondsworth, England, also (1972). Heineman Educational, London.

Oxnard, C. (1974). *University of Chicago Magazine*, Winter number, 8-12.

Oxnard, C. (1975). The place for the australopithecines in human evolution: grounds for doubt? *Nature*, 258, 389-395.

Parker, S. P. (ed.) (1980). *McGraw Hill Encyclopedia of Ocean and Atmospheric Sciences*, McGraw Hill Book Company, New York.

Patten, D. W. (1970). The pre-flood greenhouse effect, In Patten, D. W. and Others, *Symposium on Creation II*, Baker Book House, Grand Rapids, Michigan, I, 11-41.

Peach, B. N. and Horne, J. (1884). The crystalline rocks of the Scottish Highlands, *Nature*, November 11, 29-35.

Penck, A. and Brueckner, E. (1909). *Die Alpen im Eiszeitalter*, Tauschnitz, Leipzig.

Price, G. M. (1926). *Evolutionary Geology and the New Catastrophism*, Pacific Press Publishing Association, Mountain View, California.

Reeves, C. (1992). A decay in the velocity of light: a statistical critique of Norman and Detterfield, *Origins*, 4 (12), 15-19.

Rehwinkel, A. M. (1967). *The Flood in the Light of the Bible, Geology, and Archeology*, Concordia Publishing House, St. Louis, Missouri.

Rice, G. E. (1983). *Luke, a Plagiarist?* Pacific Press Publishing Association, Mountain View, California.

Riegle, D. D. (1971). *Creation or Evolution*, Zondervan Publishing House, Grand Rapids, Michigan.

Ritland, R. M. *A Search for Meaning in Nature*, Pacific Press Publishing Association, Mountain View, California.

Romer, A. S. (1966). *Vertebrate Paleontology*, 3rd edition, University of Chicago Press, Chicago.

Roth, A. A. (1985). Are millions of years required to produce biogenic sediments in the deep ocean? *Origins*, 12, 48-56.

Ruse, M. (1982). *Darwinism Defended: A Guide to the Evolution Controversies*, Addison-Wesley Publishing Co., Advanced Book

Program/World Science Division, Reading, Massachusetts.

Ruse, M. (ed.) (1988). *But Is It Science? The Philosophical Question in the Creation/Evolution Controversy*, Prometheus Books, Buffalo, New York.

Schaeffer, F. A. (1969). *The God Who is There*, Hodder and Stoughton, London.

Schumm, S. A. (1977). *The Fluvial System*, John Wiley and Sons, New York.

Schwarzbach, M. (1964). Criteria for the recognition of ancient glaciations. In Nairn, A. E. M. (ed.) *Problems in Paleoclimatology*, Interscience Publishers, London, 81-85.

Setterfield, B. (1987). 'Geological Time and Scriptural Chronology: A Supplement to the Invited Research Report The Atomic Constants, Light and Time', Box 318, Blackwood, South Australia, 5051.

Setterfield, B. (1989). The atomic constants in light of criticism, *Creation Research Society Quarterly*, 25, 190-197.

Singer, C. (1966). *A Short History of Scientific Ideas to 1900*, Clarendon Press, Oxford.

Slusher, H. S. (1973). *Critique of Radiometric Dating*, Creation-Life Publishers, San Diego, California.

Slusher, H. S. (1974). *Clues Regarding the Age of the Universe*, Institute of Creation Research Impact Series, No. 19. El Cajon, California.

Smith, J. M. (1988). Did Darwin get it right? In Ruse, M. (ed.) *But Is It Science?* Prometheus Books, Buffalo, NY, chapter 12, 195-201.

Stickling, J. A. (1972). A statistical analysis of Flood legends, *Creation Research Society Quarterly*, 9 (3), 152-155.

Strahler, A. N. (1969). *Physical Geography*, 3rd edition, John Wiley and Sons, New York.

Strangway, D. W. (1970). *History of the Earth's Magnetic Field*, McGraw Hill, New York.

Sundquist, E. T. (1987). Ice core links CO_2 to climate, *Nature*, 329, 389-390.

Teilhard de Chardin, P. (1959). *The Phenomenon of Man*, Collins, London.

Tier, W. H. (1970). Creation: the only reasonable explanation of natural phenomena, In. Patten, D. W. and Others *Symposium on Creation*, II, Baker Book House, Grand Rapids, Michigan, VII, 135-151.

Thom, A. (1967). *Megalithic Sites in Britain*, Clarendon Press, Oxford.

Thom, A. (1973). *Megalithic Lunar Observatories*, Clarendon Press, Oxford.

Thom, A. and A. S. (1978). *Megalithic Remains in Britain and Brittany*, Clarendon Press, Oxford.

Thorarinsson, S. (1966). *Surtsey: the New Island in the North Atlantic*, Viking Press, New York.

Thornbury, W. D. (1954). *Principles of Geomorphology*, John Wiley and Sons, New York.

Troitskii, V. S. (1987). Physical constants and the evolution of the universe, *Astrophysics and Space Science*, 139, 389-411.

von Fange, E. A. (1974). Time upside down, *Creation Research Society Quarterly*, 11 (1), 13-27.

Walker, A. and Leakey, R. E. F. (1978). The hominids of east Turkana, *Scientific American,* 239 (2), 44-56.

Ward, Rita R. (1971). The study of English Micraster research, In Lammerts, W. E. (ed.) *Scientific Studies in Special Creation*, Presbyterian and Reformed Publishing Co., Philipsburg, Pennsylvania, chapter 16, 184-197.

Wells, A. K. and Kirkaldy, J. F. (1966). *Outline of Historical Geology*, Thomas Murby, London.

West, R. G. (1972). *Pleistocene Geology and Biology*, Longmans, London.

Wheeler, G. (1978). *Deluge*, Southern Publishing Association, Nashville, Tennessee.

Whitcomb, J. C. (1964). *The Origin of the Solar System*, Presbyterian and Reformed Publishing Company, Philipsburg, Pennsylvania.

Whitcomb, J. C. (1974). *The World that Perished*, Evangelical Press, London.

Whitcomb, J. C. and Morris, H. M. (1974). *The Genesis Flood*, Presbyterian and Reformed Publishing Company, Philadelphia; and Baker Book House, Grand Rapids, Michigan.

White, A. J. M. (1978). *What About Origins*, Dunestone Printers, Newton Abbott, England.

White, A. J. M. (1985). *How Old is the Earth?* Evangelical Press, Welwyn, Herts.

Whitelaw, R. L. (1970a). Radiocarbon confirms biblical creation (and so does potassium-argon). In Lammerts, W. E. (ed.) *Why Not Creation?* Presbyterian and Reformed Publishing Company, Philadelphia, 90-100.

Whitelaw, R. L. (1970b). Radiocarbon and potassium-argon dating in the light of new discoveries in cosmic rays. In Lammerts, W. E. (ed.)

Why Not Creation? Presbyterian and Reformed Publishing Company, Philadelphia, 101-105.

Whittow, J. B. (1984). *The Penguin Dictionary of Physical Geography*, Harmondsworth, England.

Wilder-Smith, A. E. (1974). *Man's Origin, Man's Destiny*, Telos-International, distributed by Marshall, Morgan, and Scott, London.

Wilder-Smith, A. E. (1981). *The Natural Sciences Know Nothing of Evolution*, Creation-Life Publishers, San Diego, California.

Wood, J. E. (1978). *Sun, Moon, and Standing Stones*, Oxford University Press, Oxford.

Woolley, L. C. (1952). *Ur of the Chaldees*, Penguin Books, Harmondsworth, England.

Young, D. A. (1977). *Creation and the Flood: An Alternative to Flood Geology and Theistic Evolution*, Baker Book House, Grand Rapids, Michigan.

Young, D. A. (1982). *Christianity and the Age of the Earth*, Zondervan, Grand Rapids, Michigan.

Zajdlerowa, Z. (1989). *The Dark Side of the Moon*, 3rd edition, Harvester Wheatsheaf, New York.

Zeuner, F. E. (1958). *Dating the Past: An Introduction to Geochronology*, Methuen and Co. Ltd., London.

Zimmerman, P. A. (ed.) (1966). *Darwin, Evolution, and Creation*, Concordia Publishing House, St. Louis, Missouri.

Zimmerman, P. A. (1971). The spontaneous generation of life, In Lammerts, W. E. *Scientific Studies on Special Creation*, Presbyterian and Reformed Publishing Company, Philipsburg, Pennsylvania, chapter 28, 317-327.

Zuckerman, S. (1970). *Beyond the Ivory Tower*, Taplinger Publishing Company, New York.

INDEX

About the Author . . .

COLIN MITCHELL

Dr. Mitchell studied at both Oxford and Harvard Universities and has a PhD in Soil Geography from the University of Cambridge.

After experience as a soil surveyor in the Middle East, Dr. Mitchell lectured in Geography at the University of Reading where he continues to be an Honorary Fellow.

At Reading, Dr. Mitchell taught Physical Geography and Soil Science, with an emphasis on survey and mapping and the use of photography from aircraft and satellites. He was responsible for a programme of desert studies involving research and field classes in North Africa.

Dr. Mitchell is a consultant on agricultural development projects to the UN Food and Agriculture Organization, and to a number of national governments.

Since 1985 he has also been working as an independent consultant in soil science and land elevation. He co-authored *Terrain Evaluation* (Longmans, London. 1991) with John Howard. With four colleagues, Colin Mitchell wrote the standard work *Physical Geography* (Longmans). In addition he has contributed a number of specialist chapters to books and published more than fifty scientific papers.

Dr. Mitchell has lectured and written articles on Creationism for twenty years.

He is married to Clemency, a doctor in general practice in Berkshire. They have three sons and one daughter, all now in their twenties. Dr. Mitchell teaches a regular Bible class and is a keen amateur gardener and photographer.